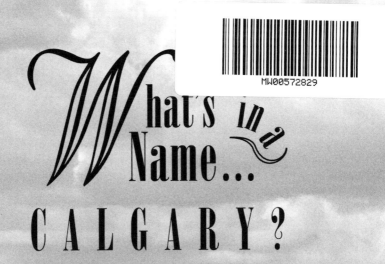

What's in a Name... CALGARY?

A Look at the
People Behind
Place Names
in Calgary

Donna Mae Humber

THE CITY
OF CALGARY

© 1995 The City of Calgary, Public Information Department

Canadian Cataloguing in Publication Data

Humber, Donna Mae.
What's in a Name...Calgary?

ISBN 1-55059-124-X

1. Names, Geographical—Alberta - Calgary. 2. Calgary (Alta.)—History.
I. Calgary (Alta.) II. Title

FC3679.5.H85 1995   917.123.'38'0014   C95.910521-2   F1079.5.C35H85 1995

Detselig Enterprises Ltd.
1220 Kensington Road N.W., Unit 210
Calgary, Alberta
T2N 3P5

All rights reserved. No part of this book may be reproduced in any form or by any means without permission in writing from the publisher.

Printed in Canada

Acknowledgements

This book would not have been as complete as it is without the help of so many people who offered their knowledge, expertise and guidance. I would like to thank each and every one of them and apologize to those I have missed.

No one interested in local history should overlook Calgary's two most valuable resources: the Local History Room of the Main Branch of the Calgary Public Library and the Glenbow Museum Library. A special thank you to Jennifer Bobrovitz and Marianne Fedori of the Public Library, and Lindsay Moir and Kathryn Myhr of the Glenbow Library, for their efforts in helping me find the necessary materials.

Thanks to Captain John Grodzinski and Wray Hughes of the Museum of the Regiments for all the time they spent filling me in on the military history and personnel recognized in the naming of the streets of Currie and Harvey Barracks. Thanks to Harry Sanders and the rest of the staff of The City of Calgary Archives for their assistance. Thanks to Sandy Handy of the Calgary Public School Board for her help and encouragement, to Simone Grattan and Colleen Rioux of the Calgary Separate School Board for their assistance in completing the information on separate schools, to Cathy Nickel of Mount Royal College for her help with information on the college's place names, and to Ron Linden for sharing his knowledge and expertise on early Calgary. A special thank you to Hugh Dempsey, who offered guidance and direction during the research and writing of this book.

And most of all, a big thank you to my daughter, Carley, for giving me the inspiration which began this project, to my husband, Allyn, for encouraging me to begin and to keep going when things got tough, and to my sons, Jamie and Colin, who put up with a lot of inconvenience around home while mom was busy on the phone or at the computer.

Detselig Enterprises Ltd. appreciates the financial assistance from the Department of Canadian Heritage and The Alberta Foundation for the Arts, a beneficiary of the Lottery Fund of the Government of Alberta, for its 1995 publishing program.

Preface

Seeing this book in print is seeing a tangible answer to prayer and I am grateful to God for helping me to see this project to completion.

Doing the research has been an adventure and an education. It has been fulfilling to discover hundreds of Calgarians, past and present, who have contributed to making this city a wonderful place to call home. As a Calgarian, I was filled with a tremendous sense of pride as I read about so many people who, in one way or another, gave of themselves to make life in this city easier and more pleasurable for others. And I chuckled when I discovered some of Calgary's characters who have given our city a personality second to none.

Many Calgarians have been recognized by having something in the city named after them. But there are so many others whose names are unknown except to those who are history buffs. I think of Fred Kanouse, the first semi-permanent white resident of the Calgary area, and John Glenn, one of Calgary's earliest settlers; of Jean Drever Pinkham, one of Calgary's outstanding pioneer women, and John Ingram, our first chief constable. And there are Mary and Catherine Barclay, founders of the Canadian Youth Hostel Association, O.H. Patrick, the driving force behind the creation of the dinosaur park at the Calgary Zoo, and John Kanerva, creator of the dinosaur models. The list goes on and on.

I want to acknowledge each Calgarian whose name deserves to be honoured and I hope that in some small way this book will be a tribute to all Calgarians who strive to make our city the best possible place to live. Calgarians, I salute you!

Table of Contents

Identification of front cover photographs:

1. Chief David Crowchild *(Crowchild Trail)*
    Glenbow Archive File #NA-667-432a
2. Marion Carson *(Marion Carson Elementary School)*
    Glenbow Archive File #NA-2980-2
3. James Lougheed *(Lougheed Building)*
    Glenbow Archive File #NA-3918-14
4. Freddie McCall *(McCall Drive)*
    Glenbow Archive File #NA-3511-6
5. John Ware *(John Ware Building)*
    Glenbow Archive File #NA-101-37
6. Ernest Manning *(Ernest Manning High School)*
    Glenbow Archive File #NA-2922-14
7. Nellie McClung *(Nellie McClung Centre)*
    Glenbow Archive File #NA-273-2
8. Mary Dover *(Dover Subdivision)*
    Glenbow Archive File #NA-2307-34
9. William Reader *(Reader Rock Gardens)*
    Glenbow Archive File #NA-504-5
10. Emily Murphy *(Murphy Road)*
    Glenbow Archive File #NA-273-3
11. Sam Livingston *(Sam Livingston Building)*
    Glenbow Archive File #Na-94-1
12. Deerfoot *(Deerfoot Trail)*
    Glenbow Archive File #NA-250-3
13. Alice Jamieson *(Jamieson Avenue)*
    Glenbow Archive File #NA-2315-1
14. Paddy Nolan *(Nolan Road)*
    Glenbow Archive File #NA-1371-1
15. Louis Riel *(Louis Riel Elementary/Junior High School)*
    Glenbow Archive File #NA-504-3

Panoramic photograph of Calgary
    Glenbow Archive File #PE-36-1

Background photograph of sky:
    Ian Tomlinson©/Take Stock Inc.

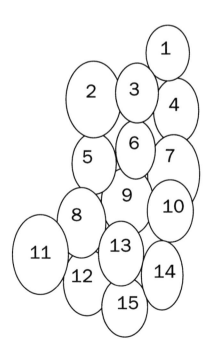

Introduction

This book began as a look at the stories behind the people whose names appear throughout Calgary gracing our streets, buildings, parks, bridges and subdivisions. But it soon evolved into much more. So many other names have fascinating stories behind them that needed to be shared, many of them rich in Calgary history. However, space restrictions meant that not every story could be told, not every name origin could be explained. But how could one choose? Thus we went back to people and those things named in their honour. Many of these people share a part of Calgary's history and many reflect the influence of the native culture on our heritage. Others reflect our European heritage, particularly our historical ties to Great Britain. Still others were important in Canadian history. All share the distinction of making such contributions to their society that they will be forever remembered.

For the most part, there is documentation behind the names, however, in some cases, speculation and general consensus proved to be the best, or only, evidence. It is unfortunate that for many names no suggestion of the origin could be found, and thus those names were omitted. There are still many tales that need to be told which are beyond the scope of this book, and hopefully will be compiled into a future volume.

But what of the name "Calgary" itself? Although it is not named for a person, it is important to look at the name's origin. This is especially true as there has always been some dispute about the meaning of the name Calgary. On February 29, 1876, Colonel A.G. Irvine, Assistant-Commissioner of the NWMP, asked Colonel James Macleod for help in naming the fort. Macleod suggested Fort Calgary. He had relatives with a small castle called Calgary House located on Calgary Bay on the Isle of Mull, Scotland, a beautiful spot which he had visited. There was another Calgary located on the Isle of Skye, close to Macleod's grandfather's farm. Col. Irvine believed the word Calgary meant "clear running water" in Gaelic, but this has been disproved. The name may have come from the Gaelic term "Cala-ghearridh," "Cala" meaning "harbour" or "bay" and "ghearridh" meaning "enclosed pasture" or "farm." Thus, a proper meaning may be "bay farm" or "bay pasture." However, numerous other translations have been offered during the past century.

Most of the buildings listed in this book are public in nature. However, there are some which are private structures, such as apartments and lodges. Those included in the book are named after people of distinction or who have historic significance.

Examining the process by which Calgary's streets, public buildings, parks and landmarks are named, has been, to some degree, frustrating. Each division of the Civic government and each school board has its own specific procedures for making such decisions. Although the naming procedures seem quite clear, the names chosen sometimes seemed questionable. And once names were chosen, the background as to the "who's" and "why's" was often lost in the sea of information and paper that comprises any large bureaucracy.

The naming of some facilities, schools, streets and subdivisions did not always fit the criteria used at the time and naming policies have changed over the years. For instance, during the 1950s, subdivision development changed from the grid system and numbered streets — which had been the norm — to named streets and curved layouts. Some subdivisions developed at that time have street names that do not seem to fit with the name of the community. For instance, the streets in Southview were named after trees. However, The City soon required that streets be named beginning with the same letter as the subdivision name. As development boomed, all usable letters were taken, so the regulations again were changed so that streets must be numbered or given names beginning with the first three letters or the same prefix as the subdivision name.

Another policy, introduced in 1987, allows the streets in a subdivision to be named based on a theme. The subdivision and street names must be accepted by the Planning and Building department and to date only the subdivision of Monterey Park, with its California theme, has received City approval.

In some of the older subdivisions, developers appear to have tried to find street names that in some way reflect Calgary's past. Brentwood is a good example. In others, developers appear to have co-ordinated street names by some other method. For instance, most of the streets in Cambrian Heights have British names, all beginning with the letter "C." In other cases it is not clear whether the names were used for a purpose or simply because they fit the naming criteria. For example, were Armstrong, Allison, and Avery in Acadia named after real people or places, or were they simply common proper names which begin with the letter "A"? Because some developers are no longer in existence, and records concerning the "why's" of street naming have not generally been kept, it was not always possible to confirm the origin of a street's name. Some we will probably never know. As a result, many entries include a qualification such as "perhaps," or "may have been."

In many cases developers chose street names by looking on a map for communities, counties, or physical features whose names might fit with their subdivision. Names from British Columbia, Alberta, Saskatchewan, California and Great Britain are common.

It is fascinating to see how Canada's British heritage is reflected in so many street names. Dozens of streets in both old and new subdivisions have the same names as villages and hamlets in England, Scotland, Ireland and Wales. In North Glemore Park, Highwood, Westgate and Wildwood, a large portion of the names are of English origin. In Killarney, all of the street names are Irish.

Major Facilities

City policy states that only major facilities commonly used by the public, such as parks, swimming pools and arenas, should be officially named. Buildings used entirely by The City administration are generally identified by their geographic location or by their use. Exceptions may be made to honour long-time, respected employees who were connected with the service provided from that particular building.

When a decision is made to name a facility, several considerations are kept in mind. The name must be different from other facilities and should indicate the geographic area in which the facility is located. Buildings may be named after historic sites or pioneers who once owned the land. The name may recognize organizations or citizens who have made a major contribution to the activity for which the facility is primarily used. And, names can be chosen to honour a citizen's long-term, distinguished contribution in a particular area, or to recognize those who were instrumental in the development of the facility.

When considering names of individuals, only nominations from recognized organizations are accepted. The nominees must no longer be active in their field and they may be deceased.

Bridges in the city of Calgary are named after prominent individuals or for their geographic area.

Streets

The policy for naming streets depends on the type of street being named. Freeways are given Aboriginal names, expressways are named for geographic locations and major arteries are generally named after prominent individuals. If a major artery travels across the city, a name that is meaningful in more than one area is required. Therefore, the name of a subdivision cannot be used for an artery that travels a significant distance beyond the subdivision's boundaries. A private road in a private development can be named anything. However, if it is to be a mailing address, The City must approve the name.

Subdivisions

The names of subdivisions are chosen by the developer and submitted to The City planning department for approval. Although The City requires some sort of justification for the name on the basis of historic or geographic significance to the area, the name is generally chosen primarily for its marketability. Developers have become quite adept at finding a rationalization for their choice of names. Ease in naming the streets of a subdivision is also taken into consideration.

Schools

Calgary public schools are named by a committee comprised of three trustees – two appointed and one in whose ward the school to be named is located. The School Naming Committee meets with two representatives of the school community and, in consultation with the community, makes recommendations to a confidential committee of the Board of Trustees and the School Board administration. The first elementary school in a district is generally named after the community.

Subsequent schools are named after a person of recognized stature. Elementary-junior high schools, junior high schools and senior high schools are named after persons of recognized stature.

When considering the name of an individual, persons who are retired or deceased are looked at first. Before a name is used, consent of the individual or immediate family is obtained.

The Separate School Board has no official policy for naming schools. However, in practice, a committee meets to examine names that have been brought forward for consideration. Representatives from the school board and a local priest are included. The names considered are generally those of saints, those tied to Catholic tradition, or individuals active in Catholic activities in the district. In the past, the name chosen has been one whose first letter coincides with the first letter in the name of the subdivision, wherever possible. However, this has become increasingly difficult and is no longer common practice.

Listings

The names in this book are presented in alphabetical order. To assist readers in identifying what has been named after a person, the following icons have been designed to represent:

Arts & Culture   Parks   Streets

Buildings   Schools   Subdivisions

Bridges   Sports & Leisure

CALGARY

A

A.E. Cross Junior High School   3445 - 37 Street S.W.

Alfred Ernest Cross was a Montrealer who moved west seeking to make his fortune. He began as a ranch hand and veterinarian at the Cochrane Ranch, but seeking a more challenging life, he soon left to begin ranching on his own. He built a quarter-section homestead west of Nanton into the huge A7 Ranch. After an injury forced him to move into Calgary, Cross decided that the city needed a brewing industry to meet the changing liquor laws. He studied brewing in Eastern Canada and returned to found the Calgary Brewing and Malting Company. This ultimately became one of the city's major industries. Cross was also one of Calgary's "Big Four" (see Big Four Building). At the official opening of A.E. Cross Junior High School in 1961, one of the speakers was Mary Dover, a former city alderman and daughter of A.E. Cross.

Abbot Avenue   Bridgeland, N.E.

Abbot Avenue was possibly named after Abbot Pass at Lake Louise. The pass was named after Phillip Stanley Abbot, a member of the Appalachian Mountain Club who died there in 1896 after a fall on Mount Lefroy.

Abbott Place   Acadia, S.E.

Abbott Street was the original name of 2nd Avenue South. The name disappeared when the city changed from named to numbered streets in 1904. Originally the streets in downtown Calgary were named after officials of the Canadian Pacific Railway and others with ties to the CPR. Sir John Joseph Caldwell Abbott (1821-93) was called to the bar in 1847 and created Queen's Counsel in 1862. He was standing counsel to the CPR from 1880 to 1887. Upon the death of Sir John A. Macdonald on June 18, 1891, Abbott became prime minister of Canada. He served until December 1892 when he resigned due to ill health. The name Abbott Place appears today in Acadia, perhaps in recognition of the old street name.

Aberdeen Road   **Acadia, S.E.**

Aberdeen Road was named either for Lord Aberdeen, governor general of Canada from 1893 to 1898, or Aberdeen, Scotland. The name means "the place at the mouth of the Don." The river was named after Devona, a Celtic goddess.

Adams Crescent   **Acadia, S.E.**

It is likely this street was named after one of three Adams important to Calgary history. One was Samuel H. Adams (1878-1975), a city alderman from 1915 to 1921 and mayor from 1921 to 1922. Another is Ernest D. Adams (1868-1960), a well-known horseman in western Canada who came to Calgary in 1901. He worked with the Calgary Exhibition even before the first Stampede in 1912 and was an honourary life director of the Calgary Exhibition and Stampede. The third is Harvey K. Adams (1877-1968), who came to Calgary in 1919 and worked as a livestock commission agent. He served as a director of the Calgary Exhibition and Stampede and was an honourary member of the Southern Alberta Old Timers and Pioneers Association.

Addison Place   **Acadia, S.E.**

Addison Place may have been named for James Addison, a pioneer Calgary contractor. His firm, Addison and Davey, built many of Calgary's public buildings, including City Hall, the Cathedral Church of the Redeemer and Central School (Carl Saffran Centre). Addison died in 1931 at the age of 88.

Adelaide Street   **Ramsay, S.E.**

Adelaide Street was named after Addie Wood, one of the daughters of Wesley Fletcher Orr, who was the original owner of the land on which the street is located. Orr served as a city alderman, from 1884 to 1891 and 1892 to 1894. He also had the distinction of being the first mayor of The City of Calgary, serving two terms from 1894 to 1895 and 1896 to 1897. (See Maggie Street.)

Albany Place   **Acadia, S.E.**

This street name was likely chosen after Albany, the capital of New York state. Granted its charter in 1686, Albany was named after the Duke of York and Albany, who later was crowned King James II.

Albert Park   **S.E.**

Albert Park was named after Albert Smythe, a real-estate "super-salesman" who claimed that the area was to be developed into an exclusive subdivision. The villages of Albert Park, Gilbert Park, Hubalta and Forest Lawn were combined in 1934 to create the Town of Forest Lawn; the town was annexed by The City of Calgary in December 1961.

Alberta Avenue   **Ramsay, S.E.**

Most of the streets in the Ramsay-Grandview area originally had names, rather than numbers. Those on the hill, such as Alexander Street, Constance Avenue, Margaret Avenue, Elizabeth Street, William Street and Alberta Avenue, have retained their names, which were likely those of landowners, their family members or developers and builders. However, the streets below the hill, which are laid out on a grid, have been given numbers. Many of the numbered streets were also originally named after the landowners in the area or their families.

Alcott Crescent, etc.   **Acadia, S.E.**

These streets may take their names from American author Louisa May Alcott, whose book Little Women has become a literary classic.

Alexander Calhoun Branch Library   **3223 - 14 St. S.W.**

Alexander Calhoun came to Calgary from Ontario in February 1911 as the city's first librarian. He remained in that position for 34 years and his work helped to make the Calgary Public Library a vital part of life in the city. He believed that the most important role of the library was in education and Calgary became the first city in Canada to establish school libraries, due in large part to Calhoun's influence. He contributed greatly to cultural life in Calgary and was instrumental in the opening of the Allied Arts Centre in 1946, the first centre of its kind in North America. He was the first president of the Alberta division of the Canadian Society of the Control of Cancer (now the Canadian Cancer Society) and a founding member of the John Howard Society (1947) and the Golden Age Club (1949). Calhoun died in 1979, ten months short of his 100th birthday.

Alexander Crescent   **Rosedale, N.W.**

The origins of this name are unclear. However, there are several likely candidates. The most prominent Alexander associated with Calgary history was Earl Alexander of Tunis, governor-general of Canada from 1946 to 1952, who visited the city in July 1946 to officially open the Calgary Exhibition and Stampede. He returned to the city for the Stampede again in 1950. The governor-general was a football fan and joined with Calgary supporters at the Royal York Hotel in Toronto in 1948 in celebrating the Calgary Stampeders' Grey Cup victory. Two local Alexanders were Henry Bruen "Harry" Alexander and his cousin, George, who were pioneer builders and real estate developers in Calgary. Together they also built Calgary's first waterworks system, which was later taken over by The City. H.B. Alexander was a charter member of the Ranchmen's Club and was one of the city's early sportsmen. He died in Africa in 1932 at the age of 71.

Alexander Street   **Ramsay, S.E.**

See Alberta Avenue.

Alexandra Centre   9 Avenue and 9 Street S.E.

One of the first schools in Calgary, Alexandra Centre now functions as a centre for medical and social services for the Inglewood and Ramsay communities. The present building was constructed in 1906 to replace a small frame school house built in 1891, which had been known as East Ward School. The name was changed between 1906 and 1908 to Alexandra School after the consort of King Edward VII, who began his reign in 1901. Queen Alexandra gave much time and money to aid the poor. The school closed in 1963 and renovations to Alexandra Centre began in 1975.

Alex Ferguson Elementary School   1704 - 26 Street S.W.

Alexander Hamilton Ferguson was born in Scotland and served with the British military in India and South Africa. He was twice a member of the honour guard to Queen Victoria. He came to Canada in 1905 and to Calgary in 1909 where he was appointed sergeant major in the 103 Battalion. He joined the Calgary Board of Education as a physical education instructor in 1910. One of his great accomplishments was in the instruction of rifle shooting and many of his students became expert marksmen. He was a promoter of all sports and officiated at most athletic meets held in the city. In his 34 years with the school board he instructed over 100,000 children, to many of whom he was known as "Fergie." He was still employed with the school board at the time of his death in 1944. In 1951 an award for the best male high school athlete in city schools was created in his honour, with a trophy being presented each year.

Alex Munro Elementary School   427 - 78 Avenue N.E.

Alex Munro was born in Scotland in 1895. He began his gardening career at age 17, working as an apprentice gardener on several large Scottish estates. After serving with the British Army in World War I, he moved to Calgary in 1920. He joined The City's nursery staff in 1923 and became head gardener in 1929. In 1949 he was appointed superintendent of the parks department, a position he held until he retired in 1960. In 1955 Munro began writing a popular weekly horticultural column in the Calgary Herald and in 1961 published The Calgary Herald Gardening Book. It sold more than 18,000 copies, remarkably high for a non-fiction work in Canada. In 1960 a plaque honouring Munro was erected in the rock garden on 10th Street above Riley Park. Munro died in 1966.

Alex Walker Tower   124 - 15 Avenue S.E.

Scottish-born Alex Walker enlisted in the original 50th (Calgary) Battalion in 1915 and served through World War I as a sergeant. He was seriously wounded at the Battle of the Somme in 1916. He joined the Great War Veterans Association in 1918 and worked toward the establishment of the Canadian Legion, which was formed in 1926. He became president of the Calgary Branch Legion (now No. 1) in 1935 and was elected Alberta command president in 1937. He was the first non-commissioned officer to serve as Dominion president of the Legion and the only person to serve three consecutive terms from 1940 to 1946. He worked with the government through World War II to ensure benefits for returning servicemen and was made a Commander of the Order of the British Empire in 1943. Walker died in Victoria in 1977 at the age of 91.

Alice M. Curtis Elementary School   9711 Academy Drive S.E.

Alice Marion Curtis was born in Ireland and taught school in Ontario before coming to Calgary in 1905. She established the first Home and School Association west of Ontario in 1912, known then as the Connaught Mothers' Club. She held many offices during her long association with the HSA and was made a life member in 1945. In 1951 she was elected as a life member of the Canadian Home and School and Parent Teacher Federation. Curtis died in Vancouver in 1957 after taking ill during a visit there.

Allan Crescent   Acadia, S.E.

Allan Crescent may have been named for Alexander Allan (1857-1927), a Scot who came to Calgary in 1884 to establish a dry goods business. He served on the town council from 1887 to 1889 and also was on the school board. In 1900 Allan became Calgary's first collector of customs, a post which he held until 1911.

Amherst Street   Mount Royal, S.W.

Most of the streets in Mount Royal were named after people who played a significant role in the history of French Canada. Jeffery Amherst (1717-1797) was the British army officer in charge of the campaigns which led to the capitulation of Montreal and the end of French rule in Canada. As a result of his success in North America, he was knighted in 1761 and made 1st Baron Amherst in 1776.

Anderson Apartments   S.W. - S.E.

Built in 1912 as a bachelors' hotel, the Anderson Apartments have served as an excellent example of early Calgary quality apartment living for over 80 years. It was built by Alexander Victor Anderson, who came to Alberta in 1883 and worked in the machinery business. After he built the apartment block, Anderson occupied one of the suites and managed the building until his death in 1920 at age 57.

Anderson Road   S.W. - S.E.

Between 1913 and 1960, Harry T. Anderson farmed a quarter section of land through which Anderson Road now passes. Anderson was instrumental in bringing such services as electricity and telephones to the area. In the early 1950s a group of citizens who wished to recognize his efforts successfully lobbied to have the road named in his honour.

Andrew Davison Building   133 - 6 Avenue S.E.

This building, which houses the Calgary Police Service, is named after Andrew Davison. Davison served as Calgary's mayor for 16 years, through the Great Depression and World War II - the longest term for a mayor in Calgary's history. He began his career in civic politics as an alderman in 1921 and was elected mayor by acclamation in 1929. He was re-elected by acclamation five times. Due to ill health, Davison retired to Vancouver in 1945, where he died in 1963.

Andrew Davison Elementary School   **9603 - 5 Street S.E.**

See Andrew Davison Building.

Andrew Sibbald Elementary School   **1711 Lake Bonavista Drive S.E.**

Andrew Franklin Sibbald was born in 1833 in Barrie, Ontario. He first aspired to be a carpenter, then a farmer, but after losing a hand in an accident he returned to school to train as a teacher. In 1875 Rev. George McDougall visited Ontario and invited Sibbald to become the first teacher of the Stoney Indians. Sibbald and his family arrived at Morley, Alberta in October 1875, after 104 days of travel. Sibbald was one of the first teachers in Alberta and assisted in the building of the first Morley church and the first Methodist church in Calgary. He taught at Morley until 1896, then tried ranching, and at age 75 moved to Banff and took up carpentry, erecting several houses in the town. Sibbald died in Banff in 1934 at the age of 100 and was buried at Morley.

Anne Avenue   **Brittania, S.W.**

This street is named after Princess Anne, the second child of Queen Elizabeth and Prince Phillip, who was an infant when the subdivision of Brittania was developed. Each of the streets in Brittania was given a name which in some way is associated with the British royal family, since Brittania is the ancient Roman name for Great Britain.

Annie Foote Elementary School   **6320 Temple Drive N.E.**

Annie Graham Foote was born in Elora, Ontario in 1855 and taught for a number of years in Ontario before joining the Calgary school board teaching staff in 1893. She taught at South Ward and Haultain Schools until 1911. In 1913 she accepted the nomination of the Local Council of Women to run as their candidate for the school board. She was elected and served from 1914 to 1917 as the first female trustee. After she retired from teaching, Foote remained in Calgary for a number of years. She returned to her home in Ontario in 1929 and died there in 1945.

Annie Gale Junior High School   **577 Whiteridge Way N.E.**

Annie Gale (1879-1970) immigrated to Calgary from England with her husband in 1912. Appalled by social conditions, she soon became an active social reformer. Her reputation became so great that she was easily elected to city council in 1918, becoming the first female alderman in Calgary and the British Commonwealth. She was highly respected as an alderman and was the first woman in Canada to hold the position of acting mayor. She was a member of council from 1918 to 1923 and was elected to the public school board in 1924, but was defeated in a bid to enter provincial politics in 1921.

Archie Boyce Arena   **Stampede Park, 13 Avenue and 6 Street S.E.**

Archie Boyce moved with his family from Ontario to Alberta in 1906. After serving in World War I, he became involved in auctioneering and purchased a farm through the Soldiers' Settlement Board. He was a charter member of the Auctioneers' Association and conducted sales throughout Alberta until 1956. In that year he sold his shares in the Olds Auction Mart and retired to Calgary.

Armstrong Crescent   **Acadia, S.E.**

Armstrong Crescent may have been named for William Charles Gordon Armstrong (1865-1951), a northwest surveyor who came to Calgary from England in 1892 and surveyed much of the northwest area of the city. In 1903 he became quartermaster of G Squadron, Canadian Mounted Rifles, which was the first military unit to be established in the North-West Territories. Armstrong became a lieutenant-colonel in 1910 and commander of the 103 Calgary Rifles. As an alderman from 1909 to 1913, he helped develop the city's street numbering and electric light systems. He was one of Alberta's pioneer motorists, and was active in the Alberta Motor Association for many years. Before his death, Lt.-Col. Armstrong was one of the oldest living Calgarians to have served during World War I.

Assiniboine Road   **Acadia, S.E.**

One of many streets in Calgary with an Aboriginal name, Assiniboine refers to the nation scattered throughout western Canada and the northern United States. The Stoney Indian tribe, west of Calgary, are Assiniboines.

Astoria Crescent   **Acadia, S.E.**

This street name may have been taken from the port city of Astoria, Oregon. The city was named after its founder, American industrialist John Jacob Astor.

Athlone Road   **Acadia, S.E.**

Athlone Road was likely named for Alexander Augustus Frederick William Alfred George Cambridge, Earl of Athlone (1874-1957). In 1914 Athlone was to have been appointed governor-general, but requested that his name be withdrawn so he might serve in the military during World War I. Athlone served as Canada's governor-general from 1940 to 1946, and was the second member of the royal family, after the Duke of Connaught, to serve in this capacity. He was the husband of the Princess Alice, granddaughter of Queen Victoria.

Austin Road   **Acadia, S.E.**

This street likely takes its name from the city of Austin, capital of Texas. Austin was named for Stephen F. Austin, founder of many of the English-speaking settlements in Texas while it was still a part of Mexico.

Austin Nixon Manor   **10660 Elbow Drive S.W.**

Austin H. Nixon was a member of Southwood United Church, under whose auspices this senior citizens' home operates. He was on the committee that initiated this building project. He died shortly after construction commenced and the facility was named in his memory.

CALGARY

B

Bagot Avenue   **Mount Royal, S.W.**

Sir Charles Bagot (1781-1843) was the governor general of British North America from 1841 to 1843.

Baines Bridge   **Bow River at Zoo Road S.E. and 12 Street S.E.**

When the Calgary Zoo opened in 1929, Tom Baines was appointed as labourer in charge of the animals and became curator later that year. Between 1929 and 1938, Baines was the only permanent staff hired by the zoo and worked tirelessly to make it a success. In 1961 he became the first Canadian to serve as president of the North American Association of Zoological Parks and Aquariums. By the time he retired in 1964, Baines had become an internationally known figure in the zoological world and the Calgary Zoo had developed into a world-class facility. Baines also was known and beloved by thousands of Calgary students for his entertaining visits to Calgary schools. (Also, probably, Baines Road in Brentwood.)

Baker Crescent   **Brentwood, N.W.**

This street may have been named after I.G. Baker & Company, the original supplier of provisions to the North-West Mounted Police at Fort Calgary. Isaac Baker, owner of the company, played a significant role in the settlement of Alberta. Under company foreman D.W. Davis, this American company helped build the fort. When it was finished, they built a company store, the first in the settlement. I.G. Baker & Company remained in business in Calgary until 1891.

Baker House   **230 - 5 Avenue S.E.**

Developed to house those displaced by urban renewal, Baker House was funded by the Canadian Mortgage and Housing Corporation and is administered by the Calgary Housing Authority. Because of the number of bachelor suites, it is now mostly occupied by seniors. It was named after Ethel Baker (1878-1977), who was at the official opening in 1970. Baker came to Calgary in 1910 and spent many years lobbying the federal government to introduce pensions for senior citizens. She served as secretary of the Alberta Old Age Pension Society and was named citizen of the year in 1952-53.

Baldwin Crescent   Bel-Aire, S.W.

This street may take its name from Stanley Baldwin, British prime minister in 1923 from 1924 to 1929 and 1935 to 1937.

Bannerman Drive   Brentwood, N.W.

Bannerman is a prominent name in Calgary's past. Brothers Joseph and James Bannerman came to Calgary in 1883 to open a flour and feed business. Joseph served on Calgary's first city council in 1894 and was a member of the third legislature of the North-West Territories from 1894 to 1896. James was postmaster in 1884 when the townsite of Calgary was laid out. He re-located the post office across the Elbow River from the original site at the request of the Canadian Pacific Railway. As a reward, the CPR gave him two free lots and a $100 bonus. James Bannerman also served as alderman from 1886 to 1887, 1889 to 1890 and 1891 to 1892.

Bannister Road   Midnapore, S.E.

Bannister Road is one of the original streets whose name was registered when the town of Midnapore was developed in 1913. The streets were named after some of the town's first citizens. A.E. Banister (sometimes spelled Bannister) established a ranch in the area in 1884. His son, Harold, was mayor of Midnapore from 1932 to 1933.

Banting and Best Elementary School   1819 - 66 Avenue S.E.

Frederick Grant Banting (1891-1941) was a Canadian doctor and scientist who, with the aid of Charles Herbert Best (1899-1978) and James B. Collip, began seeking a cure for diabetes at the University of Toronto in 1921, under the direction of Dr. J.J.R. Macleod. One of the greatest medical discoveries of the 20th Century occurred in 1922 when they isolated insulin and demonstrated its effect on diabetes after only eight months of research. In 1923 Banting and Macleod received the Nobel Prize and Banting was knighted in 1934. Best was a physiology student when the discovery of insulin was made. He became director of the University of Toronto physiology department in 1929 and director of the Banting and Best Department of Medical Research in 1941.

Barclay Mall   3 St. S.W. between Riverfront Avenue
                                                   and 7 Avenue

The original name of 3 St. S.W. was Barclay Street, named after W.D. Barclay, a construction engineer with the CPR. Part of his job was to find suitable locations for stations in the railway's western division so he was likely involved with locating the CPR station in Calgary and Calgary's main streets. Originally the streets in central Calgary were named after prominent CPR employees. Barclay Mall was created and named in 1984.

Barlow Trail   **N.E. - S.E.**

Three suggestions have been put forward concerning how Barlow Trail got its name. One is that it was named after Noel Barlow, a World War II flying ace and bush pilot who lives in Carseland. Another is that the street was built close to a CNR siding or small station called Barlow, located at the south end of Barlow Trail. The station was probably named after a man named Barlow who was involved in financing a railroad in the 1840s that eventually amalgamated with the CNR. A third suggestion is that it was named after Dr. Alfred E. Barlow, a prominent geologist who lost his life in a marine disaster on the St. Lawrence River in May 1914.

Barr Road   **Brentwood, N.W.**

Rev. Isaac M. Barr, a Canadian-born British clergyman, along with another minister, George Exton Lloyd, organized a group of 2,200 British colonists to settle in the area of Lloydminster in 1903. The group was commonly known as the Barr Colonists. The settlement scheme was organized to encourage British settlement of the Canadian west to offset the large number of settlers coming from the United States. The street may have been named for the minister or for the colony.

Barrett Drive   **Brentwood, N.W.**

There were two Barretts of significance in southern Alberta and Barrett Drive was likely named for one of them. Elizabeth A. Barrett was a Methodist teacher from Ontario who came west in 1875. She worked among the Crees at Whitefish Lake and later with the Stoney Indians at Morley. She was one of the witnesses to the signing of Treaty No. 7 and taught school at Fort Macleod. She died at Morley in 1888. R.A. Barrett was a prospector and adventurer who panned for gold in the North Saskatchewan River at Edmonton and was employed at the Indian Department's farm at Fish Creek, south of Calgary, from 1879 to 1881. He then moved to Helena, Montana, where he spent the rest of his life.

Barron Building   **610 - 8th Avenue S.W.**

Lawyer-brothers Jacob B. and Abe L. Barron came to Calgary in 1911 and practiced law together from 1919 to 1936. Jacob then went into the theatre business and owned the Grand, Uptown, and Odeon Theatres. He also operated the Palace Theatre from 1923 to 1927. In 1949, he constructed Calgary's first large office building to accommodate oil companies following the oil boom. The new building was soon occupied by Mobil, Shell and Sun oil companies and Calgary was established as the headquarters of the oil industry in western Canada. Abe continued to practice law after his brother left the firm, first on his own, and then with his son. He was made a Queen's Council in 1945 and was a founding member of Calgary's Petroleum Club. Both brothers died at the age of 77, Jacob in 1965 and Abe in 1966. (It is likely that Barron Crescent in Brentwood is also named after these brothers.)

Batchelor Crescent   Brentwood, N.W.

There are two prominent Batchelors in Calgary's past after whom this street might have been named. George D. Batchelor came to Calgary from Kent, England, in 1908. He served as an alderman from 1921 to 1923. His son, Dudley E. Batchelor (1906-78), began working for the Electric Light Department of The City in 1926. He later became City treasurer, head of the finance department. From 1954 to 1959 he was commissioner of finance and from 1959 to 1963 served as chief commissioner. He retired in 1963 after serving The City of Calgary for 31 years.

Baylor Crescent   Bayview, S.W.

This street may share its name with Baylor University in Waco, Texas, which was named after its founder, Robert Baylor.

Beaconsfield Crescent, etc.   Beddington, N.W.

There are seven streets in Beddington with the name Beaconsfield. They may take their name from British prime minister Benjamin Disraeli, who was created 1st Earl of Beaconsfield by Queen Victoria in 1876. He served as prime minister in 1868 and from 1874 to 1880.

Bearspaw Drive   Brentwood, N.W.

According to legend, Stoney chief, Masgaahsid, or Bearspaw, became a warrior when he avenged his mother's murder by killing a Blood Indian. Over the next several years, his people frequently clashed with the Blood, Blackfoot and Sarcee tribes. However, he was later influenced by Methodist missionary Rev. John McDougall to follow the path of peace and when Treaty No. 7 was negotiated in 1877, he signed on behalf of his band. The chief was first honoured in 1954 when Calgary Power built the Bearspaw Dam on the western edge of the city.

Beaupre Crescent   Bowness, N.W.

Beaupre Crescent was named after Beaupre Lake, which is located northwest of Calgary. The lake was named for Louis Beaupre, a French-Canadian settler who, with his Metis wife, bought squatter's rights in the area. He ranched and did some logging. The naming committee enjoyed the humour in their choice of the name "Beaupre" (pronounced "Bow-pray") as their mandate included instructions that all streets should begin with "Bow."

Beil Avenue   Brentwood, N.W.

Beil Avenue was likely named for Charles "Charlie" Beil (1894-1976). Beil worked as a cowboy in the American West until, in 1922, he met American cowboy artist Charlie Russell (see Russell Road) who encouraged him to make use of his natural artistic talent. For a short time Beil studied art in California and then worked with Russell until his death in 1928. He came to Canada in 1930 and settled in Banff where he died in 1976. Beil was known throughout the world for his art. He worked on models for the original dinosaurs at the Calgary Zoo and between 1932 and 1967 created a series of trophies for the Calgary Exhibition and Stampede. He was a recipient of an honourary doctorate from the University of Calgary, was an honourary member of Cowboy Artists of America and a member of the Order of Canada.

Bell Street   **Harvey Barracks, S.W.**

Arthur Henry Bell (1871-1956) was born in Ireland and served with the British army before coming to Canada in 1903. He re-entered military service in 1906 as a lieutenant in the Royal Canadian Mounted Rifles and came to Calgary with the army in 1911. When war broke out he commanded the 31st Battalion (Bell's Bulldogs) overseas until April 1918, when he was made brigadier-general, commanding the 6th Canadian Infantry Brigade. He was in command of Military District No. 13, Calgary, from 1919 to 1925. He was appointed adjutant-general of Canada in 1929, and retired as major-general in 1933.

Bell Street   **Brentwood, N.W.**

There were several Bells for whom this street could have been named. Ralph A.G. Bell was a citizen of Calgary from 1882 until his death at age 92 in 1953. He was in the NWMP and served during the Riel Rebellion. He was also the force's ferryman in Calgary and thus greeted the pioneers coming to Calgary before the arrival of the railway. Bell retired from the Mounted Police in 1886 and was one of Calgary's earliest implement dealers. Another possibility is Max Bell, who was a Calgary businessman and philanthropist (see Max Bell Theatre). A third, less likely possibility is Ernest Leopold Bell, one of Calgary's early residents. He came to Calgary with a survey party in 1881 and was attached to the NWMP for some years, breaking horses for the force. He was a member of the Steele's Scouts during the rebellion of 1885, went to the Klondike during the gold rush, and later lived in Ontario where he died in 1937 at the age of 74.

Bennett Crescent   **Brentwood, N.W.**

Bennett Crescent may have been named in recognition of R.B. Bennett, the only Canadian prime minister to have lived and worked in Calgary. (See R.B. Bennett Elementary School and Viscount Bennett Centre).

Benton Drive   **Brentwood Heights, N.W.**

It is possible that this street was named for Benton, Alberta which in turn was named for the Benton Trail, which ran from Fort Benton, Montana to Fort Macleod, Alberta in the 1870's. Fort Benton was named for Thomas Hart Benton, a senator from Missouri.

Betty Mitchell Theatre   **Lower Floor, Jubilee Auditorium,**
                                      1415 - 14 Avenue N.W.

Betty Mitchell (1912-1976) was one of the most prominent promoters of amateur theatre that Calgary has known. She became involved in dramatic productions during her undergraduate years at the University of Alberta in Edmonton. Her greatest interest was in directing and she became proficient and well-known in this field. She taught drama at Western Canada High School from 1932 to 1961 and was instrumental in the formation of the Calgary Theatre Guild in 1932 and Workshop 14 in 1944. Both were important to the development of theatre in Calgary. In 1965, Workshop 14 merged with the newly formed Musicians and Actors Club to become MAC 14. Three years later the company, now professional, changed its name to Theatre Calgary.

Beveridge Block   138A - 7 Avenue S.E.

The Beveridge family arrived in Calgary from Ontario over a 21-year period. Eldest son Thomas arrived in 1885, his younger brother Stephen in 1886, parents Peter and Mary in 1887 and middle son Francis in 1906. All three brothers ranched in the Springbank area and later became well-known real estate figures in the city. Among the buildings built by the brothers were the Beveridge Building and the Flat Iron Building in Chinatown, apparently a small copy of its namesake found in Manhattan.

Big Four Building   Stampede Park, 13 Avenue and 6 Street S.E.

It is most appropriate that one of the major buildings found on the Calgary Exhibition and Stampede grounds is named after Calgary's "Big Four" - Archie McLean, Pat Burns, George Lane and A.E. Cross. These four guaranteed the expenses of the first Calgary Stampede in 1912 which totalled $100,000. Without their generosity, perhaps the world famous event would never have started. Archie McLean (1860-1933) was one of Alberta's major ranchers and a popular member of the Alberta legislature for the Lethbridge and Taber constituencies from 1910 to 1921. Patrick Burns (1856-1937) was an entrepreneur at heart. He and his brothers left their home in Ontario to begin farming in Manitoba, but buying and selling others' cattle was more in his line. He was soon selling beef to feed the construction crews building the CPR and followed the progress of the railway west, arriving in Calgary in 1890. Here he founded P. Burns and Company Ltd., which became one of the largest meat-packing firms in Canada. He also acquired many ranching properties from which he supplied beef to his packing plant. Burns was appointed to the Senate in 1931. George Lane (1856-1925) was the owner of the famous Bar U Ranch southwest of High River. He had the greatest breeding farm for Percheron horses in the world. A.E. Cross was a rancher and founder of the Calgary Brewing and Malting Company (see A.E. Cross Junior High School).

Birkenshaw Apartments   605 - 13 Avenue S.W.

This apartment building was named for the Birkenshaw home which stands next door (621 - 13 Avenue S.W.) William H. Berkenshaw (note the difference in spelling) was president of W.R. Brock and Company, one of the largest wholesale houses in Canada. He also served as president of the Calgary Board of Trade in 1914. Berkenshaw built his home in 1908 and lived there until 1910, when the house was sold to O.S. Chapin, a Chicago-born implement and carriage dealer. Berkenshaw moved back into the house in 1927 and re-purchased it in 1928. He moved again in 1929 to the Ranchmen's Club where he resided until 1936. The house was converted to apartments in 1930 and to a clubhouse for the apartment residents in 1980. It was designated as a Provincial Historical Resource in 1981.

Bishop Carroll High School   4624 Richard Road S.W.

Most Rev. Francis P. Carroll was born in Toronto in 1890 and ordained as a Catholic priest in 1917. He served at St. Augustine's Seminary for 18 years, as professor, vice-president and president. He was appointed Bishop of Calgary in 1935, arriving in Calgary in March 1936. He resigned in 1966 due to ill health and died a year later.

Bishop Grandin High School   111 Haddon Road S.W.

Vital Justice Grandin (1829-1902) was born in France and was ordained in the Order of Mary Immaculate in 1854. He arrived in St. Boniface, Manitoba that year and began ministry in a diocese stretching from the Arctic to the American border and from Lake Superior to the Rockies. He was made a bishop at age 28 after serving as a missionary for three years and in 1871 he was named bishop of St. Albert, responsible for the area which now comprises Alberta and much of Saskatchewan. He was the first Catholic bishop of Alberta and possibly the first bishop west of St. Boniface. Never in good health, his condition deteriorated in the last five years of his life and he died in his residence in St. Albert (now an historic site) in 1902.

Bishop Kidd Junior High School   1420 - 28 Street S.E.

Rt. Rev. John Thomas Kidd, D.D., (1868-1950) was Bishop of Calgary from 1925 until he was transferred to London, Ontario in 1931. He was the second Roman Catholic Bishop of Calgary and during his tenure, 35 new churches or chapels and four separate high schools were built.

Bishop McNally High School   1050 Falworth Road N.E.

The Most Reverend John Thomas McNally, D.D. was born at Hope River, Prince Edward Island in 1871. After completing various levels of education, he was sent in 1892 to study for the priesthood as one of the first students of the Canadian College in Rome. Ordained in 1896, he served in various locations until 1913 when he was appointed as the first bishop of the newly formed Diocese of Calgary. Known for his energy and common sense, Bishop McNally dealt effectively with many controversies and concerns in establishing the fledgling diocese. He remained Bishop of Calgary until 1924, whereupon he became Bishop of Hamilton. In 1937, he was appointed as Archbishop of Halifax where he served until his death in 1952.

Bishop Pinkham Junior High School   3304 - 63 Avenue S.W.

William Cyprian Pinkham (1844-1928) was born in St. John's, Newfoundland, but grew up and was educated in England. He was ordained as an Anglican priest at the Red River settlement of St. James in 1869, becoming the youngest priest in the diocese of Rupert's Land. In 1887 he was consecrated Bishop of Saskatchewan and his area expanded to include Calgary. He became a member of the board of education for the North-West Territories in 1887 and was unanimously voted chairman, a position he held for several years. He moved to Calgary in 1889. In 1903 the diocese was divided and Bishop

Pinkham was given Calgary as his seat of administration. He still oversaw an area of 100,000 square miles. He remained bishop of Calgary until his retirement in 1926.

Blackfoot Trail   **N.E. - S.E.**

Blackfoot Trail is named to recognize the Blackfoot tribe. It lies approximately along the trail used by the Blackfoot from about 1800 to 1870 to travel from the southern plains to the fur trading posts at Rocky Mountain House and Edmonton.

Blakiston Drive   **Brentwood, N.W.**

This street was likely named for Lieutenant T.W. Blakiston, the magnetic observer on the Palliser Expedition (see Captain John Palliser Elementary School and Palliser Hotel). Having an interest in ornithology, he also recorded many species of birds. After having a disagreement with Palliser, he left the expedition and eventually submitted a report of his own.

Blessed Kateri Tekakwitha Elementary School   **1005 Abbotsford Drive N.E.**

Tekakwitha (1656-80) was a Mowhawk Indian from New York state who was left an orphan at age five when her family died of smallpox. Her mother had been a Christian and her influence remained with the child. When she was baptized into the Catholic church at age 20, she was given the name Kateri, Mohawk for "Katherine." She was severely persecuted for her decision to become a Christian. There are many accounts of her appearing to the living after her death and of her miraculous interventions on their behalf. She was beatified in 1980.

Blow Street   **Brentwood, N.W.**

This street was possibly named after Dr. Thomas Henry Blow who, along with Rev. George Kerby and others, was responsible for bringing post-secondary education to Calgary. Blow was instrumental in the opening of Calgary College, which was incorporated in 1912. Unfortunately, it did not have degree-granting status. Even as a Conservative MLA, Dr. Blow was unable to obtain that status for the college and it closed. Dr. Blow was an eye, ear, nose and throat specialist, the only one in Calgary for a number of years.

Bob Bahan Pool and Fitness Centre   **4812 - 14 Avenue S.E.**

Born and raised in the Albert Park area of Calgary, Bob Bahan devoted much of his life to sport. He excelled at golf and was the city's juvenile golf champion in 1956. He attended the University of Colorado on a golf scholarship and later the University of Calgary where he played hockey. He later taught school in Forest Lawn and also coached minor hockey. Bahan died in an airplane accident in 1970. The pool was named in recognition of his contribution to and encouragement of minor sport in Forest Lawn.

Bob Edwards Building   **Southern Alberta Institute of Technology II Campus, 2015 Centre Avenue E.**

The SAIT II Campus building houses many apprenticeship programs. Bricklayers, painters, carpenters and heavy duty mechanics all receive part of their training here. The old Alberta Liquor Control Board warehouse was bought by SAIT for the sum of $1 and named most appropriately after Bob Edwards, Calgary's most famous and outspoken imbiber. (See Bob Edwards Junior High School.)

Bob Edwards Junior High School   **4424 Marlborough Drive N.E.**

Robert (Bob) Chambers Edwards was the founder and editor of the Eye Opener, a satirical newspaper well known both in the Calgary area and nationally. It began in High River in 1902, and moved to Calgary in 1904. Edwards used satire as a form of social criticism and nothing escaped the wrath of his pen. At the time of his death in 1922, he was a Conservative MLA for Calgary, a term begun in 1921. Edwards is well remembered as one of Canada's great humourists.

Boulton Road   **Brentwood, N.W.**

Boulton Road may have been named for John and Mary Ann Boulton, pioneer Alberta farmers, who lived near Medicine Hat from 1887 until 1941 when they retired to Calgary. Another possibility is Calgary pioneer Thomas Boulton (1875-1936), who came to the city in 1890. He worked on a number of large southern Alberta ranches, including William Roper Hull's 25 Ranch, the Oxley and the Cochrane. He was killed in a Calgary traffic accident.

Bowlen Street   **Brentwood, N.W.**

This street is likely named for John James Bowlen. (See J.J. Bowlen Provincial Building.)

Boyce Crescent   **SAIT Campus, 1301 - 16 Avenue N.W.**

J.F. Boyce served as principal of SAIT from 1917 to 1918. In 1985, most of the streets of SAIT were named after former principals.

Braden Crescent   **Brentwood, N.W.**

This street was probably named after Thomas B. Braden who, along with Andrew M. Armour, began publishing the Calgary Herald in 1883 as a weekly newspaper. The two men were connected with The Herald for just one year, selling it to Hugh St. Quentin Cayley, later a prominent lawyer. Braden (1851-1904) grew up on the farm next to Armour. The two came to Calgary along with their printing equipment on one of the first CPR trains to arrive in Calgary from the east. They set up their newspaper business in a tent on the banks of the Elbow River. The yearly subscription cost was $1. After selling The Herald, Armour moved to Medicine Hat where he founded the Medicine Hat Times and from there to California, where he died in 1904. Braden returned to newspaper work in 1885, when he founded The Calgary Tribune. He rejoined The Herald in 1894 and left to begin a real-estate and insurance business just before his death. He was also Calgary's Dominion Government meteorological observer.

Brantford Crescent, etc.   **Brentwood, N.W.**

These streets may take their name from the city of Brantford, Ontario, which was named in honour of the Mohawk chief, Joseph Brant, who founded a village there in 1784.

Branton Junior High School   **2102 - 20 Street N.W.**

William A. Branton came to Calgary from England in 1905 at the age of 16. After spending two years studying at Brandon College in Manitoba, he joined the Calgary school board staff in 1911. He began as an employee of building superintendent, Hugh McClennan, became his assistant in 1912 and was appointed building superintendent and architect in 1920, holding the latter post for 34 years. During that time he travelled widely, studying school buildings and bringing about considerable change to Calgary schools, from the sandstone structures of the early part of the century, to the post-World War I cottage schools, to the glass and stucco structures of the 1950s. The 17 cottage schools built in Calgary were two-room, two-storey wooden structures designed to fit in with the surrounding homes. They were intended for later conversion to rooming houses for the city's large single male population. However, after World War I, demographics changed and the conversions never occurred.

Braxton Place, etc.   **Braeside, S.W.**

Perhaps these streets take their name from Braxton County, West Virginia. It, in turn, was named for Carter Braxton, a signatory of the American Declaration of Independence.

Brazeau Crescent   **Braeside, S.W.**

There are many locations around Jasper, Alberta named for Joseph E. Brazeau, an employee of the Hudson's Bay Company. He was the chief trader at Rocky Mountain House and was invaluable to the Palliser Expedition as an interpreter because he spoke six different Aboriginal languages. The Brazeau family's link to Calgary comes through Joseph's son, John, who was an interpreter for the NWMP in Calgary. His wife, Louise, was the force's first matron for the Calgary detachment and their son, Joseph, rode in the first Calgary Stampede in 1912. The latter was known in rodeo circles as "Calgary Red." This street was likely named in recognition of the Brazeau family.

Brebeuf Elementary/Junior High School   **5030 Northland Drive N.W.**

In 1626 Jean de Brebeuf, a French priest, became the first Jesuit missionary in what is now Ontario. He was the inspiration for 24 other Jesuit priests to come to the mission of Huronia along the shores of Lake Huron, and thousands of Aboriginal people were converted to Catholicism. He was martyred when Iroquois warriors from across Lake Ontario attacked the Huron settlements on March 16, 1649. He was beatified in 1925; his feast day, better known as the feast of Canadian Martyrs, is October 9.

Brecken Road   Brentwood, N.W.

Brecken Road was probably named for Paul R. Brecken (1886-1960), who died while serving in his 13th year as a City alderman. Brecken was a high school teacher and vice-principal of Crescent Heights High School who served on city council, and was an MLA for three years. He was active in the Kiwanis Club, Canadian Club, Royal Canadian Legion and church affairs, and was named the Jaycees' citizen of the year for 1951.

Breen Crescent, etc.   Brentwood, N.W.

These streets may have been named for Peter J. Breen, who died a hero. He drowned while rescuing an assistant fire chief from the Bow River in 1929.

Breton Bay, etc.   Brentwood Heights, N.W.

These streets may have been named for Cape Breton, Nova Scotia, or for Breton, Alberta, a village named after Douglas C. Breton who was MLA for Leduc from 1926 to 1930.

Brewster Hall   University of Calgary, 2500 University Drive N.W.

Brewster is the name of a prominent Banff family who are well known for their transport company. Fred Brewster, the best known member of the family, was a mining engineer whose vast knowledge of the Rockies was used by such organizations as the Smithsonian Institution and the United States Department of Biological Survey. He spent a large part of his life working to make the mountains around Jasper more accessible to visitors. Brewster Hall was likely named in recognition of the Brewster family. All of the university residences have names linked to the Rocky Mountains.

Brisebois Drive   Brentwood, N.W.

Inspector Ephrem Brisebois (1850-90) was one of the first nine men recruited when the North-West Mounted Police was formed in 1873 and was its first French-Canadian officer. In 1875, as commander of F Troop, he and 50 men were sent to establish a new fort between Fort Macleod and the Red Deer River country. The site chosen was at the confluence of the Bow and Swift (now Elbow) Rivers. The fort was finished by Christmas of 1875. The commander unofficially named it Fort Brisebois but his superiors did not concur. There was general dissatisfaction with Brisebois' leadership and the winter had been marked by a mutiny and poor morale. Early in 1876, Col. Macleod suggested that it be named Fort Calgary. Brisebois resigned from the force later in 1876. He became active in Conservative politics in Quebec and then spent the rest of his life as the land registrar at Minnedosa, Manitoba.

Brockington Road   Brentwood, N.W.

The street was probably named for Welsh-born Leonard Brockington, a Calgary lawyer who, by the end of his lifetime had become an internationally known figure. He was The City of Calgary's solicitor from 1921 to 1935, became first chairman of the Canadian Broadcasting Corporation in 1936 and worked as a special advisor to Prime Minister

MacKenzie King during World War II. He also worked as a specialist in arbitration of labour disputes and was Rector of Queen's University. Brockington was a personal friend of Sir Winston Churchill and an honourary Sarcee chief. He considered his most significant honour to be the conferral of an honourary degree from the University of Wales in 1953 on the same day as Queen Elizabeth II. Brockington died in 1966.

Brown Crescent   Brentwood, N.W.

Brown was fairly common name in southern Alberta. The street may have been named after John George (Kootenai) Brown (1839-1916), an English frontiersman who was the first settler in the Waterton Lakes area in 1868. When Waterton Lakes became a National Park, Brown became acting superintendent. He was the first to search for oil in Alberta, but was only interested in finding enough to lubricate the axles on his wagon. Brown received his nickname (originally spelled Kootenaie) because he traded with and spoke the language of the Kootenaie Indians. There were three people with the surname Brown who served as alderman in Calgary: Henry Brown from 1895 to 1897, Magnus Brown from 1910 to 1912, and George M. Brown from 1937 to 1949. Two other Browns were prominent in Calgary history. One was Robert A. Brown, who was superintendent of the Calgary electric light and street railway departments from 1911 to 1937 and who discovered oil in Turner Valley in 1936. The other was Maurice L. Brown, founder of the Community Chest in Calgary (now the United Way), national director of the Air Cadet League of Canada and director of the Calgary Stampede.

Buchanan Elementary School   3717 Centre Street N.

Dr. Frank G. Buchanan was a provincial inspector of schools and served as both assistant superintendent and later as superintendent of schools in Calgary from 1935 until retiring in 1951. His years as superintendent saw the introduction of junior high and composite high schools into the Calgary school system. Dr. Buchanan died in Vancouver in 1981 at the age of 95.

Buckmaster Park   16 Street and 22 Avenue S.W.

Found in the subdivision of Bankview, the park is named after Dr. Harvey Buckmaster and his wife, Margaret. Planning for the park began in the mid-1980s when a study of inner-city communities indicated that Bankview had the least park space per resident of any city community. The community association felt that the park should be named after the Buckmasters in recognition of almost two decades of volunteer work in the community. They helped create a redevelopment plan for Bankview and worked for many years to get more park area for the community. Dr. Buckmaster was a nuclear scientist at the University of Calgary before his retirement in 1992. Buckmaster Park opened in 1990.

Bulyea Crescent, etc.   Brentwood, N.W.

These streets were probably named for George Hedley Vickers Bulyea (1859-1926), who was Alberta's first lieutenant-governor from 1905 to 1915.

Burbank Crescent, etc.   **Burns Industrial Park, S.E.**

This name was possibly chosen for Burbank, Alberta, a former CNR station which is thought to have been named after a famous American horticulturist, Luthur Burbank.

Burgess Drive   **Brentwood, N.W.**

Burgess Drive may have been named after A.M. Burgess, deputy minister of the interior for the federal government. In 1884, he was partially responsible, along with Colonel James Walker, for Calgary's acquisition of a fairground on the site of what is now Victoria Park.

Burns Avenue   **S.E.**

This street is named after Patrick Burns (see Big Four Building).

Burns Building   **237 - 8 Avenue S.E.**

Named after Patrick Burns (see Big Four Building), the Burns Building was built between 1911 and 1912 as an office building and retail market for the P. Burns Company. Originally planned and built as a two-storey structure, it was actually completed with six storeys in 1913, making it one of the finest buildings of its size in western Canada. It had a marble-columned interior and was equipped with the finest in lighting, heating and ventilation systems. The building was slated for demolition in the early 1980s, but due to public demand it was restored and renovated at a cost of $4.5 million. It reopened in 1984 and now houses a restaurant and office and retail space.

Burns Stadium   **Corner of Crowchild Trail and 24 Street N.W.**

Burns Stadium is the home of the Triple A Pacific Coast League Calgary Cannons Baseball Club. Originally called Foothills Stadium, it was refurbished when it was leased by the Cannons in 1985 and was expanded in 1987. It was further expanded in 1994-95, and re-named Burns Stadium. The name is in recognition of the support given to the Cannons by Burns Foods Ltd. (see Big Four Building). The Cannons, in turn, made a substantial contribution to little league baseball in Calgary and agreed to maintain the little league field which lies north of Burns Stadium.

Burnsland   **S.E.**

The areas of Burns Avenue and Burnsland are both named after Senator Patrick Burns (see Big Four Building). His stock yards and meat packing plant were both located in Burnsland.

Butler Crescent   **Brentwood, N.W.**

E.N. Butler was a prominent architect in Calgary from 1906 to 1912. He supervised the completion of city hall and the construction of numerous other city buildings, including the Grain Exchange - the first building in Calgary to be built of reinforced concrete.

CALGARY
C

Cabot Street   **Mount Royal, S.W.**

John Cabot was an Anglo-Italian explorer whose arrival in North America in 1497 was the first recorded landfall on the continent since the Vikings. He was attempting to reach Asia by sailing west across the Atlantic. Cabot Street was named in his honour.

Cadogan Road   **Cambrian Heights, N.W.**

The origins of this street name are unclear. Cadogan is a Welsh family name which was originally Cadugan, after Cadugan of the Battle Axe, who was chief of the Cadugan clan during the rule of one of the earliest Princes of Wales. Most of the streets in Cambrian Heights have names of British origin. There is also an Alberta town called Cadogan.

Calf Robe Bridge   **Bow River on Deerfoot Trail S.E.**

Ben Calf Robe (1890-1979), a Blackfoot Indian, was well known in Calgary as an enthusiastic supporter of the Calgary Stampede. He was present at the first Calgary Stampede in 1912 and when it became an annual event in 1923, he was hired as interpreter, a job he held until 1940. His buffalo and wolf design tepee was a familiar sight at the Stampede's Indian village. Calf Robe was an original organizer of the Indian Association of Alberta and served as a councillor of his tribe. As a farmer, he was the first Indian to use horses to break land on the Blackfoot reserve. It is appropriate that this particular bridge, built in 1980, was named after Ben Calf Robe for at that time he was the last surviving native student of the Calgary Indian Industrial School (1896-1907), which was demolished to make way for the Deerfoot Trail.

Cameron Avenue   **Mount Royal, S.W.**

There were two important Camerons in Calgary's history and this street was probably named after one of them. One was Arthur L. Cameron, alderman in 1894 and from 1896 to 1897, and mayor in 1898 and from 1907 to 1908. The other was John McKinley

Cameron, K.C. (1879-1943), a lawyer from Nova Scotia who came to Calgary in 1911. He became one of the city's best known defense counsels.

Canmore Road   **Banff Trail, N.W.**

As with most of the named streets in this area, Canmore Road is named for one of the places through which the old Banff highway passed. The town of Canmore was the first divisional point for the CPR west of Calgary Its name was probably chosen by Donald Smith, Lord Strathcona (see Strathcona Street) in honour of Malcolm III of Scotland who defeated Macbeth and reigned from 1057 to 1093. Malcolm was known as Canmore, a Gaelic word which means "big head" or "height."

Cannon Road   **Charleswood Heights, N.W.**

It is possible that Cannon Road was named for Raymond A. Cannon, a lawyer who came to Calgary in 1929. He served as a separate school trustee in 1940 and as superintendent of separate schools from 1941 to 1964.

Cappy Smart Elementary School   **5808 Madigan Drive N.E.**

Cappy Smart Elementary School was named after James "Cappy" Smart (1865-1939), one of Calgary's most colourful historical figures who was a firefighter and later became fire chief. Smart joined the fire department in 1885 and was elected chief in 1898. He served as chief for 25 years, retiring in 1933. He was a very civic-minded man and was president of numerous city associations as well as provincial, national and international firemen's associations. His lively personality and sense of humor were well known to both Calgarians and others from far afield. He was one of the first fire chiefs in Canada to motorize his fire brigade. That, and his efforts to educate the public about fire prevention, were perhaps his greatest contributions.

Captain John Palliser Elementary School   **1484 Northmount Drive N.W.**

John Palliser was the leader of a scientific expedition which explored Western Canada from the Cypress Hills to the Rocky Mountains between 1857 and 1860. The expedition was sponsored by the Royal Geographic Society and the Imperial Government and its purpose was to map the area, to consider its agricultural and mineral potential, and to consider transportation routes. Palliser concluded that the area of southeast Alberta and southwest Saskatchewan, now known as Palliser's triangle, would never be arable agricultural land as it was too dry. Without the introduction of dry farming methods and irrigation, this may have been true. Palliser's report became an important document and drew much attention to the Canadian West.

Cardell Street   **Renfrew (St. George's Heights), N.E.**

There was a Cardell family, involved with the railroad, who moved to Canmore in 1884 and later to Calgary. It is possible that Cardell Street is named after them.

Cardinal Newman Elementary/Junior High School   16210 Lake McKenzie Boulevard S.E.

John Henry Newman (1801-1890) was the son of an English banker who was raised as an Anglican. His religious studies eventually led to his conversion to the Catholic faith. When he became a priest, this action was looked upon with suspicion by many Catholics and with anger and hatred by many of his former faith. He finally felt this burden lifted from him when he was made a cardinal by Pope Leo XIII in 1879.

Cardston Crescent   Foothills Estates, N.W.

Cardston Crescent is likely named after the town of Cardston in southern Alberta. It was founded in 1887 by Charles Ora Card and is the site of Canada's only Mormon temple.

Carleton Street   Mount Royal, S.W.

Sir Guy Carleton was governor of Quebec from 1768 to 1778 and from 1785 to 1795. He oversaw the passing of the Quebec Act in 1774, and administered it so that it supported the Roman Catholic church and retained French civil law, steps which created the Quebec of today.

Carlyle Road   Chinook Park, S.W.

William Levi Carlyle was manager of the EP Ranch near High River for 23 years. The ranch was owned from 1919 to 1960 by HRH Edward, Prince of Wales, later to become the Duke of Windsor. He named the ranch EP after his signature, which meant Edward Prince. Carlyle managed the ranch until 1942, when he left to become the managing director of the Hillcrest-Mowhawk Collieries at Bellevue, Alberta. He had been director and vice-president of the collieries since 1922. Carlyle retired to Calgary in 1943 and died here in 1955 at the age of 85.

Carmangay Crescent   Collingwood, N.W.

Carmangay is a village northwest of Lethbridge. Its name is a combination of Charles W. Carman owner of the land, and his wife Gertrude, whose maiden-name was Gay. This street may be named for the village.

Carnarvon Way   Cambrian Heights, N.W.

Carnarvon Way was probably named either for Carnarvon, Wales or Lord Carnarvon (1831-90), secretary of state for the colonies. Carnavon introduced the British North America Act to the British House of Commons in 1867. Most of the streets in Cambrian Heights have names that are British in origin.

Carney Road   Charleswood, N.W.

Carney Road may have been named for Augustus Carney, who came to Calgary with his wife Ann in 1883, and farmed the land where the Union Cemetery now stands. He was active in civic affairs and was elected as the first president of the Calgary Agricultural Society in 1884.

Carroll Place   1540 Northmount Drive N.W.

A senior citizens' home, Carroll Place is named for Most Rev. Francis P. Carroll. (See Bishop Carroll High School.)

Carter Place   602 - 1 Street S.E.

Carter Place, a senior citizens' apartment complex, was built as a joint venture of the Anglican Cathedral Church of the Redeemer and St. Francis Catholic Church, on land owned by the Anglican church. The two churches created the Trinity Foundation to oversee its construction. David Carter, who was Dean of the Anglican Diocese of Calgary and Rector of the Anglican Cathedral Church of the Redeemer when the project began, was president of the Trinity Foundation board of directors from 1974 to 1977. Carter Place opened in 1977. David Carter became a Conservative MLA in 1979 and served as Speaker of the House for the Alberta Legislature from 1986 to 1993.

Cartier Street   Mount Royal, S.W.

Jacques Cartier (1491-1557) explored the St. Lawrence region on three voyages between 1534 and 1542. On his voyage in 1535 he christened a small part of Quebec "Canada," which often leads to his being credited with the discovery of Canada. He charted the St. Lawrence River in 1535, enabling France to settle the North American interior.

Casson Green   University of Calgary Family Housing, N.W.

When the University of Calgary Board of Governors named the streets of the family housing units, they wanted to honour famous Canadians. They chose the names of five of Canada's Group of Seven artists, as they felt that using the names from one group of people would create a sense of unity for the project. Founded in 1920, the Group of Seven described themselves as modern artists and worked together primarily as landscape artists until they disbanded in 1933. A.J. Casson joined the group in 1926 after the resignation of Franz Johnston, one of the original members.

Catherine Nichols Gunn Elementary School   6625 - 4 Street N.E.

Catherine Nichols Gunn was a nurse who came to Calgary in 1913 and went overseas during World War I to join the nursing staff at a hospital in France. In 1922 she joined The City health department as a school nurse in the north section of the city. She remained for 30 years, retiring in 1952. Catherine Nichols Gunn died in 1979 at the age of 92. The school opened in 1972.

Cavanaugh Place   Foothills Estates, N.W.

Cavanaugh Place may have been named for Lt.-Col. Lawrence Arthur Cavanaugh who came to Calgary in 1912 and founded an auto supply company. He began his army career in 1924 and served as commander of the Calgary Regiment from 1934 to 1938, when he transferred to the officers' reserve. He retired from the military in 1946 and was awarded the Jubilee Medal and Coronation Medal. Cavanaugh served as a director of the Canadian

National Institute for the Blind, as president of the Calgary Board of Trade and as a governor of the board of directors of the Stampeder Football Club.

Cayuga Crescent, etc.   **Foothills Estates, N.W.**

As with the streets in neighbouring Collingwood and Charleswood, all the streets in Foothills Estates begin with "C." Where possible, The City likes developers to use names of well-known Calgarians, Aboriginal people, or names denoting geographical features. The Cayugas are one of six Aboriginal tribes whose names grace the streets of the area, the others being Cherokee, Chippewa, Cheyenne, Chilcotin and Comanche. The Cayugas are one of the five nations of the Iroquois confederacy and lived along the shores of Cayuga Lake in New York.

Cecil Swanson Elementary School   **4820 Rundlewood Drive N.E.**

Cecil Swanson was born in London, England in 1889 and came to Canada in 1908. He was ordained as an Anglican priest in 1912 and spent the next five years as a missionary in the Yukon. He laboured in a number of parishes including St. Stephen's Church in Calgary from 1932 to 1940. Swanson retired in Calgary in 1960 as archdeacon emeritus. He then served as honourary associate rector of Christ Anglican Church in Calgary. He held honourary degrees from St. John's, Winnipeg, Wycliffe College, Toronto, the Theological College of British Columbia, and the University of Calgary. He was made a member of the Order of Canada in 1978. Archdeacon Swanson, known affectionately to many as "Swanny," was well known for his wit and was a popular speaker. He died in 1984.

Champlain Street   **Mount Royal, S.W.**

Samuel de Champlain was a French explorer whose discoveries along the St. Lawrence between 1603 and 1615 led him to be called the "father of New France." He was appointed governor of New France in 1633 and held the position until his death in 1635.

Charles Avenue   **Brittania, S.W.**

This street is named after Charles, the first son of Queen Elizabeth and Prince Phillip, and heir to the British throne, who was a child when this subdivision was developed. (See Anne Avenue.)

Cherokee Drive, etc.   **Charleswood, N.W.**

The Cherokee are a branch of the Iroquois family found in the southeastern United States. (See Cayuga Crescent.)

Cheyenne Crescent   **Foothills Estates, N.W.**

The Cheyenne are part of the Iroquois family inhabiting the western American plains. (See Cayuga Crescent.)

Chief Crowfoot Centre   2634 - 12 Avenue N.W.

Crowfoot was a Blackfoot chief who was known as a peacemaker and wise leader. He negotiated Treaty No. 7 in 1877 in which his tribe surrendered its hunting grounds in exchange for a reserve and other benefits, and which kept his people at peace during the Riel Rebellion of 1885. He was honoured by the prime minister and made a triumphant tour of eastern Canada the following year. When he died in 1890, Crowfoot had become one of the country's most famous chiefs. The Chief Crowfoot Centre, used since 1985 as the police department training centre, was originally an elementary school opened in 1955. Present at the official opening were Chief Joe Crowfoot, grandson of Chief Crowfoot, and, quite by coincidence, Chief Dame Flora MacLeod, 28th chief of the MacLeod clan of Scotland. One of her clansmen, Col. J.F. Macleod, was the NWMP negotiator of Treaty No. 7.

Chief Justice Milvain Elementary School   3428 - 42 Street N.E.

James Valentine Hogarth Milvain, QC, LLD, was a Calgary lawyer who, in 1955, argued and won the last Canadian case heard by the British courts (the judicial committee of the Privy Council in London). His career as a lawyer spanned 32 years. In 1959 he was appointed to the Supreme Court of Alberta and became Chief Justice of the trial division in 1968, Alberta's first native born chief justice. He resigned in 1979 at the mandatory retirement age of 75. He was named an officer of the Order of Canada in 1987 and was awarded an honourary doctorate by the University of Calgary in 1989. Chief Justice J.V.H. Milvain School opened in 1982.

Chilcotin Road   Charleswood, N.W.

The Chilcotin are a tribe of Athapaskan-speaking Indians in northern British Columbia. There is also a river in British Columbia called the Chilcotin. (See Cayuga Crescent.)

Child Avenue   Renfrew (St. George's Heights), N.E.

Child Avenue may have been named for James T. Child, partner with James L. Wilson in the architectural firm of Child and Wilson. The firm was engaged as town engineers from 1890 until 1894. James T. Child served as city engineer again from 1908 to 1912.

Chippendale Drive   Charleswood, N.W.

Thomas Chippendale (1718-1779) was an English furniture designer and cabinet maker. He was one of the first to develop a specific English style in furniture. This may be the origin of the street's name.

Chippewa Road   Foothills Estates, N.W.

The Chippewa are a tribe of Indians in eastern Canada and the United States. They are also known as the Ojibwas. (See Cayuga Crescent.)

Chris Akkerman Elementary School   **5004 Marbank Drive N.E.**

Chris Johannus Akkerman (1900-1978) came to Canada from Holland in 1920. He farmed in various Alberta locations before moving to Forest Lawn in 1939. He owned a trailer manufacturing plant, was one of the first manufacturers of overhead truck campers and held the patent on one of the first tent trailers. He was elected to the Forest Lawn town council in 1954 and served in that position until 1958 when he was appointed acting mayor. He was elected mayor the following year and held that position until mid-December 1961, when he and the town's six councillors resigned from council in protest of Forest Lawn's annexation by The City of Calgary.

Christie Park   **S.W.**

The subdivision of Christie Park is named after the family who were the original owners of the property. The first of the family to come to Calgary was Nat Christie. The rest of the family followed in 1902, after the death of their father. The three Christie brothers, Nat, Mack and Stoney, operated the Ontario Laundry from 1903 to 1949, the biggest laundry operation west of Winnipeg, and Calgary's first power laundry. The family was well known in Calgary for their community involvement. (See Nat Christie Park.)

Christie Road   **Charleswood, N.W.**

Christie Road is likely named for the Christie family, prominent early Calgarians. (See Christie Park and Nat Christie Park.)

Christine Meikle School (Special Ed)   **64 - 12 Street N.E.**

Christine Meikle was born in Scotland and came to Calgary at age 17. After two years of nurses' training in Montreal she returned to Calgary to be married. In 1946 she gave birth to twins, one of whom was mentally handicapped. She sought out a facility to educate her handicapped son, but found that nothing was available. In 1952 she founded and became first president of the Calgary Association for Retarded Children, now called the Calgary Association for the Mentally Handicapped, and opened a school in her home. The Kitchen School, as it was called, met there for the first year. It then moved to a series of locations before the opening, in 1958, of the Christine Meikle School, with Mrs. Meikle as principal. It was the first school for the mentally handicapped in Canada built with government funds. In 1969, the Calgary Public School Board took over operation of the school and its partner, the Emily Follensbee School. In 1973, the year of her retirement at age 65, Mrs. Meikle received an honourary doctorate from the University of Calgary and was awarded the Order of Canada.

Churchill Drive   **Chinook Park, S.W.**

Churchill Drive is likely named for British prime minister and statesman Sir Winston Churchill. (See Sir Winston Churchill High School.)

Clarence Block   120 to 124 - 8 Avenue S.W.

The Clarence Block, built in 1899, is the second building by this name to stand on this spot. The first, built in 1890, was destroyed by fire. It was owned by Senator James Lougheed and was named after one of his sons. It housed the law office of Lougheed and his partner, R.B. Bennett, who later became Canada's Prime Minister. A building named after a second son, Norman, stands next door to the west. Unfortunately, most of the original character of the building has been covered by modern renovations.

Clarence Sansom Community School   5840 - 24 Avenue N.E.

Clarence Sansom was born in New Brunswick and came to Calgary following his graduation from the University of New Brunswick in 1907. He was appointed principal of Central School, later re-named James Short School. He moved to Medicine Hat the following year and was a principal, inspector and superintendent in various districts until transferring to the staff of the Calgary Normal School in 1919. He began his graduate studies in 1920 and received his Ph.D. from the University of Chicago. He returned to the staff of the Calgary Normal School in 1927 where he had a long and distinguished career. He intended to retire in 1945, but when the normal school became the Faculty of Education he remained on staff, becoming director of the faculty in 1946. He retired in 1947 and died in Calgary in 1950.

Clarke Road   Chinook Park, S.W.

Simon John Clarke (1852-1918) was a member of Calgary's first town council, elected in December 1884. The first meeting of council was held in his saloon. A year later, Clarke was sentenced to six months at hard labour for refusing to allow a search of his "temperance" saloon for intoxicants. In later years, he served as a City commissioner and as superintendent of Banff National Park.

Clem Gardner Elementary School   5915 Lewis Drive S.W.

Born in 1885 in Manitoba, Clem Gardner moved to the Calgary area with his family at age one. They settled on a farm at Pirmez Creek, west of Calgary, where Gardner grew up to be a first-class horseman. He won the all-round Canadian cowboy championship at the first Calgary Stampede in 1912 and continued to compete in rodeos at the Stampede and around the country until well past the age of 50. His ranch survived the lean years of post-World War I and the Depression to prosper after World War II and into the 1950s. For many years he supplied rodeo stock to the Calgary Stampede. Gardner never retired and was in the saddle, checking cattle, on the day he died in 1963. The Boy Scouts' camp near Bragg Creek, Camp Gardner, is also named after him.

Cleveland Crescent   Manchester, S.E.

Cleveland Crescent may have been named for Wellington Cleveland, who came to Calgary in 1888 and later farmed north of the city for 30 years before his death in 1933. It may also have been named for Cleveland, Ohio, or U.S. President Grover Cleveland.

Cochrane Road   **Banff Trail, N.W.**

As with most of the named streets in this area, Cochrane Road is named for one of the areas through which the old Banff highway passed. Cochrane is a town west of Calgary which is named for the Cochrane Ranch, established there by Senator H.M. Cochrane of Hillhurst, Quebec. The ranch house erected there in 1881 was the first in Alberta.

Colborne Crescent   **Mount Royal, S.W.**

Sir John Colborne was lieutenant-governor of Upper Canada from 1828 to 1834 and acted as governor-general from November 1838 to December 1839. He then returned to Britain where he became 1st Baron Seaton and, as a member of the House of Lords, spoke against the act to unite the two Canadas.

Coleman Road   **Charleswood Heights, N.W.**

This street was possibly named for Coleman, Alberta which had been named by A.C. Flummerfelt, president of the International Coal and Coke Company, after his youngest daughter. There also was a John Coleman, a former mountie, who hauled freight between Edmonton and Calgary during the town's earliest years.

Coleridge Crescent, etc.   **Cambrian Heights, N.W.**

These streets were likely named for British Romantic poet, Samuel Taylor Coleridge. (See Carnarvon Way.)

Collicutt Street   **Chinook Park, S.W.**

This street was likely named for Frank Collicutt, a pioneer Alberta rancher who worked as a cowboy for Pat Burns. His own herd at the Willow Spring Ranch won many awards and Collicutt was president of many cattle breeders' associations. In 1955, at the age of 79, he received an honourary doctorate from the University of Alberta. Collicutt was also an honourary life director of the Calgary Exhibition and Stampede.

Colonel Baker Place   **Riverside, N.E.**

Originally, the address of the Canadian National Institute for the Blind (CNIB) was 1216 Memorial Drive N.E. When the northeast leg of the LRT was built, the Memorial Drive access was cut off and the small street behind the building became its new access. The street was re-named Col. Baker Place in honour of Lieutenant-Colonel Edwin A. Baker (1893-1968), one of a group of seven blind and sighted people who founded the CNIB in 1918. In 1914, Baker became the first Canadian officer to lose his sight during World War I. Baker served on the CNIB National Council until 1920, when he resigned to join the staff. He served as general secretary and later as managing director. He held both positions until 1962 when, upon retiring, he was re-elected to the council. He was serving as CNIB honourary president at the time of his death.

Colonel Belcher Hospital   1213 - 4 Street S.W.

Robert Belcher (1849-1919) was born in England and served in the British army for five years before coming to Canada and becoming a constable in the first contingent of the North West Mounted Police. He served in various western posts, including having command of the Chilkoot Pass and Dawson City detachments during the Yukon's gold rush years of 1897 to 1899. He was one of the Canadian officers sent to represent the country at Queen Victoria's diamond jubilee in 1897. Belcher served in the South African War as a volunteer in the Strathcona's Horse Regiment. He left the Mounted Police in 1908 and soon accepted command of the 19th Alberta Dragoons, with rank of lieutenant-colonel. He held this rank until 1912, when he was promoted to command of the 5th Cavalry Brigade. He saw some service in Europe during World War I and was in charge of a military information bureau when he died unexpectedly in 1919.

Colonel Irvine Junior High School   412 Northmount Drive N.W.

Acheson Gosford Irvine (1837-1916) was commissioned in the Canadian militia in 1864. He served during the Red River Rebellion of 1869-70 as major, 2nd Battalion, Quebec Rifles. He remained in Manitoba after the collapse of the rebellion as commander of the occupying forces. He retired from the army with the rank of lieutenant-colonel in 1875 and the same year was appointed assistant commissioner of the North West Mounted Police. He was commissioner from 1880 to 1886, commanding the force during the Riel Rebellion of 1885. From his retirement from the force in 1886, until shortly before his death, he was warden of the Stony Mountain Penitentiary. He received the Imperial Service Order in 1902.

Colonel J. Fred Scott Elementary School   171 Whitehorn Road N.E.

J. Fred Scott (1892-1982) served in the Canadian army during World War I. During the inter-war years, he practiced law but remained in the military and joined the peacetime cavalry eventually serving as commander of the 15th Alberta Light Horse Regiment. He commanded the Calgary Highlanders Regiment from the time of its mobilization shortly before the beginning of World War II. He returned to Canada in 1942 to teach the senior officers' course at the Royal Military College in Kingston, Ontario. He founded Canada's first battle drill school at Vernon, B.C., for which he received the Order of the British Empire. He returned to Calgary in 1945 where he practised law for over 30 years.

Colonel James Walker Building   SAIT Campus, N.W.

Colonel James Walker (1847-1936) was an officer with the North West Mounted Police who served at a number of western posts including Calgary. He left the force in 1881 to work for the Cochrane Ranch and later opened Bow River Mills. When the CPR reached Calgary in 1883, he supplied it with timber for railway ties and bridges. He also acquired land in what is now east Calgary where he built and sold a large number of houses at fair prices in spite of the possibility of making large profits through speculation. Thus this area of the city developed rapidly. In 1884 Walker was chosen as head of a committee of six citizens whose task was to oversee the affairs of the community until Calgary could be incorporated as a town. He was first president of the Calgary Exhibition, organized the first school and was a school board trustee for 15 years. In 1975 Col. Walker was named Calgary's Citizen of the Century. When he died, he was the last surviving officer of the first detachment of the NWMP to come west in 1874. The Colonel James Walker Building, built in 1985, was named in recognition of the fact that the site of SAIT's first classes was Colonel James Walker School. SAIT held its classes at the school from 1916 to 1922. (See Colonel James Walker Park.)

Colonel James Walker Park   **114 - 7 Avenue S.W.**

The elevated park next to the Alberta Government Telephones Building is named after Colonel James Walker, a veteran mounted policeman and the owner and operator of Calgary's first telephone switchboard in 1885. The park was opened in 1973 on top of a two-storey building as a public service by AGT, which wanted to give Calgarians another green space in the concrete core of the city. A special feature of the park is the gargoyle statues that were salvaged when the old Greyhound Building was demolished. (See Colonel James Walker Building.)

Colonel Macleod Elementary/Junior High School   **1610 - 6 Street N.E.**

Colonel James Farquharson Macleod was born on the Isle of Skye in 1836. As assistant commissioner of the NWMP, he led a contingent from Manitoba to Southern Alberta where he commanded the forces which established Fort Macleod and Fort Calgary. He became commissioner in 1876 and a year later he negotiated Treaty No. 7 with the Stoney, Blackfoot, Blood, Peigan and Sarcee Indians. He resigned in 1880 to become magistrate and judge of the North-West Territories. He transferred to Calgary shortly before his death in 1894 and lived at 1011 - 4 Avenue S.W. Present at the official opening of the school in 1956 was his son, Norman.

Colonel Sanders Elementary School   **226 Northmount Drive N.W.**

Gilbert Edward Sanders was born in British Columbia in 1863. He was educated in England and at the age of 17 returned to Canada to attend the Royal Military College at Kingston. He began his career with the NWMP in 1884 and was posted to Fort Macleod and Calgary. He also served during the Riel Rebellion, the Boer War and World War I, earning the Distinguished Service Order during the Boer War and other decorations in World War I. He was police magistrate in Calgary from 1919 to 1932, and although somewhat eccentric, he earned a reputation for dispensing justice fairly. He helped to found the city Corps of Commissionaires. Col. Sanders died in the Colonel Belcher Hospital in 1955.

Colonel Walker Community School   **1921 - 9 Avenue S.E.**

This school is named after Colonel James Walker. (See Colonel James Walker Building and Colonel James Walker Park.)

Columbia Place   **Foothills Estates, N.W.**

The dictionary defines Columbia as "poetically, the personification of the United States of America" (after Christopher Columbus). In Canada, the name is also found in British Columbia and the Columbia River.

Comanche Road   **Foothills Estates, N.W.**

The Comanches are a branch of the Iroquois family who lived in what is now Kansas but later were moved to a reservation in Oklahoma. (See Cayuga Crescent.)

Congregation House of Jacob Mikveh Israel Synagogue   1613 - 92 Avenue S.W.

Jacob Diamond, a liquor merchant in Calgary from 1889 until his retirement in 1913, is considered to be the first Jewish resident of Alberta. Born in Russia with the surname Tabarisky, he emigrated to Canada in 1879 and came to Calgary with his wife Rachel in 1888. The city's first synagogue was founded by Diamond and was thus referred to as the "House of Jacob." In the mid-1980s, the Koschitzky foundation donated money to help rebuild the synagogue and thus the name was changed to also honour Israel Koschitzky. The word Mikvah means "hope."

Connaught Community School   **1121 - 12 Avenue S.W.**

When the cornerstone of this school was laid in 1912, among those present was His Royal Highness, the Duke of Connaught, after whom the building was named. The duke was the third son of Queen Victoria and served as governor general of Canada from 1911 to 1916. Today Connaught School is Calgary's second oldest school still in operation. The community of Connaught is also named in honour of the Duke and Connaught Drive in Cambrian Heights is likely named after him. (See Carnarvon Way.)

Conrad Crescent, etc.   **Charleswood Heights, N.W.**

These streets may have been named for Charles E. Conrad or his older brother, William G. Conrad, partners in the Montana trading firm of I.G. Baker and Company (see Baker Crescent). Charles became Canadian manager of the firm after the arrival of the NWMP and opened stores in Calgary and Fort Macleod. William looked after the financial side of the business and in 1882 bought 20 acres of Calgary land near the present Victoria Park for the firm. The CPR named an Alberta station after Charles and in 1884 the name Conrad was given to a downtown street by the CPR. This changed to 7th Street East in 1904. The Charleswood streets may have been named in recognition of the earlier Conrad Street.

Constable Place, etc.   **Foothills Estates, N.W.**

These streets may take their name from English landscape artist John Constable (1776-1837), regarded as one of England's foremost painters.

Constance Avenue   **Ramsay, S.W.**

See Aberta Avenue.

Copithorne Road   **Foothills Estates, N.W.**

This street was probably named for the Copithorne family who are well-known in the Calgary area. The original Alberta Copithornes were Irish brothers John and Richard, who settled in the Jumping Pound area in 1887. The family continued to ranch around the Calgary area throughout the next century and many Copithornes also lived in Calgary: Clarence Copithorne served as provincial highways minister; W.H. (Danny) Copithorne was president of the Calgary Exhibition and Stampede from 1992 to 1994; and Ken Copithorne is Reform Party MP for the Macleod riding as of April 1995.

Copot Arena   **6715 Centre Street N.W.**

The Thornhill Arena was re-named by The City in 1990 to honour Murray T. Copot for his 35-year involvement in community work and minor hockey. He began coaching minor hockey in 1955 and served as president of the Calgary Minor Hockey Association and the Alberta Amateur Hockey Association. In 1993, he was named Calgary's 40th Sportsman of the Year by the Calgary Booster Club.

Cornell Place, etc.   **Cambrian Heights, N.W.**

Most of the streets in Cambrian Heights have been given names that are British in origin. However, no British "Cornell" could be found. It is possible that the streets were named for Cornell University, located in Ithaca, New York, which was named after its founder and chief benefactor, Ezra Cornell.

Cornwallis Drive   **Cambrian Heights, N.W.**

This street is likely named for General Charles Cornwallis, commander of the British forces during the American Revolution who surrendered to the American troops at Yorktown. It could also be named for Edward Cornwallis, a British soldier who became the governor of Nova Scotia and founded the city of Halifax.

Coronado Place   **Monterey Park, N.E.**

Francisco Vasquez de Coronado (1500-54) was a Spanish explorer of the American southwest. In keeping with the California theme of Monterey Park, the name Coronado Place reflects California's Spanish history. There is a community called Coronado in California located on an island in San Diego Bay.

Cosgrove Street   **Foothills Estates, N.W.**

Dick Cosgrove, a rancher from Rosebud, northeast of Calgary, won 10 world championships at the Calgary Stampede chuckwagon races before he retired in 1947 to become the Stampede's Arena Director. It is likely that Cosgrove Street was named in his honour.

Costello Boulevard   **Christie Park, S.W.**

Dr. Michael C. Costello, mayor of Calgary from 1915 to 1918, came from a true Calgary pioneer family. His father, John William Costello (1842-1918), immigrated to Canada from Ireland around 1860. He arrived in Calgary from Ontario in 1883. His wife Elizabeth and their five children arrived that August aboard the first passenger train to Calgary. A sixth child, Elizabeth Lillian (Lil), was born in December 1883, the first white girl born in Calgary. Her cousin, John Calgary Costello, born a month earlier, was the first white boy. In 1884 John Costello was hired to be the first teacher at Calgary's first school, held in Boynton Hall. He taught for only a year, but later was a member of the school board. His son Thomas was one of Calgary's first doctors. The Costello family was also instrumental in the building of the Holy Cross Hospital.

Craig Road   **Chinook Park, S.W.**

Craig Road may have been named for George W. Craig, City engineer from 1913 to 1923. Or it may have been named for pioneer James Craig (1851-1938), who came to Alberta in 1884. In his early years in Alberta, James ran the Alberta Hotel in Calgary. He was The City's immigration officer from 1910 until his retirement in 1920.

Craigie Hall   **University of Calgary, N.W.**

Originally called Calgary Hall, Craigie Hall was re-named in memory of Peter Craigie, University of Calgary Vice President (Academic), who died of injuries suffered in an automobile accident in 1985. A theological scholar, Dr. Craigie joined the university in 1974 as a professor of religious studies. He became Dean of Humanities in 1979 and was appointed Vice President (Academic) in June 1985. He was named best instructor on the arts and science faculty in 1974 and given a superior teacher award by students in 1976. In 1981 he received an honourary Doctor of Divinity degree from St. Stephen's College, University of Alberta.

Crawford Road   **Charleswood Heights, N.W.**

Crawford Road may have been named after a number of notable Calgarians. Thomas H. Crawford was a city alderman from 1922 to 1925. Arthur Crawford was an early rancher in the Cochrane area. George L. Crawford, QC, is a prominent Calgarian who has served on the board of directors of numerous businesses and charities, including as president of the Calgary Exhibition and Stampede. William A. Crawford-Frost, and his son, Arthur, were both Calgarians of note. Crawford-Frost Sr. retired to Calgary in 1937 and was known internationally as an inventor, writer and thinker. Arthur Crawford-Frost, one of Canada's most successful Hereford breeders, served as president of the Calgary Exhibition and Stampede from 1953 to 1956.

Cromwell Avenue   **Foothills Estates, N.W.**

Cromwell Avenue may take its name from Oliver Cromwell (1599-1658), a prominent figure in British history. Cromwell was instrumental in the beheading of Charles I, and served with the title of Lord Protector of Great Britain and Ireland in the first parliament after the death of Charles.

Cross Bow Auxiliary Hospital   1011 Centre Avenue E.

This hospital was named after two prominent Calgary doctors. Dr. Wallace Warren Cross (1887-1973) was a Social Credit member of the Alberta Legislature from 1935 to 1957. He was Minister of Health from 1935 to 1957 and Minister of Health and Public Welfare from 1944 to 1953. Dr. Malcolm Ross Bow was appointed Deputy Minister of Public Health and chairman of the Provincial Board of Health of Alberta in 1927. When the auxiliary hospital opened in 1961, the names of Drs. Cross and Bow were combined in a title suggested by the Minister of Health, Dr. J. Donovan Ross.

Cross Crescent   Chinook Park, S.W.

This street got its name from the Cross family. Alfred Ernest Cross was a prominent Alberta businessman and rancher (see A.E. Cross Junior High School.) His son Jim was part of the group who owned the Chinook Polo Grounds, which stood where the subdivision of Chinook Park now stands. The street was given its name by City council in 1960.

Cross House Garden Cafe   1240 - 8 Avenue S.E.

The Cross House Garden Cafe is housed in the original Calgary home of pioneer Alfred Ernest Cross (see A.E. Cross Junior High School) and is designated as a Provincial Historic Resource.

Crowchild Trail   N.W. - S.W.

David Crowchild (1899-1982) was a Sarcee Indian who, after his election as chief in 1946, became a well-known figure in Calgary. He and his wife Daisy were fully committed to fostering good relations between the city and his tribe. He was a longtime secretary of the Indian Association of Alberta and an active supporter of several Calgary organizations, such as the Calgary Pioneers and Old Timers Association. He was a close friend of John Laurie (see John Laurie Boulevard), who he took as his adopted brother. Chief Crowchild was present at the opening of the road and bridge bearing his name in March 1971.

Crowfoot Way, etc.   Crowchild Ranch, N.W.

All of the five streets surrounding the Crowfoot Plaza shopping area are named after Crowfoot, chief of the Blackfoot tribe. He negotiated Treaty No. 7 in 1877, and is one of only two chiefs who signed the treaty to be honoured by having a city street or structure named after him, the other being Bearspaw, a Stoney chief. (See Chief Crowfoot Centre.)

Currie Barracks   S.W.

Sir Arthur William Currie was the first full general in the Canadian army. He was promoted to commander of the Canadian Corps in 1917, its first Canadian commander. He is best known for his planning and leadership during the last one hundred days of World War I. He achieved the rank of general when he returned to Canada in 1919.

Cushing Bridge   **Bow River at 17 Avenue S.E.**

W.H. Cushing (1852-1934) came to Calgary from Ontario in 1883. He opened a sash and door factory which developed into one of the leading businesses in the province. He served six terms as alderman, beginning in 1890, and was mayor from 1899 to 1900. When Alberta became a province in 1905, Cushing was elected to the legislature as a Liberal member and appointed Minister of Public Works. He resigned that post in 1910 and became the first chairman of Mount Royal College's Board of Governors, a post which he retained until 1926 when he became honourary chairman. When Cushing died, his political, educational and philanthropic endeavours were remembered by Calgarians, as flags throughout the city flew at half-mast for a day.

CALGARY

D

Dalhousie   **N.W.**

Chosen by The City, the name Dalhousie was selected for its Canadian flavor after George Ramsay, the 9th Earl of Dalhousie and governor-in-chief of British North America from 1820 to 1828. As lieutenant-governor of Nova Scotia, he founded Dalhousie University in Halifax in 1818. Dalhousie was also the name of one of the Turner Valley oilfields.

David D. Oughton Elementary School   **1511 - 34 Street S.E.**

David D. Oughton (1862-1956) came to Calgary from Ontario via Michigan in 1902. He began farming east of Calgary and was one of the first trustees of the Bow River School Board which opened its first school in January 1906. Of the first six students, two were Oughton's sons. Oughton continued his interest in education and donated the land upon which stands the school which bears his name. The David D. Oughton School opened in 1953.

David Shelton Park   **Dovercrest Way and Dovercrest Road S.E.**

David Shelton was a 10-year-old boy who died after being struck by lightning while riding his bicycle in August 1990. When a mural was being painted on the wall of a nursery school that adjoins a tot lot, his friends asked the artist if he might include a picture of David. Community members took up the idea of remembering him in some way and petitioned city council to name the tot lot after him. Approval was given in December 1990.

David Thompson Elementary School   **9320 Arbour Crescent S.E.**

A cartographer and surveyor who worked for both the Hudson's Bay Company and the North West Company, David Thompson is believed to be the first white man to visit the site of what would eventually become Calgary. In 1787, he wintered in a Peigan Indian encampment on the Highwood River south of Calgary. In 1801 he made a second visit to the area and crossed the Bow River near Calgary on his way southwest to the Highwood River.

Deane House   806 - 9 Avenue S.E.

This historic house was built in 1906 for NWMP Superintendent Richard Burton Deane. Deane was born in India in 1848 and came to Canada in 1882. In 1883 he was appointed an inspector for the NWMP, promoted to superintendent in 1884, and was the officer directly in charge of Louis Riel during Riel's imprisonment in Regina. Deane came to Calgary as commanding officer in 1906, hoping to enjoy his new home with his wife Martha. However, she died before the house was finished. He retired and left for England following the death of his second wife, Mary, in 1914, and died in Italy in 1930. Deane was the first policeman in the West to apply available scientific knowledge to solving crimes. The house was designated a Registered Historic Resource in 1978 and was restored and opened to the public as a tea house in 1985.

Deerfoot Trail   N.E. - S.E.

Deerfoot was a Blackfoot who became famous as a long distance runner in the 1880s. His real name was Api-kai-ees in Blackfoot, or "Scabby Dried Meat." The name Deerfoot was coined by his promoters in 1886 when he defeated a number of professional runners in Calgary. He became famous locally but his victories were also reported in American sporting journals. His running career ended shortly after he was cheated in a fixed race and he spent the rest of his life in and out of jail. He died of tuberculosis in the Mounted Police infirmary in Calgary in 1897.

Devenish Design Centre   908-17 Avenue S.W.

The Devenish Design Centre began as a 57-suite executive apartment building constructed of Alberta sandstone and brick by real estate promoter Oscar G. Devenish in 1911. When it was built, it was one of the most up-to-date apartment complexes in western Canada, featuring 2 1/2 metre-wide hallways and trim of wood and brass. Each suite was equipped with disappearing wall beds so that a bedroom by night became a living room by day. It was declared an historic site by the provincial government in 1981 and converted into a retail centre in 1982 by interior designer Christopher Maier.

Doll Block   116 - 8 Avenue S.E.

The Doll Block was built by L.H. Doll in 1907 to house his jewellery store. It was a beautiful building, with the first and second floor windows of bevelled glass. Today it is notable for the third storey bay window, with leaded glass and sandstone trim.

Don Bosco Elementary/Junior High School   13615 Deer Ridge Drive S.E.

Saint John Bosco (1815-88) was an Italian priest. He was born John Bosco but is commonly known as Don Bosco, "don" being Italian for "father." Ordained in 1841, his primary interest was the welfare of children. He helped to revolutionize how children were taught; the three tenets of his philosophy of teaching being kindness, reason and religion. While he is not well known here, his methods of teaching have been widely used in Europe.

Dorchester Avenue **Mount Royal, S.W.**

After Sir Guy Carleton (see Carleton Street) began his second term as governor of Quebec in 1886, he was given the title Baron Dorchester.

Douglas Harkness Community School **6203 - 24 Avenue N.E.**

Douglas Scott Harkness was the first Calgary teacher to enlist in the armed forces when war was declared in 1939. He ended the war as a lieutenant-colonel in the Royal Canadian Artillery, having received the George Medal for courage, gallantry and devotion to duty. He began his political career when elected to the House of Commons as a Progressive Conservative member for Calgary in 1945. He resigned from the cabinet in 1963 and retired from political life in 1972, having served three different Calgary ridings. He later served as chairman of the board of governors of the Glenbow-Alberta Institute.

Dover **S.E.**

Although the subdivision was probably named after the city on England's south coast, it would have been appropriate had it been named after Mary Dover (1905-94), a prominent Calgary native. Daughter of Calgary pioneer A.E. Cross and granddaughter of Col. James Macleod, Dover was an outstanding Calgarian in her own right. In 1946 she received the Order of the British Empire for her service in the Canadian Women's Army Corps during World War II. She served as a city alderman from 1949 to 1953 and from 1956 to 1960, and was on many civic committees. She was active as a Stampede volunteer and in many areas of Calgary society. Besides her O.B.E., Dover was also a recipient of an honourary doctorate from the University of Calgary and the Order of Canada. In 1960, Dover moved to a country home near Millarville which she named Oksi Hill, Blackfoot for "a good place."

Dr. Carl Safran Centre (Continuing Ed.) **930 - 13 Avenue S.W.**

Carl Safran trained as a teacher after serving in World War II, receiving his doctorate in education in 1951. His main interest was in special education. He worked in the guidance and special education department of the Calgary school board for 11 years before becoming its superintendent in 1966. He was chief superintendent from 1972 to 1977.

Dr. Carpenter Circle **SAIT Campus, N.W.**

In 1985 most of the streets on the SAIT campus were named after the institution's early principals. Dr. William Carpenter served as principal from 1924 to 1941.

Dr. E.P. Scarlett High School **220 Canterbury Drive S.W.**

Dr. Earle Parkhill Scarlett (1896-1982) spent his early years in Ontario and did post-graduate work in the United States. He came to Calgary in 1930 on the advice of Prime Minister R.B. Bennett, who had once lived in the city. Scarlett was an academic who became involved in public speaking on a variety of topics throughout the city and prompted the formation of the Medical Historical Society in 1932. He was head of the Calgary Associate Clinic and contributed frequently to medical journals. His literary and artistic interests were broad in scope and his activities in these areas made him well-known. He was honoured with election to the University of Alberta board of governors and was chancellor of the university from 1952 to 1958.

Dr. E.W. Coffin Elementary School   5615 Barrett Drive N.W.

Ernest W. Coffin was born on Prince Edward Island in 1875, received his Bachelor of Arts degree from Dalhousie University in 1902, and then worked as headmaster of a school in the West Indies. He earned his Ph.D. in 1909 and joined the staff of the Calgary Normal School the same year. He was principal of the school from 1911 until his retirement in 1940, at which time he was senior normal school principal in Alberta. Aside from his work as principal, he served on curriculum committees for the Department of Education. He was a member of the University of Alberta Senate for many years and was active in home and school associations. He died in 1963. Dr. E.W. Coffin School was built in 1967 and re-opened in 1975 following a fire in 1974.

Dr. Gladys McKelvie Egbert Community School   6003 Madigan Drive N.E.

Born in Winnipeg, Gladys McKelvie moved to Calgary as a child. At age 12, she became the first Canadian to win a three-year scholarship to the Royal Academy of Music in London. In 1938 she was made a Fellow of the Royal Academy, one of only 150 people world-wide. A pianist who could have had a concert career, she chose to teach instead and was regarded as one of the world's best music teachers. She taught both students and teachers in Calgary from 1922 until her death in 1968. Her husband, Gordon Egbert, was a justice of the Supreme Court of Alberta.

Dr. Gordon Higgins Junior High School   155 Rundlehill Drive N.E.

Gordon Higgins came to Calgary from New Brunswick in 1954 to practice internal medicine, specializing in diabetes. He founded the Calgary camp for diabetic children, one of the first in Canada, the same year. He was a member of the Calgary board of health from 1965 to 1967, a public school board trustee from 1963 to 1970, and a member of the Senate of the University of Calgary from 1972 to 1975. As a school board trustee, he was a strong supporter of school library programs. Dr. Higgins retired to Nova Scotia. Four memorial awards, presented annually in the form of Sir Winston Churchill commemorative coins, were made to the school system by Dr. Higgins. The school named in his honour opened in 1977 as an elementary school and after renovations, was redesignated as a junior high school in 1982.

Dr. Gordon Townsend School   Alberta Children's Hospital, 1820 Richmond Road S.W.

Gordon Townsend was born in New Brunswick then moved with his family to Saskatchewan. He received his M.D. from McGill University and did post-graduate work in Michigan and Montreal. He came to Calgary in 1940 to aid and eventually take over the practice of Dr. R.B. Deane, Alberta's first bone specialist. He worked with children at the Alberta Children's Hospital, became chief of staff at the Rockyview Hospital, was a consultant at the Foothills Hospital, and an honourary member of the medical staff at the Holy Cross and General hospitals. He even, on occasion, set broken bones of animals, including a thoroughbred colt, which went on to win races.

Dr. J.K. Mulloy Elementary School   7740 - 10 Street N.W.

Dr. John (Jack) Knox Mulloy was born in Ontario, came to Calgary in 1910 and attended the Calgary Normal School. He worked as a teacher in the Stettler area for a brief time before entering the faculty of medicine at the University of Alberta in 1912. His education was interrupted by a stint in the military during World War I and he did not graduate from McGill University until 1921. He then practised medicine in Cardston for 17 years. In 1940 he became medical superintendent of the Colonel Belcher Hospital, where he remained until his retirement in 1956. He was a public school board trustee in Calgary from 1953 to 1963. He was the first to x-ray Aboriginal people for tuberculosis and assisted in the establishment of TB sanitaria in Alberta. He was made an honourary chief of the Blood tribe in 1963 and given the name of Running Rabbit. Dr. Mulloy died in 1969 at the age of 76. The school that bears his name opened in 1970.

Dr. Norman Bethune Elementary School   315 - 86 Avenue S.E.

Born in Ontario in 1890, Norman Bethune served with the Canadian army, the British navy and the Canadian Flying Corps in World War I, then worked as a doctor in Toronto, Detroit and Montreal. During the Depression he began to question the medical profession and eventually society as a whole, which he felt was not taking proper care of the poor. He turned to socialism and went to Spain in 1936 to serve with the Loyalists during the Spanish Civil War. He went to China in 1938 and worked with the 8th Route Army, which eventually brought Mao Tse Tung to power. A national hero in China, he died from an infection caused when he cut his finger during surgery in 1939. As a doctor, Norman Bethune improved the techniques of thoracic surgery, developed several new surgical instruments and established the first mobile blood transfusion unit to operate in the front lines of battle. The school opened in 1972, closed in 1984 and re-opened in 1994.

Dr. Oakley School   3904 - 20 Street S.W.

Geraldine Oakley was born in Stratford, Ontario and received her medical training at the University of Toronto. She came to Calgary in 1912 and in 1917 was appointed medical health officer for Calgary schools. When the school clinics merged with The City of Calgary Health Department in 1935, she became assistant medical officer in charge of schools, a position she held until her death in 1948. Dr. Oakley Elementary/Junior High School opened in 1959. During the 1980s it operated as the Oakley Centre for gifted and talented students and now deals primarily with children with learning difficulties.

Dr. Vernon Fanning Extended Care Centre   **722 - 16 Avenue N.E.**

Born and educated in Alberta, Dr. Vernon Fanning (1932-72) practiced medicine in Calgary for 14 years. He founded both the Acadia-Fairview and Willow Park clinics and joined the medical staff of Calgary Auxiliary Hospital and Nursing Home District No. 7 (now known as Carewest) in 1962. After serving in a variety of offices including vice-president, he was elected president of the medical staff in 1969. He then served as past-president from December 1970 until his death in a plane crash at Ghost Lake in June 1972. He served as chairman of the committee which planned the facility named in his memory.

Durham Avenue   **Mount Royal, S.W.**

John George Lambton, 1st Earl of Durham, was the governor-in-chief and lord high commissioner to British North America for five months during 1838. It was his responsibility to prepare a report on the rebellions in Canada during 1837. His famous Durham Report led to the uniting of Upper and Lower Canada. Lord Durham, broken in health, returned to England and died there in 1840.

CALGARY

E.H. Crandell Building
SAIT Campus, N.W.

Edward Henry Crandell came to Calgary in 1899 from Brampton, Ontario, where he had been mayor. He began his career here in the life insurance business but became interested in minerals and oil. He was president of the Discovery Oil Company which drilled near Waterton Lakes. In 1905 he opened a brick plant on the western outskirts of Calgary which he operated for 30 years. The Great Depression led to its closing. Today the name of his plant, Brickburn, can be seen along the railroad tracks in Edworthy Park. Crandell also owned the Calgary Tent and Mattress Company, served on the Calgary school board from 1905 to 1907, served as school board chairman in 1907, sat on city council from 1913 to 1915, and contested a seat for the provincial legislature for the Conservative party. Mount Crandell in Waterton Lakes National Park also bears his name. Crandell died in Calgary in 1944. He was chosen to be honoured by SAIT because the opening of his brick and sandstone company changed the face of Calgary, since now buildings could be built of brick as well as wood and sandstone.

Earl Grey Elementary School
845 Hillcrest Avenue S.W.

Albert Henry George Grey (1851-1917) grew up at Windsor Castle and was private secretary to Prince Albert and Queen Victoria. In 1894 he succeeded his uncle as the fourth Earl Grey. He was a politician and diplomat who served as governor general of Canada from 1904 to 1911 at the time when Alberta and Saskatchewan became provinces. He was very popular with Canadians and was one of the few governors general of that time to complete a full term. In 1909 he donated the Grey Cup, the trophy which is now awarded annually to the Canadian Football League champions. The original Earl Grey School was built in 1912 and a gymnasium was added in 1953. The original was demolished and a new school built in 1968. (Also, Earl Grey Crescent in Mount Royal.)

Earl Grey Golf Club   **6540 - 20 Street S.W.**

The golf course was founded in 1919 by Major Duncan Stewart, a Calgary lawyer. Originally five-holes in length, and later expanded to nine, it was laid out on the south side of Earl Grey School, and thus received its name. With city expansion, the course moved in 1930 and again in 1933 to its present site beside the Glenmore Reservoir.

Ed Corbett Park   **Renfrew Drive and Russett Road N.E.**

Ed Corbett, "Mr. Fastball," was active for many years in the Calgary and District Softball Association and served as president of both the Alberta and Canadian softball associations. He founded the Alberta Umpires Association and was named to the Alberta Sports Hall of Fame in 1966.

Edinburgh Road   **Brittania, S.W.**

The official title of Prince Phillip, husband of Queen Elizabeth II, is the Duke of Edinburgh. Edinburgh is also a city in Scotland whose name means "fortification at a place called Eidyn." (See Anne Avenue.)

Edison Drive   **Elboya, S.W.**

Edison Drive was probably named for Thomas Alva Edison, inventor of the telephone. It may, however, have been named for the Edison district, north of Edmonton.

Edwards Place Senior Citizens Apartments   **344 - 9 Avenue S.E.**

Operated by the provincial department of Municipal Affairs, the senior citizens' complex is named after Robert C. "Bob" Edwards, editor of the Calgary Eye Opener and a member of the Alberta legislature from 1921 until his death in 1922. (See Bob Edwards Elementary School.)

Edworthy Park   **5050 Spruce Drive S.W.**

In the early 1880s this area was part of the Cochrane Ranch. In 1883 Thomas Edworthy received homestead title to the land which he called the Shaganappi Ranch. He irrigated the land with water from a small spring on the hillside to run a market garden. He also branched into ranching and operated a sandstone quarry. Edworthy died of typhoid in 1904. In 1960 the ranch was purchased by The City of Calgary for the proposed Shaganappi Trail extension and as a possible site for a sewage treatment plant. A park was created in the interim. Edworthy Park has become a popular community park. The original Edworthy log cabin has been incorporated into a nearby home. Edworthy Park was once a favorite campsite for Aboriginal people and Metis.

Elizabeth Road   **Brittania, S.W.**

Elizabeth Road is named for Queen Elizabeth II. (See Anne Avenue.)

Elizabeth Street   **Ramsay, S.E.**

See Alberta Avenue.

Elveden Centre   **717-7 Avenue S.W.**

Considered Calgary's first real skyscraper, the 20-storey Elveden House (pronounced "Eldon House") was built in 1957 by the Guinness organization. British in origin (makers of world famous Guinness stout), the multi-million dollar company has projects world-wide. When Elveden House was built, it was twice as high as any building in Calgary. City council had previously decided that building height should be restricted to 12 storeys, so the Guinness firm had to win a battle with City Hall before beginning construction. The cornerstone was laid by 23-year-old Arthur Francis Benjamin Guinness, Viscount Elveden. In 1964 a third tower was built and named Guinness House. Today the three-tower complex is known as Elveden Centre.

Emily Follensbee Centre   **5139 - 14 Street S.W.**

Emily Follensbee was the first elected secretary of the Calgary Association for Retarded Children, now the Calgary Association for the Mentally Handicapped, when it was formed by Christine Meikle in 1952. When Meikle's home school opened in 1953, Follensbee became a regular volunteer. She was elected secretary of the Provincial Association for the Mentally Handicapped in 1954 and became a staff member at the Calgary School for Retarded Children, now the Christine Meikle School. The Emily Follensbee School opened in 1964 and came under the operation of the public school board in 1969. An expanded facility, the Emily Follensbee Centre, opened in 1984.

Ernest Manning High School   **3600 - 16 Avenue S.W.**

Ernest Charles Manning came to Calgary from Saskatchewan to attend the Prophetic Bible Institute where he came under the influence of William Aberhart. He began his political career in the newly organized Social Credit party and was elected to office in 1935. He became provincial secretary and upon Aberhart's death in 1943, succeeded him as premier of Alberta. During his 25 years of leadership, Manning had one of the most effective governments in Canada. When he retired in 1968, it had wiped out the provincial debt and had implemented some of the most progressive legislation in the nation. Manning was appointed to the Canadian Senate in 1970. He was named a Companion of the Order of Canada in 1969 and was the first recipient of Alberta's Order of Excellence in 1979.

Ernest Morrow Junior High School   **1212 - 47 Street S.E.**

Ernest Morrow was born in his family home in Forest Lawn in 1913. When Forest Lawn was incorporated in 1940 he was elected to the village's first council and school board. He became mayor in 1941 and served in that office for seven years. The school, named in his honour for services to the community, is located on land which he once farmed. Ernest Morrow died in 1986.

Ernie Starr Arena   **4808 - 14 Avenue S.E.**

Ernie Starr was born in Wales and served with the British Army medical corps during World War I. He came to Calgary in 1920 and worked as an orderly at the Calgary General Hospital. He left in 1931 to found Starr's Ambulance Service, which he owned and operated until 1946. It eventually became part of a City-owned service. Mr. Starr served on the Calgary school board in 1933 and 1934 and as an alderman from 1940 to 1947, 1949 to 1950, 1952 to 1957 and 1958 to 1966. In recognition of his more than a quarter century of public service, The City opened the Ernie Starr Arena in 1969. Starr died in Vancouver in 1981 at the age of 91.

Ethel M. Johnson Elementary School   **255 Sackville Drive S.W.**

Ethel M. Johnson came to Calgary from Ontario in 1918. She served on the Calgary public school board for 12 years, rarely missing a meeting, as well as numerous committees of the Alberta School Trustees Association. She was active in politics, serving as president of the Alberta Women's Liberal Association, and in community and church affairs. She was on the executive of the Scarboro Community Association and president of the United Church Women. She was a life member of the Calgary Council of Women and of the Calgary Women's Liberal Association. Johnson died in 1966.

Eugene Coste Building   **SAIT Campus, N.W.**

When the buildings at SAIT were re-named in 1985, the Power House was given a most appropriate name - the Eugene Coste Building. Eugene Coste (1859-1940), a geologist and engineer, discovered gas at Bow Island in 1908. He created the Canadian Western Natural Gas, Heat, Light and Power Company, and brought gas to Calgary through a 171-mile long pipeline. Coste was president and managing director of the company from 1912 to 1921. The Coste mansion in Mount Royal (2208 Amherst Street S.W.) was considered one of the finest in the city. It was the home of the Calgary Allied Arts Council from 1946 to 1959 and is now a private residence. Eugene Coste Elementary School is also named in his honour.

Eugene Coste Elementary School   **10 Hillgrove Crescent S.W.**

See Eugene Coste Building.

Exshaw Road   **Banff Trail, N.W.**

As with most of the names streets in this area, Exshaw is named after one of the places through which the old Banff highway passed. The hamlet of Exshaw was named after a director of the cement company which operated there, who was a son-in-law of Sir Sanford Fleming.

F.E. Osborne Junior High School   **5315 Varsity Drive N.W.**

Frederick Ernest Osborne (1878-1948) was born in Ontario and came to Calgary in 1905. That year, he opened Osborne's, a book, stationery and school supply store. It became one of the leading stores of its kind in western Canada and was in operation until it was destroyed by fire in 1966. Osborne served as an alderman from 1919 to 1920 and from 1923 to 1924, and was mayor of Calgary from 1927 to 1929. He was president of the Calgary Board of Trade, served in various capacities with the Rotary Club, and was a member of the University of Alberta Board of Governors. In 1947 he received an honourary doctorate from the University of Alberta and was made an officer of the Order of the British Empire in recognition of his chairmanship for Alberta of the national war finance committee during World War II.

Father Damien Elementary School   **2619 - 28 Street S.E.**

Damien de Veuster was born in Belgium in 1840. He travelled to Hawaii as a missionary brother in 1863, was ordained as a priest in 1867 and was then sent to the leper colony on the island of Molokai. Originally he was to serve there for three months as part of a rotation with other priests, but he stayed for 16 years, providing the lepers with food, clothing, medical care, education and spiritual comfort. He eventually contracted leprosy himself and died in 1889. He was declared Venerable in 1977 and was beatified on May 15, 1994. He is now referred to as Blessed Damien de Veuster.

Father David Bauer Arena   **2424 University Drive N.W.**

Father David Bauer is a name synonymous with amateur hockey in Canada. He played hockey as a child and coached as an adult. After becoming a priest with the Basilian Fathers in 1953, he continued encouraging his players to combine a formal education with their love of hockey. He was instrumental in the formation of a national amateur hockey team in 1962, coached the Canadian team at the 1964 Olympics, and led the 1968 team to a bronze medal. Father Bauer continues to teach at St. Mark's College,

University of British Columbia, and has aided in the development of amateur hockey in Japan and Austria.

Father Doucet Elementary School   65 Shannon Drive S.W.

Leon Doucet (1847-1942) came to Canada from France in 1868 and was ordained as a priest in 1870. He began his work as a priest around the St. Albert area, nursing the Aboriginal people through an epidemic of smallpox which almost cost him his life. He then came south to work with the Blackfoot tribe near Calgary, to whom he devoted a large part of his life. He was the first white man to settle in Calgary and personally greeted the NWMP when they crossed the Bow River to establish the fort. When a chapel was built at Fort Calgary in 1877, he was the first priest in charge. He later carried on the work of Father Lacombe at Midnapore, retiring shortly before his death.

Father James Whelihan Elementary School   70 Sunmills Drive S.E.

James Austin Whelihan was ordained as a Catholic priest in 1930. He came to Calgary in 1933 as a member of the Basilian Fathers, a teaching order. He was well known in Calgary for his football coaching skill, taking his St. Mary's High School team to the provincial high school championships three times. He coached junior football, in and out of school, in Calgary for 37 years, until his retirement in 1969. He also coached other high school sports and became director of athletics for Calgary separate schools. In 1954 he was named the Calgary Booster Club's Sportsman of the Year, and in 1985 was inducted into the Order of Canada. Father James Whelihan died in 1986 at the age of 84, the last of the original Basilian Fathers to come to Calgary.

Father Lacombe Senior High School   3615 Radcliffe Drive S.E.

Albert Lacombe (1827-1916) spent nearly 70 years as an Oblate priest among the Aboriginal people in Western Canada. He was one of the most beloved missionaries of his time, serving faithfully at various parishes and often travelling to eastern Canada and Europe to raise funds for the missions. He founded the community of St. Albert and the Lacombe Home in Midnapore, now the Lacombe Centre, where he resided at the time of his death.

Father Scollen Elementary/Junior High School   6839 Temple Drive N.E.

Born in County Fermagh, Ireland, Constantine Scollen (1841-1902) was the first English-speaking missionary in Alberta. Arriving in St. Albert in 1862, Father Scollen was originally a lay missionary. He made perpetual vows with the Oblate order in 1865 and was ordained as a priest in 1873. Father Scollen was the first teacher in Alberta and the first missionary to what is today the Diocese of Calgary. Working closely with Father Lacombe and Bishop Grandin, he served as Superior of the Southern Missions from 1873 to 1882. He was a witness to Treaty No. 6 with the Cree and Treaty No. 7 with the Blackfoot. Father Scollen is credited with the founding of Our Lady of Peace, the first chapel in the Calgary Diocese. Today, a cairn, built in part with stones from the original chimney, stands on the site of the chapel, located along Highway 22. A plaque commemorates Father Scollen's work.

Fisher Road, etc.   **Fairview Industrial Park, S.E.**

These streets may have been named for one of a number of Fishers associated with the Calgary area. Willliam Chauncey Fisher, a prominent Calgary lawyer, came to Calgary in 1912 to article with the law firm of Lougheed, Bennett and Company. He was active in the oil industry at the time when oil was discovered in Turner Valley, founded Ducks Unlimited and was active in the Alberta Fish and Game Association. He won the Julian Crandall Award for Conservation and died in 1979 at the age of 92. Charles W. Fisher of Cochrane was the first speaker of the Alberta legislature, occupying the speaker's chair from 1905, when Alberta became a province, until his death in 1919. August O. Fisher came to Calgary in 1899. He managed a ranch at Morley for David McDougall until 1902 when he moved to the Calgary area to farm the land on which the airport now stands. He was also involved in Calgary real estate until 1916 when he moved to Didsbury. He retired to Calgary in 1937.

Fleetwood Drive   **Fairview, S.E.**

Fleetwood Drive may take its name from the town of Fleetwood, Lancashire on the west coast of England. The town was founded by Sir Peter Fleetwood in the early 19th Century.

Flowerdew Avenue   **Harvey Barracks, S.W.**

Gordon Muriel Flowerdew was born in England in 1885 and when he came to Canada in 1903 he lived at Duck Lake, Saskatchewan. He enlisted in the British Columbia Horse Regiment in 1914 and later transferred to the Lord Strathcona's Horse (Royal Canadians) Regiment. During the battle at Morieul Wood, France on March 30, 1918, Lieutenant Flowerdew led his cavalry troops in a charge against two enemy lines, breaking them and sending the Germans into retreat. This was one of the last cavalry charges in history. Flowerdew died of wounds suffered during the attack and was posthumously awarded the Victoria Cross.

Foster Road   **Fairview, S.E.**

Foster Road may have been named for Ellen Foster, co-founder of Calgary's SPCA. At age six Foster came from Lancashire, England to homestead in Alberta with her family. Her experiences of watching the cruel trapping methods in the frontier West began her life-long concern for animals. With the help of others, she founded a local chapter of the SPCA in 1922. She was honoured by the society in 1965, when a new wing of the SPCA building, designed to house more than 100 cats, was named the Ellen Foster wing. She died in 1975.

Fountain Road   **Fairview, S.E.**

Fountain Road may have been named for H. Harold Fountain, who came to Calgary in 1931. He taught at Western Canada High School for 27 years before becoming the first principal of Henry Wise Wood High School in 1959. He remained there until his retirement in 1968. Fountain died in 1993 at the age of 88.

Fowler Drive
SAIT Campus, N.W.

The streets and buildings on the SAIT campus were re-named in 1985. Most of the streets received the name of one of SAIT's early principals. Dr. James F. Fowler served as principal from 1941 to 1952. (See James Fowler High School.)

Francis Klein Centre
240 - 92 Avenue N.E.

The Most Rev. Francis J. Klein (1911-1968) became the 5th Bishop of Calgary on April 25, 1967, Previously, he was the Bishop of Saskatoon. After nine months and nine days as Bishop of Calgary, he died of a heart attack following surgery. The Francis Klein Centre, a senior citizens' lodge, is sponsored jointly by St. Cecilia's Church and the Knights of Columbus. When the centre was being planned, the name was chosen after a contest was held among the members of St. Cecilia's board and the Knights of Columbus.

Frank McCool Arena
1900 Lake Bonavista Drive S.E.

Native Calgarian Frank McCool had a very short, but distinguished career as a goalie with the Toronto Maple Leafs. Winner of the outstanding rookie award in 1944, he also played in the 1945 Stanley Cup. While pursuing his hockey dream, he started a newspaper career as a part-time newsboy. When injuries forced him to retire from hockey, he became assistant publisher and general manager of the Calgary Albertan. He also served as president of the Calgary Tourist and Convention Association and was very active in many aspects of minor sports in Calgary until his death in 1974 at age 54.

Franklin Drive
Fairview, S.E.

This street was possibly named after Sir John Franklin. (See Sir John Franklin Junior High School.)

Franklin Industrial Park
N.E.

Franklin Park industrial area and Franklin Park Mall are named for Franklin Reuben, owner of the land on which they are built.

Fraser Road
Fairview, S.E.

There are a number of Frasers after whom this street might have been named. One possibility is Simon Fraser (see Simon Fraser Junior High School). It may also be named for G.L. Fraser, a fruit-seller in Calgary, who owned the city's first sports establishment, Fraser's Rink, built in the early 1880s. It was popular as both an ice and roller rink and for the competitive events held there. A third possibility is Angus Fraser, second manager of the Hudson's Bay Company in Calgary. John A.W. Fraser was a Calgary pioneer who owned many properties on Royal and 17th Avenues and ranched on his XC Ranch at Jumping Pound. And another pioneer, James Fraser, came to Calgary in 1885 and joined the police force when it was formed. After he resigned from the police force he joined the sheriff's office as a bailiff, a position he held until he retired in 1929.

Fred Parker Elementary School   360 - 94 Avenue S.E.

Fred Parker was born in England and attended an art and technical school before coming to Canada in 1910. He worked in Edmonton as a draftsman then came to Calgary in 1914 as an instructor in industrial arts at the Calgary Normal School. Parker left in 1917 to take charge of the manual training department of the high schools of Calgary. He then decided to work as an academic teacher and was appointed vice-principal of Stanley Jones School and later principal of Earl Grey School. He served as president of the Alberta Teachers' Provincial Alliance in the 1920s and as a city alderman from 1948 to 1956.

Fred Seymour Elementary School   809 Willingdon Boulevard S.E.

Fred Seymour (1913-1968) began his teaching career in 1933. He taught in Calgary for 11 years and in 1951 was appointed to the staff of the Alberta Teachers' Association (ATA) as assistant executive secretary. He had previously served terms as a Calgary representative and president of the association. He worked for the ATA for 15 years, as editor of the magazine, head of the teacher welfare department and on numerous committees. In 1968 he was given the position of executive secretary, but died before he could assume his new post.

Frobisher Boulevard   Fairview, S.E.

Frobisher Boulevard is likely named for Sir Martin Frobisher (1539-1594), a British mariner who, in his search for the Northwest Passage in 1576, discovered Frobisher Bay on Baffin Island. He was knighted in 1588 for heroism in the British battle against the Spanish armada.

Frontenac Avenue   Mount Royal, S.W.

Louis de Buade, Compte de Frontenac (1622-1698) was governor general of New France from 1672 to 1682 and from 1689 to 1698. He expanded the territory under French control in spite of orders to confine French settlement to areas with maritime access to France. Most of the streets in Mount Royal were named for people who had a significant role in the history of French Canada.

Fulham Street   Fairview, S.E.

Better known as Mother Fulham, Caroline Fulham was a well-known character in early Calgary. She was a woman who raised pigs, had a caustic tongue, a penchant for drink, poor personal hygiene, and who was often in trouble with her neighbors. One story about Fulham occurred when she was treated for a sore ankle. The doctor took one look at her dirty leg and exclaimed, "By George, I'll bet a dollar that there's not another leg in Calgary as dirty as that one!" Mother Fulham took the bet, removed her other stocking and claimed her prize. The street may take its name from this colourful Calgary citizen, or from Fulham, a district in London, England, whose name means "Fulla's riverside grassland."

Fullerton Road   **Fairview, S.E.**

This street may have been named for Ernest Redpath "Jake" Fullerton (1882-1975), who was born in Marquette, Michigan, while his family was en route to Calgary. They arrived by covered wagon in 1883. Fullerton became one of the Calgary area's best known heavyweight boxers and was the light-heavyweight boxing champion of western Canada. He began ranching in the Bragg Creek area in 1913 and made Bragg Creek a summer resort area when he opened an eight-sided dance hall at his dude ranch. Fullerton retired to Victoria in 1945 and returned to Calgary in 1967.

CALGARY

G

G.W. Skene Elementary School   6226 Penbrooke Drive S.E.

George Wilbert Skene, Q.C. (1883-1979) came to Calgary in 1911 to article with a local law firm after graduating from Queen's University. He practiced law in Calgary for 78 years until his death at age 96. He was a member of the Calgary Public School Board from 1940 to 1944 and its chairman in 1944. He was counsel for the board for 29 years. He also served as president of the Calgary Bar Association and chairman of the board for Wood's Christian Home.

Gainsborough Drive, etc.   Glamorgan, S.W.

These streets may have been named for Thomas Gainsborough (1727-1778), one of the first, and perhaps greatest, of what is known as the English School of painters. He is best known for his landscapes and also painted portraits. Or the streets may get their name from the market town of Gainborough in the county of Lincolnshire, England.

Galbraith Drive   Glamorgan, S.W.

Galbraith Drive may have been named for Daniel Harcourt Galbraith (1878-1868), a well-known poet who lived in the town of Bowness. Galbraith came to Alberta from Ontario in 1903 and farmed near Vulcan. In the early 1930s he lost his sight, but continued farming until he retired to Bowness in 1945. He was a member of the Alberta Legislature from 1921 to 1930, made a fellow of the London Royal Society of Arts in 1955 and had many of his poems published.

Garden Crescent   Glencoe, S.W.

James H. Garden arrived in Calgary from Scotland in 1902. He was a carpenter by trade and was well known in Calgary as a general contractor. He served three terms as alderman between 1910 and 1923 and was elected City commissioner in 1915. He served in Europe during World War I, returning to Calgary in 1919. After his last term as alderman he continued to be active in city politics and sat on the board of governors of Mount

Royal College until his death in 1945. Garden's brother, Rev. John H. Garden (1893-1961), was the first student to enroll at Mount Royal College when it was established in 1910. He served on the college's board of governors from 1926 to 1961 and was its second principal from 1942 to 1958 following George Kerby, its founder. He was the honourary principal from 1959 to 1961. John H. Garden Meditation Centre at Mount Royal College is named in his honour.

Garrick Drive   Glamorgan, S.W.

Garrick Drive may have been named for Joseph Garrick, one of the earliest pioneer ranchers in southern Alberta, who came to Alberta in the 1880s and ranched near Taber until his death in 1934.

General DeLalanne Lodge   113 - 18A Street N.W.

Brigadier James Arthur DeLalanne, C.B.E., M.C. with bar, E.D., D.A., C.A. was born in the Westmount district of Montreal in 1897. He earned his B.A. at McGill University in 1919 and as a civilian worked as a chartered accountant. He joined the Princess Patricia's Canadian Light Infantry (PPCLI) in 1915 and served as a captain in the 60th Canadian Infantry during World War I. He was wounded three times and received the Military Cross with bar. He began World War II as a major, became a brigadier in 1943, and a vice adjutant general in 1945. After the war he resumed his career as an accountant and served in numerous capacities including: president of the PPCLI Association; chairman of the board of governors of the Canadian Corps of Commissionaires, Montreal Division; chairman of the Canadian Paraplegic Association, Quebec Division; mayor of Westmount; governor of McGill University and numerous Canadian Legion activities. Brigadier DeLalanne died in 1988. The General DeLalanne Lodge for senior citizens is run by the Canadian Legion, North Calgary Branch.

George Blundun Arena   5020 - 26 Avenue S.W.

George John Blundun (1907-1988), Calgary's 1985 Sportsman Of the Year and a member of the Alberta Sports Hall of Fame, began his love affair with skating as a hockey player. However, after moving to Calgary in 1945 and watching figure skating at the Glencoe Club in 1950, he switched to ice dancing. He was forced to give up skating himself after a fall in 1960, but he went on to judge world championship competitions, wrote a handbook on ice dancing and served as president of the Canadian Figure Skating Association. He was also responsible for the beginning of Skate Canada, first held in Calgary in 1973. He came out of retirement to chair the figure skating committees for Skate Canada in 1987 and the 1988 Olympics.

George Boyak Nursing Home   1203 Centre Avenue N.E.

George Boyak (1895-1990) was a farmer from the Rockyview district who was well known for his many years of public service. One of his many projects was to assist in the creation of the Calgary Rural Hospital District. District taxpayers received basic hospital care for one dollar a day with the provincial and municipal governments paying the balance. The district's first nursing home built in the 1960s was named after him.

George C. King Home   807 - 6 Street S.E.

George Clift King was a constable in the NWMP in 1875 when "F" troop was sent to the Red Deer River to meet Sir Selby Smyth, head of the Canadian Militia. The troop then turned south to build a post at the confluence of the Bow and Elbow rivers. King was assigned to find a suitable ford across the Bow River from the north and became the first mountie to set foot on the site of what would become Fort Calgary. After being discharged from the NWMP in 1877, he managed the I.G. Baker & Co. store at Fort Calgary, became the town of Calgary's first postmaster and in 1886 was elected as its second mayor.

George Craig Boulevard   Calgary International Airport, N.E.

George Eric Gwynne Craig was the second manager of the Calgary airport from 1945 to 1958, a time which saw tremendous growth in the airline industry. When he assumed the position, Trans-Canada Airlines (TCA) was the only carrier that flew to Calgary, flying from Lethbridge through Calgary to Edmonton. In 1949 TCA began a second east-west main line through the city. Craig was also airport manager when the first modern airport terminal in Canada opened in Calgary in 1956.

George Moss Park   74 Avenue and 24 Street S.E.

George Moss (1883-1952) came to Canada from England in 1906, and moved to Calgary in 1913. He helped to organize the Ogden-Millican Community Association and was its secretary for 39 years. The park was created through Moss' efforts to provide a recreation area for the vast number of unemployed during the Depression years. The community of Ogden honoured his memory by naming the park after him in 1970.

George Murdoch Building (Parkade)   SAIT Campus, N.W.

When the buildings at SAIT were re-named in 1985, the new names were chosen to reflect Calgary's heritage. George Murdoch was Calgary's first mayor, elected in 1884 in a hotly contested campaign, and re-elected the following year. (See Murdoch Manor.)

George R. Gell Park   16 Avenue and 43 Street N.W.

George Richard Gell (1888-1990) came to Canada from his native England in 1904. He arrived in Calgary in 1910, where he was employed with a real estate firm. In 1915 he began work in the stores division of the Calgary school board and became secretary-treasurer of the board in 1941, a job he held until his retirement in 1956. He was an active volunteer with the Calgary Cadets and the Calgary Zoo. The Gell home was the second house in Montgomery, which was then known as Shouldice. It was built by his father-in-law and remained the family home for 50 years. In 1982 the land on which the homestead stood was named the George R. Gell Park by The City of Calgary.

Georges P. Vanier Junior High School   509 - 32 Avenue N.E.

Born in Montreal, Georges Philian Vanier (1888-1967) was both a soldier and a diplomat. He was the first French Canadian and first Roman Catholic governor general of Canada, serving from 1959 to 1967. He served in World War I, where he lost a leg, and later became a major general. He also served as the Canadian ambassador to France from 1945 to 1953.

Georgia Street   **Glendale Meadows, S.W.**

Georgia Street may take its name from the state of Georgia in the southern United States. Georgia was the last of the English colonies to be established in America and takes its name from King George II of Great Britain.

Georgina Thomson Branch Library   **51 Cornell Road N.W.**

Georgina H. Thomson (1892-1963) began her career as a teacher. She joined the staff of the Calgary Public Library in 1923 and remained for 34 years, until her retirement in 1957. For 30 years she was in charge of the reference department. Shortly before her death, she became an author when her book of reminiscences, Crocus in Meadowlark Country, was published.

Gissing Drive   **Glenbrook, S.W.**

Roland Gissing came to Alberta from England in 1913 at the age of 16. He dreamed of becoming a cowboy and eventually managed to get a job as a cowhand on a ranch near Crossfield. For 10 years he worked, at the same time sketchings scenes around the ranch as a hobby. After moving near Cochrane in the 1920s, he began to pursue his painting seriously. Self-taught, his greatest pleasure was painting nature. Gissing oil landscapes became exceedingly popular and before his death in 1967 he had achieved international recognition.

Gladstone Gardens, Gladstone Road   **Glamorgan, S.W.**
                                                      Hillhurst, N.W.

These two streets were most likely named for William Ewart Gladstone (1809-98) who served as British Prime Minister from 1868 to 1874, 1880 to 1885 and 1892 to 1894. Many cities across Canada have streets named to honour this famous political leader. A Gladstone of note in Alberta history was William "Billy" Gladstone, a Calgary Metis who acted as an interpreter for the Mounted Police. He translated for Crowfoot when he met Sir John A. Macdonald at Gleichen on his trip west in 1886.

Gladys Ridge Road   **Glendale Meadows, S.W.**

Gladys is a small locality southeast of Calgary. It was named for Gladys Harkness who operated the first post office in the area from 1890 to 1894. The area north of Blackie, Alberta, is referred to as the Gladys Ridge district. The ridge itself rises east of the Highwood River. This is likely to be the origin of this street name.

Goddard Avenue   **Greenview, N.E.**

Goddard Avenue may have been named for Gilbert Goddard, an Englishman who came to southern Alberta in 1888. He became manager of the Bow River Horse Ranch west of Calgary where he raised Clydesdales and French coach horses. He became a well-known horse breeder. The street may also have been named after Goddard, Alberta, a small community which was once found southeast of Lethbridge. It was named after Ernest Goddard, one of the earliest settlers in the area.

Graham Drive   Glenbrook, S.W.

Graham Drive may have been named for the Graham family of Morley and Calgary. The family came west from Ontario in 1883 and ranched near Morley. They also ran the Morley Trading Company. Son John went to Edmonton in 1886 where he married Clara Hardisty, daughter of Senator Richard Hardisty, first senator of the North West Territories (before Alberta became a province), and granddaughter of Rev. George McDougall. Clara Hardisty (1868-1933) was the first white girl born in what would become Alberta. The Grahams came to Calgary in 1908. After Clara Graham's death, John Graham married her cousin, Lillian, also a grand-daughter of Rev. George McDougall. A second Graham, son Fred, served as sheriff of Calgary from 1910 to 1938, and as a judge of the Calgary small debts court. Coincidentally, his wife, Jean McDougall Graham, was also a granddaughter of Rev. George McDougall, and was one of the first white children born in the Calgary area. Her mother was the first white woman in Calgary. The other Graham sons, Thomas and William, were also long-time residents of the Calgary area.

Grant Crescent   Glendale, S.W.

The crescent was possibly named after Grant Pass, on the Alberta-B.C. border. The pass was named for George Munro Grant (1853-1902) who was secretary to an expedition headed by Sir Sanford Fleming in 1872 which travelled from the Atlantic to the Pacific looking for a possible route for a transcontinental railway. In addition, there were two Grants important to Calgary's early history. James Grant was a Calgary public servant who came to the city in 1883 and was friend or acquaintance of the majority of the city's populace until his death in 1904. Archibald Grant arrived in 1884 and opened a hardware store in partnership with E.R. Rogers. He was one of the city's first aldermen.

Grant MacEwan Elementary School   180 Falshire Drive N.E.

John Walter Grant MacEwan was born in Brandon, Manitoba in 1902. Before coming to Calgary in 1951, he was a professor of animal husbandry at the University of Saskatchewan and dean of agriculture and home economics at the University of Manitoba. His contributions to the city of Calgary and the province of Alberta are outstanding. He served as an alderman in Calgary from 1953 to 1963 (except for 1959), and as mayor from 1963 to 1966, completing the term of Mayor Harry Hays (who resigned to enter federal politics), and then serving a second term. He was a Liberal MLA from 1955 to 1959 and provincial Liberal leader from 1958 to 1960. In 1966 he became Alberta's lieutenant-governor, a position he held for two terms, until 1974. In 1966 MacEwan received an honourary doctorate from the University of Alberta. After his retirement he taught Western Canadian History at the University of Calgary. For 36 years he wrote a column called "Our Past" for the Calgary Herald until 1992, when, at age 90, and after 1,854 columns, he decided to retire. An author of more than 30 books, mostly historical, Dr. MacEwan continues to do research and to bring Alberta's and Canada's history alive.

Graves Bridge   Bow River at Glenmore Trail S.E.

Arthur Garnet Graves (1877-1973) immigrated to Canada from England in 1897. He was a City alderman from 1905 to 1908, and a City commissioner from 1908 to 1921 and 1923 to 1932. As Commissioner of Public Utilities, he was involved in the development of The City's electric public transportation systems. In 1970 at the age of 92, Graves performed the ribbon cutting ceremony at the opening of the bridge.

Grier Avenue   Greenview, N.E.

Grier Avenue may have been named for David J. Grier (1857-1935), who joined the NWMP in 1877 and became a rancher and farmer near Fort Macleod in 1881. He was one of the first commercial wheat producers in Alberta when he introduced a strain called Red Fife in 1883. He also was a founding member of the Western Stock Growers Association and a candidate for the Alberta legislature.

Guy Weadick Elementary School   5612 Templehill Road N.E.

Guy Weadick (1885-1953), a Wild West Show performer, came to Calgary in 1912 to promote a week-long rodeo - the first Calgary Stampede. He returned in 1919 to organize a Victory Stampede in celebration of the end of World War I. When the Stampede became a permanent part of the annual Calgary Exhibition in 1923, Weadick was hired as manager. He remained in this position until 1932 when he left after a disagreement with the exhibition board of directors. He then operated the Stampede Ranch, west of High River, and later retired to California.

CALGARY

H

H.D. Cartwright Junior High School   **5500 Dalhart Road N.W.**

Herbert (Bert) Daniel Cartwright came to Calgary from Ontario in 1906. After receiving his M.A. degree from the University of Alberta, he worked for three years as a school inspector and then became principal of Rideau Junior High School - the first junior high school in Alberta and a school which he helped organize. He later served as principal at Balmoral Junior High School and Crescent Heights High School before his retirement in 1959. He was an honourary life member of the Alberta Teachers' Association, which sponsored a scholarship in his honour. Cartwright died in 1967 and the school that bears his name was officially opened in 1972.

H. Kroeger Bridge   **Bow River - N.W. LRT**

As Alberta Minister Responsible for Transportation, Henry Kroeger was associated with the Calgary Transportation System and with the development of Calgary's LRT System. Kroeger was born in Moscow, Russia in 1917 and spent the first years of his life there during the Russian Revolution. He immigrated to the Consort area with his family at age nine. Kroeger was MLA for the Chinook constituency and transportation minister in the Lougheed government from 1979 to 1982. He died in September 1987.

Harcourt Road   **Haysboro, S.W.**

Harcourt Road may have been named in memory of Lt. E.H. Harcourt, a Calgarian and member of the Calgary Highlanders, who was killed on July 16, 1944, during the invasion of Normandy. Another possibility is that it was named for George Harcourt, Alberta's first deputy minister of agriculture from 1905 to 1915 and assistant dean of agriculture at the University of Alberta from 1915 to 1935.

Hardisty Place   **Haysboro, S.W.**

Richard Hardisty (1831-1889) was chief factor with the Hudson's Bay Company, a position held by both his father and grandfather before him. He lived in Calgary from 1883 to 1885. Hardisty became the first senator from the North-West Territories in 1888 and was a son-in-law of Rev. George McDougall (see McDougall Place). The CPR named an Alberta railway station after Hardisty and in 1884 gave the name to a downtown Calgary street. Hardisty Street was changed to 3rd Street East in 1904 and was not in use elsewhere when Haysboro was subdivided so the name was used again in this area.

Harley Road — Haysboro, S.W.

Harley Road may have been named for pioneer John Stuart Harley, who came to Calgary from Scotland in 1883. A blacksmith by trade, he was also employed by The City of Calgary.

Harmon Place — Haysboro, S.W.

Harmon Place may be named for Daniel Williams Harmon (1778-1843), a prominent fur trader in the northern regions of Alberta and British Columbia. His book about his travels is a basic reference on the fur trade and Aboriginal life.

Harold Panabaker Junior High School — 23 Sackville Drive S.W.

Born in Ontario in 1897, Harold Panabaker was decorated for bravery at Vimy Ridge during World War I. On his return to Canada he became a teacher and was appointed principal of James Short School in 1941 and supervisor of guidance for the school board in 1946. He later became assistant superintendent of schools and retired in 1962. In 1963, his contribution to education in Calgary was recognized when Harold Panabaker Junior High School opened and he received the distinguished service award for his contribution to education in Alberta. Panabaker died in 1977.

Harold W. Riley Elementary School — 3743 Dover Ridge Drive S.E.

Harold William Riley (1877-1946) moved to Calgary with his family (see Thomas Riley Building) in 1888, to settle on a farm in what is now West Hillhurst. When Alberta became a province in 1905, Riley, at age 27, became its first deputy provincial secretary and registrar of companies, the youngest deputy minister in Canada. He was appointed registrar of the University of Alberta when it was founded in 1908, but resigned in 1910 to return to Calgary and run Riley's Limited, an insurance business. He was elected MLA for Gleichen in 1912 and served as a Calgary alderman from 1914 to 1915 and 1932 to 1935. He served overseas as a captain during World War I with the occupation forces. In 1921 he established the Southern Alberta Pioneer and Old Timers Association and became its first secretary. He held the position until he resigned in 1943 due to ill health. He was also first secretary of the Calgary Stock Exchange and toured western Canada and the United States on behalf of the Board of Trade encouraging prospective immigrants.

Harris Place — University of Calgary Family Housing, N.W.

The streets of the University of Calgary family housing units have been named to honour five of Canada's Group of Seven artists. The Board of Governors felt that using names from one group of people created a sense of unity within the housing project. Lawren Harris was one of the founding members of the Group of Seven, formed in 1920 to introduce modern techniques to Canadian art. Of the seven original members, only Harris, who was independently wealthy, did not make his living as a commercial artist.

Harry Boothman Bridge   Edworthy Park, N.W.

The footbridge which crosses the Bow River to Edworthy Park is named in honour of Harry Boothman, superintendent and director of Calgary Parks & Recreation from 1961 until his death in 1976. Boothman was known nationally for his work in parks and recreation and in 1967 was awarded the Centennial medal for this work. That same year he was elected president of the Parks and Recreation Association of Canada. Boothman was an enthusiastic supporter of a system of trails and walkways throughout the city for hiking, jogging and cross country skiing. The Harry Boothman Bridge, which opened in 1977, connects the trails on the north side of the Bow River to those on the south.

Harry Hays Building   220 - 4 Avenue S.E.

The building housing federal government offices in Calgary is named after Harry William Hays (1909-82). Born in Carstairs, Alberta, Hays moved to a farm on the southern edge of the city of Calgary when he was 13. A cattleman and auctioneer, Hays served as mayor of Calgary from 1959 to 1963. He left his second term to enter federal politics and was Minister of Agriculture from 1963 to 1965. He was a member of the Canadian Senate from 1966 until his death in 1982. (See Hays Farm.)

Harvey Barracks   S.W.

Brigadier Fredrick Maurice Watson Harvey (1888-1980) was one of three Victoria Cross winners from the Lord Strathcona's Horse (Royal Canadians) Regiment. A native of Ireland, he joined the regiment in 1915 and received a Victoria Cross for his actions on March 27, 1917. During an attack on the village of Guyencourt, France, a party of Germans advanced and opened rifle and machine gun fire causing heavy casualties. In command of the leading troops, Lieutenant Harvey jumped the wire in the trench, shot the machine gunner and captured the gun. He came to Calgary in 1938 as commanding officer of the regiment. In 1940 he became commandant of Currie Barracks, and was promoted to brigadier and commander of the 13th Alberta Military District shortly thereafter. He retired in 1946. Sarcee Barracks, the home of the Lord Strathcona's Horse (Royal Canadians) regiment was re-named Harvey Barracks in Brigadier Harvey's honour on April 26, 1981.

Harvey Place   Haysboro, S.W.

Harvey Place may have been named for Horace Harvey (1863-1949), a Calgary lawyer who was Chief Justice of Alberta from 1910 to 1949.

Harvie Bridge   Footbridge over the Bow River
                                     connecting Southland Park and Riverbend, S.E.

This bridge is named after Eric L. Harvie, Q.C., who earned millions from mineral rights he held in both the Leduc and Redwater oilfields. These he purchased from a British land firm when it went broke. He began the Glenbow Foundation in 1955, eventually amassing a vast record of western Canadian history. The Harvie family gave the collection to the Alberta government in 1966 together with $5 million in grants. With a matching grant from the Alberta government, the Glenbow-Alberta Institute came into being. Harvie was also instrumental in the opening of Heritage Park in the mid-1960s. In recognition of these legacies to the city of Calgary, the bridge was named in his honour.

Hastings Crescent, etc.   Highfield, S.E.

These streets may have been named for Hastings Lake, Alberta, which was named after Tom Hastings, a member of the 1884 Geological Survey party. Or it may have been named for Hastings, England, site of the battle in which the Norman king William I conquered England in 1066.

Haultain Memorial Elementary School   605 Queensland Drive S.E.

Sir Fredrick Haultain (1857-1942) was a lawyer who came to Macleod, Alberta in 1884. He became a member of the North-West Assembly for Macleod in 1887, then held the seat by acclamation until 1905. Haultain was the leader of the assembly in an extended fight with Ottawa. He was asked to form a cabinet in 1891, and in 1897 when the Territories achieved responsible government, he became its first premier. Haultain remained leader until the provinces of Alberta and Saskatchewan were formed in 1905. He had wanted one large province instead of two but he elected to remain in politics in Saskatchewan. There, he was defeated and became opposition leader until 1912 when he was made chief justice of the Saskatchewan Appeal Court. Haultain was knighted in 1916 and remained as chief justice until his retirement in 1938. Haultain Memorial School opened in 1982. The original Haultain school, located at 225 - 13 Avenue S.W., opened as South Ward School in 1892. A second, larger school opened in 1906, with an annex built in 1921. In 1937, Haultain School became the first school in Canada to begin a Safety Patrol program. The school annex burned down in 1964 and the school was demolished in 1965. The original building is Calgary's oldest surviving school building. It was re-opened in 1986 as headquarters for Uncles At Large.

Hawkwood   N.W.

The district was named for the family of Arthur and Isabel Hawkwood who homesteaded an area which encompassed the west part of the Hawkwood district. The family came to Canada from England about 1913, living in Calgary before moving to the Hawkwood area. They named their house Watergrove and operated a dairy farm and market garden.

Haysboro   S.W.

This subdivision is built on the site of the farm which Harry Hays purchased from his father in 1943. (See Harry Hays Building.)

Hays Farm   8948 Elbow Drive S.W.

The Hays Farm apartment complex is situated on the site of the farm buildings which Harry Hays purchased from his father in 1943. When Hays sold his farm to Kelwood

Corporation in 1957, he retained 21 acres, which included the house and barn. The turn-of-the-century buildings were demolished in 1967 and construction of the Hays Farm apartment complex began. (See Harry Hays Building.)

Healy Drive   Haysboro, S.W.

There were at least three Healys who played a prominent role in southern Alberta history. John J. was an American trader who built Fort Whoop-Up in 1869 southwest of present-day Lethbridge and had an interest in an outpost located at Calgary. His brother, Joseph, claimed in 1882 to have discovered silver and copper at the base of Castle Mountain. Whether this was a legitimate claim, or the mine was "salted," is uncertain. But the find precipitated a mining rush and for a short time Silver City, with a population of about 1,000, was a booming mining town. As quickly as it grew, it failed. The great Castle Mountain Rush was as short as it was dramatic. Another unrelated Healy was Ebenezer, the owner of Alberta's first cheese factory which was built in 1888 on Healy's homestead near Springbank. He came west from Nova Scotia in 1882 and arrived in Calgary from Regina in 1887. He changed from dairy ranching to cheese production when an overproduction of milk in the area occurred. His dairy operated until 1896.

Henry Viney Arena   814 - 13 Avenue N.E.

Known as "the man with the big cigar," Henry Viney (1910-80) was a prominent Calgary sportscaster. He started his career in 1932 and came to Calgary in 1945 to work for CFCN radio. He travelled all over the world covering sporting events including: the World Series; Stanley Cup playoffs; summer and winter Olympics; the Kentucky Derby; and every Grey Cup final from 1948 until his retirement in 1975. He received the Foster Hewitt Award as Canada's outstanding sportscaster in 1967 and was named Calgary's Sportsman of the Year in 1976. Viney was active in promoting minor sports in the city and was in great demand as a master of ceremonies. In his younger years he was a first-class official in baseball, hockey and basketball and received both national and international recognition for his contributions to sportscasting. The Henry Viney Arena opened in 1977.

Henry Wise Wood High School   910 - 75 Avenue S.W.

Henry Wise Wood was born in Missouri and given the Christian names of Henry Wise after the governor of that state. He learned farming and the cattle business on the family homestead, then moved to the Carstairs area in 1905. He was keen to help farmers improve their economic fortunes and their status, and was president of the United Farmers of Alberta (UFA) from 1916 to 1931. The UFA formed the government of Alberta in 1921 and although Wood was offered the position of premier, he turned it down, preferring not to become involved in politics. He helped form the Alberta Wheat Pool and served as chairman of the board of directors until retiring to his Carstairs farm in 1937. He died in 1941 and was named to the Alberta Agricultural Hall of Fame in 1951.

Hillhurst (Louise) Bridge   Bow River at 10 Street N.W.

The Louise Bridge was for many years the unofficial name for the Hillhurst Bridge, named after the community of Hillhurst. Construction on the present bridge began in

1920 and it opened in 1921. Another bridge, west of the present site, was in use from 1906 until it was dismantled in 1927. It was called the Louise Bridge and its name was commonly used for the new bridge. It was likely named after Louise Cushing, deceased daughter of W.H. Cushing. (See Chushing Bridge.) Some suggest the bridge was really named after the fourth daughter of Queen Victoria, Princess Louise Caroline Alberta. However, there is no documentation to support this. A third explanation suggests that the Riley family, who owned land on the north, and the Shouldice family, landowners on the south, called the bridge Louise because both had daughters named Louise. However, there is no record of a Louise Shouldice. Due to confusion over whether the bridge was the Hillhurst Bridge or the Louise Bridge, it was renamed the Hillhurst (Louise) Bridge in 1970.

HMCS Tecumseh   **24 Street and 17 Avenue S.W.**

The first naval unit in Calgary was formed in 1923 and established permanent quarters at the present site in 1939. In 1941 all naval stations in Canada were commissioned as ships, Calgary's being given the name Tecumseh, after a Shawnee chief (1768-1813). Tecumseh was an American Indian who became a Canadian hero in the War of 1812. In his fight against the encroachment of white settlers on Aboriginal territory, he joined the British and as a brigadier-general lead about 1,000 Aboriginal warriors. He was killed at the Battle of Moraviantown in Upper Canada. The name Tecumseh means "Shooting Star." The naval reserve station was built at HMCS Tecumseh in 1943 and burned down in May 1981 with the loss of many navy artifacts and mementos. It was rebuilt along with a naval museum.

Hogarth Crescent   **Haysboro, S.W.**

Hogarth Crescent may have been named for James Hogarth, a resident of Calgary from 1910 until his death in 1969, and a veteran of three wars. A native of Scotland, he served with the British army during the Boer War and with the 56th (Calgary) Infantry Battalion during World War I. He was one of the original members of the Calgary Highlanders, formed in 1921, and served as its quartermaster during World War II. He finished his military career as a major.

Holden Place   **Haysboro, S.W.**

Holden Place may have been named after Holden, Alberta, or for F. Morgan "Tiny" Holden, of Midnapore, who was a well-known owner, trainer and breeder of thorough-bred horses for 31 years, until his death in 1966.

Holy Family Elementary School   **904 - 32 Street S.E.**

This title refers to the family of Jesus, the Virgin Mary and St. Joseph. The Holy Family is regarded by the Catholic Church as the example and model for Catholic families, demonstrating all the virtues necessary for holiness. The feast of the Holy Family is celebrated on the first Sunday after Christmas.

Holy Redeemer Bilingual Elementary School   708 - 47 Street S.E.

The term redeemer means one who pays a price for or who "buys back" someone (i.e. from slavery). In Christian terms, Jesus is the Redeemer of all mankind because by His passion, death and resurrection, we have been "bought back" or delivered from sin and restored to living in the grace of God. Thus Holy Redeemer has become, over the centuries, one of the many titles for Jesus.

Holy Trinity Elementary School   1717 - 41 Street S.E.

The central mystery of the Christian faith is that the one God, is Father, Son and Holy Spirit: Three Persons sharing one nature. This mystery, is expressed in the term "Most Holy Trinity."

Hooke Road   Haysboro, S.W.

Hooke Road may have been named for Alfred J. "Alf" Hooke (1905-92), who was the longest sitting member of the Social Credit Party of Alberta. He was a member of the original Social Credit government which swept to power under William Aberhart in 1935, and was the last member of that group still in the legislature when the party was defeated in 1971, an election in which he chose not to run. During his many years of government service he held every major cabinet post.

Hoover Place   Haysboro, S.W.

The most prominent landmark with this name is the Hoover Dam in Nevada, named for U.S. president Herbert Hoover. The street may take its name from this landmark.

Hope Street   Mount Royal, S.W.

Henry Hope was lieutenant-governor of Quebec from 1785 to 1789. He was a member of the British army who rose to the rank of brigadier general and was commissary general of troops in Canada when appointed as Quebec's lieutenant-governor, a position which he held until his death. He also administered the government of Quebec from November 1785 to October 1786 when Lord Dorchester arrived to take up his post as governor.

Hounsfield Heights   N.W.

This area was named after Georgina Hounsfield, wife of Thomas Riley, who homesteaded the land on which Hounsfield Heights and Hillhurst are located. The Riley family settled in this area in 1888. Hounsfield Heights was developed as a subdivision when the area was annexed by The City of Calgary in 1906.

Hudson Road   Highwood, N.W.

As most of the streets in the Highwood district have names which appear to be British in origin, it is likely that this road honours British explorer Henry Hudson, who was abandoned in Hudson Bay in 1611 when his crew mutinied. The Hudson River in New York is also named for him.

Hull Estates   **1200 - 6 Street S.W.**

William Roper Hull arrived in Calgary in 1883 bringing 1,200 horses from his ranch in British Columbia. While here, he signed a contract with the CPR to supply beef to the railway during construction in B.C. In 1884 he opened a butcher shop in Calgary and within two years had 15 outlets. To supply beef to his shops, he bought several Alberta ranches, with his Bow River Ranch on Fish Creek as the showpiece. The ranch house is still standing and is now used as one of the administrative buildings for Fish Creek Provincial Park. Hull also was involved in Calgary real estate. Some of the buildings he constructed were the Grain Exchange, Alberta Block, Victoria Block, Albion Block and the Hull Opera House, which was the centre of social life in Calgary at the time. The Hull Estates apartment complex is built on the site of the Hull mansion, "Langmore," which was demolished in 1970. Hull Avenue in Haysboro is likely named in his honour. (See William Roper Hull School.)

Hunt House   **806 - 9 Avenue S.E.**

The Hunt House, perhaps the oldest structure in Calgary still on its original site, is located behind the Deane House. The small log cabin was built by the Hudson's Bay Company in 1876 as a home for the company's interpreter. The house has been covered with shingles, but the roof is original. The two lean-to's are additions. The house gets its name from its last resident, William H. Hunt, who willed it to The City in 1975. The Hunt House is one of the oldest Hudson's Bay Company buildings left in Alberta and one of less than 25 structures in Alberta which pre-date 1882.

Hunter Street   **Highwood, N.W.**

The name Hunter is often associated with Enos Hunter (1883-1949), one of the three head chiefs of the Stoney Indians at Morley during the 1940s. He worked hard to see the Stoneys received more arable land and during that time additional reserves were obtained at Eden Valley and Bighorn. Chief Hunter was well-known in Calgary for the prominent part he played in the Calgary Stampede. Because most of the streets in the Highwood district have names which appear to be of British origin, it is also possible that this one was named for Hunter Street, just south of King's Cross in London.

Ian Bazalgette Junior High School   3909 - 26 Avenue S.E.

Located in the old Forest Lawn Senior High School, Ian Bazalgette Junior High School was named after the only native-born Calgarian to win the Victoria Cross. Ian Willoughby Bazalgette was born in Calgary in 1918, but left at the age of four and spent most of his life in England. He was awarded the Victoria Cross posthumously for landing a flaming aircraft in France on August 4, 1944. After keeping his damaged aircraft in the air long enough to guide bombers to their target and avoid unnecessary civilian casualties, he ordered his crew to bail out, and landed, avoiding a French village, before the aircraft exploded. Bazalgette was also awarded the Distinguished Flying Cross for outstanding service in the RAF and was named to Canada's Aviation Hall of Fame in 1973.

Ivor Strong Bridge   Bow River at Deerfoot Trail S.E.

John Ivor Strong began working for The City of Calgary in 1944 as assistant City engineer. He was commissioner of public works and utilities from 1952 to 1956, then left the civic administration in 1958 to become a partner in Strong, Lamb and Nelson Ltd. He returned in 1965 as chief commissioner, a job which he retained until his retirement in 1971.

CALGARY

J

J.H. Woods Park   Elbow Drive and 29 Avenue S.W.

The name of this park was originally Elbow Boulevard Park. It was changed to J.H. Woods Park in 1941, in recognition of a Calgary business leader and local resident who had contributed greatly to its development and to the landscaping at the north and south ends of the Hillhurst Bridge. Col. James Hossack Woods was the publisher of the Calgary Herald from 1907 to 1935. He was involved with the Boy Scouts and was the founder of Camp Woods at Sylvan Lake. The Woods Foundation, created by his estate, provided funding for the aviary conservatory at the Calgary Zoo and the establishment of Heritage Park.

J.J. Bowlen Provincial Building   620 - 7 Avenue S.W.

John James Bowlen (1876-1959) was born in Prince Edward Island and moved to Alberta where he became a prominent horse rancher. He was an MLA for Calgary for 14 years and served as house leader for the Liberal party. He was appointed lieutenant-governor of Alberta in 1950 and remained in that position until his death in 1959. The Bowlen Building, housing Provincial Government offices, was opened in October 1969.

Jack James High School   5105 - 8 Avenue S.E.

John (Jack) Wesley James was born in Ireland and immigrated to Canada with his family at an early age. Educated in Winnipeg and Calgary, he taught in rural Alberta and Calgary before serving in the RCAF during World War II. He returned to Calgary to teach in the public system after the war and by 1961 had attained the position of superinten-dent of secondary schools. He was very involved in the movement to provide vocational education for Calgary students. Calgary's third secondary vocational school, which opened in 1982, is named in his honour.

Jack Setters Arena   2020 - 69 Avenue S.E.

When this arena was built by The City in 1974, it was named after Jack Setters, who was instrumental, along with Rose Kohn and Stu Peppard, in the restructuring of minor hockey in Calgary in the early 1960s. One of his tasks was registering 10,000 minor hockey players in the city. Setters served as president of the Minor Hockey Association of Calgary and was honoured as the Calgary Booster Club's Sportsman of the Year in 1972. The arena is now owned and operated by the Millican-Ogden Community Association.

Jack Simpson Gymnasium   University of Calgary, N.W.

Many university faculty libraries, lecture theatres, etc. are known by the names of people who provided funds toward their construction. A donation was made for the gymnasium by the Simpson family in memory of Jack Simpson, an amateur sportsman, and head of CANA Construction until his death in 1984. A graduate of the University of Alberta, Simpson was senior engineer of Burns and Dutton Construction (which became CANA in 1970) during the expansion of the Physical Education Building and MacEwan Hall at the University of Calgary. He also was involved in the construction of Alberta's two Jubliee Auditoriums, both the 1954 and 1978 International Airports, the Calgary Centre for Performing Arts and the Olympic Saddledome.

Jack Singer Concert Hall   Calgary Centre for Performing Arts,
                                                                        205 - 8 Avenue S.E.

Alan and Stephen Singer were the first Calgarians to make a donation to the Calgary Centre for Performing Arts for a performance space. They presented a $1.5 million contribution in honour of their father, Jack Singer, a native Calgarian with a long-time involvement in the real estate industry. Jack Singer is an avid supporter of the arts and has sponsored a number of Broadway shows and films and Hollywood Center Studios in Los Angeles.

Jackson Place   University of Calgary Family Housing, N.W.

The streets of the University of Calgary family housing units have been named to honour some of Canada's Group of Seven artists. The U of C Board of Governors wished to use names honouring famous Canadians and felt that using names from one specific group gave a sense of unity to the housing project. Jackson Place is named in honour of A.Y. Jackson, one of the original members of the group which worked together from 1920 to 1933 to introduce modern painting techniques to Canadian art.

Jacques Lodge   2500 Bow Trail S.W.

Run by the Metropolitan Foundation of Calgary, Jacques Lodges is a senior citizens' complex opened in the mid-1960s. It was named after the Harry Jacques family who owned the property on which it is built and who donated it to the foundation.

James Fowler High School   4004 - 4 Street N.W.

James Fowler was born and educated in Scotland. He came to Alberta from Edinburgh in 1913 to teach at the Olds School of Agriculture. He joined the staff of Crescent Heights High School in 1914 and taught there for two years. When the Provincial Institute of Technology and Art (now SAIT) opened in 1916, he was appointed as a science instructor. After serving in World War I, he was a school inspector for two years before returning to the institute in 1921 as head of the science department. In 1929 he was appointed vice-principal and in 1941, principal. He received an honourary doctorate from the University of Alberta in 1949. The year after his retirement in 1952, he became executive secretary of the Community Chest (forerunner to the United Way), a position which he held at the time of his death in 1959.

James Short Memorial Elementary School   6633 - 5 Avenue S.E.

James Short was the first principal of Calgary's Central School from 1889 to 1892. He left to study law, was called to the bar in 1895, and was a crown prosecutor for 15 years. However, he continued to be closely associated with Calgary schools until 1914. He was the school board secretary, a member of the Board of Education, and its chairman from 1908 to 1909. He organized one of the first two high schools in the North-West Territories. The original school of which he was principal was a four-room wooden structure built in 1887. When the school population outgrew the structure, the school board constructed a large new building adjacent to it. Calgary's first large school, it was considered by some to be the finest west of Toronto. It was completed in 1905 and renamed after Short in 1938. This was the first time in Calgary's history that a school was named in honour of a living person. James Short died in 1942 and the sandstone school was demolished in 1969. James Short Memorial Elementary School opened in 1973.

James Short Park   115 - 4 Avenue S.W.

James Short Park sits on the site of the original James Short School. The park's centerpiece is the school's cupola, which was salvaged when the school was demolished in 1969 and displayed in Prince's Island Park from 1973 until it was moved to its present site in 1990. The cupola houses a 1904 clock, originally purchased by Pat Burns (see Senator Patrick Burns Junior High School), which was part of a building at 8 Avenue and Centre Street S. until it was demolished in 1967. Believed to be the first public clock in Calgary, it was salvaged from a local antique store. (For information on James Short see James Short Memorial Elementary School.)

Jamieson Avenue   Bridgeland, N.E.

Jamieson Avenue was probably named to honour Reuben R. or Alice J. Jamieson. As general superintendent of the western division of the CPR, Reuben was well known and widely respected throughout the west. He served as mayor of Calgary from 1909 to 1910. His wife Alice was appointed as judge of the juvenile court in Calgary in 1914, the first female juvenile court judge in the British Empire and perhaps the world. In 1916 she became magistrate of the women's court. She was also active with many women's organizations and supported campaigns to elect Calgary's first female school board member, Annie Foote, and Alberta's first female MLA, Louise McKinney. She also worked on the campaign which saw Alberta become the first province to grant women the right to vote.

Janet Johnstone Elementary School **224 Shawnessy Drive S.W.**

Janet Johnstone (1911-84), a native Albertan, came to Calgary in 1942 after teaching in a number of small Alberta communities. She taught at five Calgary schools until 1952, when she became primary supervisor for public schools. In 1964 she was promoted to assistant superintendent of elementary schools, a post she held until her retirement in 1973. The school bearing her name was opened in 1983.

Jefferies Pond **Inglewood Bird Sanctuary,**
3020 Sanctuary Road S.E.

James Edward Jefferies came to Canada from Wales in 1907. A year later he arrived in Calgary and began hauling coal. His business gradually evolved into gravel hauling and excavation and eventually to concrete products. In 1949 Jefferies donated the Colonel Walker home and surrounding land to the Alberta Fish and Game Association for the purpose of creating a sanctuary for migrating waterfowl. The land was given to The City in 1970 with the condition that it remain a natural wildlife park. It was re-named the Inglewood Bird Sanctuary. Although Jefferies died in 1955, it wasn't until 1993 that his contribution was officially recognized and Jefferies Pond was named.

Jennie Elliott Elementary School **3031 Lindsay Drive S.W.**

Mary Jane (Jennie) Elliott came west from Ontario in 1900 to experience the adventure of teaching in the North-West Territories. She taught in Olds and High River before moving to Calgary in 1920 where she taught at Central High School. After her retirement in 1940 she served three terms as a school board trustee. Elliott moved to Victoria in 1950 and died in Vancouver in 1956. She is buried in Calgary.

Jerry Potts Elementary School **3720 - 42 Street N.W.**

Jerry Potts (1840-96) was hired by the NWMP in 1874 as an interpreter and guide. He spent 22 years as an advisor to the police helping the men adapt to frontier life. Potts was born to a Scottish father and a Blood Indian mother and spent his early years living around American trading posts and with his mother's people. He seemed to live a charmed life, miraculously escaping death on a number of occasions. Potts' association with Calgary lies in the fact that he likely suggested the confluence of the Bow and Elbow Rivers as the site for the police fort.

Jimmie Condon Arena **502 Heritage Drive S.W.**

Born Demetrious Kouimgis, James (Jimmie) Apostolos Condon came to North America from Turkey in 1909, arriving in Calgary in 1911. He owned several candy stores and restaurants in the city and was an avid sponsor of amateur sports. From 1921 to 1944, teams in many sports - rugby, football, lacrosse, hockey and basketball - were known as the "Jimmies." Condon was named the Booster Club's Sportsman of the Year in 1963 in recognition of his support of amateur sports. In 1980 Jimmie and his wife Maria donated four marble statues to the University of Calgary - Socrates, his students Plato and Krito (which stand in the courtyard of the administration building) and Hippocrates (which stands in the grand mall of the university's health sciences centre). In recognition of his contribution to sports in Calgary, the Jimmie Condon Arena was opened in August 1981. Condon died a month later at the age of 92.

| **John Dutton Theatre** | **2nd Floor, W.R. Castell Central Library, 616 Macleod Trail S.E.** |

Lethbridge-born John Dutton served as the director of the Calgary Public Library (CPL) from 1979 to 1990, the fourth chief librarian in CPL history. He had 26 years' experience in library work before coming to Calgary, having served as chief librarian in Lethbridge, Toronto and Winnipeg.

| **John G. Diefenbaker High School** | **6620 - 4 Street N.W.** |

John Diefenbaker (1895-1979) moved with his family to a homestead in Saskatchewan in 1903, and received his law degree from the University of Saskatchewan in 1919. He first became a member of parliament in 1940. He was chosen leader of the federal Progressive Conservative Party in 1956 and was prime minister from 1957 to 1963. He came to Calgary for the official opening of the school in 1972. It was the third school in Canada to be named after him.

| **John Hextall Bridge** | **Bicycle/foot bridge, Bowness Road N.W.** |

John Hextall had a dream. He envisioned the Bow River valley, southwest of the curve in the river, as a subdivision for the well-to-do — a valley of country residences. To attract buyers, he developed two islands in the Bow River by widening creeks and creating a lagoon and building paths and a concession. He then erected a bridge over the river and arranged for The City to build a trolley line. As an added incentive for the trolley line to be built quickly, he gave Bowness Park to The City of Calgary. Hextall also built an electrical generating station and a waterworks system and established the Bowness Golf and Country Club where the Greenwood Village Mobile Home Park now stands. However, World War I intervened and Hextall took his family back to England. He never returned and his dream died. But the Town of Bowness, later annexed by The City of Calgary, had begun. The foot and bicycle bridge bearing Hextall's name was originally called the Shouldice Bridge, but took the name Hextall when a new traffic bridge was built in 1987.

| **John Laurie Boulevard** | **N.W.** |

John Lee Laurie (1899-1959) was born in Ontario and moved west in 1920. He was hired as English and Latin master at Calgary's Western Canada College in 1923 and moved to Crescent Heights High School in 1927. He remained there until 1956, when he retired due to ill health. He is lovingly remembered by both Aboriginal and non-Aboriginal people for his selfless interest in the plight of the Sarcee, Stoney and other Alberta tribes. He was the secretary of the Indian Association of Alberta from 1944 until his death and brought about many positive changes in the administration of Aboriginal affairs. To the Stoneys he is White Cloud, to the Sarcee he is Detanisi-tami (Sitting Eagle), and to the Blood tribe Mekaisto (Red Crow). He received an honourary doctorate from the University of Alberta and is buried in the Stoney Indian cemetery at Morley, Alberta.

John Paul II Elementary School   119 Castle Ridge Drive N.E.

The present and 264th pope in the history of the Catholic church was born Karol Wojtyla in 1920 in Poland. Originally hoping to become an actor, he worked in underground theatre during World War II and secretly studied for the priesthood. He was ordained shortly after the war when Poland was under communist rule. He became Bishop of Cracow in 1956 and served as an aide-bishop at the Second Vatican Council. Wojtyla became Archbishop of Cracow in 1965 and in 1967, Cardinal of Cracow. He was elected pope in October 1978, the first non-Italian to hold the office in 455 years.

John Ware Building   SAIT Campus, N.W.

John Ware was a slave who, when freed at the end of the American Civil War, was hired for a cattle drive from Texas to Idaho. From there he headed north on another cattle drive to High River. He was an excellent cowboy and rider and was considered to be one of the top bronc riders in the West. Less than 10 years after arriving in Alberta he had his own ranch and a herd of 200 cattle. He later moved to the Red Deer River and was killed in 1905 when his horse stumbled in a badger hole and rolled on top of him, breaking his neck. His funeral was the largest ever in Calgary at that time. The names given to the buildings at SAIT in 1985 were chosen to reflect Calgary's heritage.

John Ware Junior High School   10021 - 19 Street S.W.

See John Ware Building.

John XXIII Elementary/Junior High School   1420 Falconridge Drive N.E.

The 261st pope was born Angleo Roncalli in 1881 in Monte Berramo, Italy. The son of peasant farmers, he began studying for the priesthood as a boy. Ordained in 1904, he served as a priest in Italy, Bulgaria, Turkey, Greece and France. He became a bishop in Bulgaria in 1925, was elevated to archbishop in 1944 and was named Cardinal of Venice in 1953. In 1958, following the death of Pius XII, he became pope, taking the name of John in honour of his father and of the patron saint of his hometown.

Joliet Avenue   Mount Royal, S.W.

Louis Jolliet (1645-1700) was born in Quebec City. In 1672 he was appointed by Frontenac, the governor of New France, to explore the Mississippi River with the purpose of determining into which ocean it emptied. The French wanted to extend their empire westward and were looking for a river that emptied into the Pacific, giving them links to Asia. Upon reaching the mouth of the Arkansas River, Jolliet learned from the Aboriginal people that the Mississippi did not flow west, but south, and so he returned home. He did further exploration in Quebec before settling on Anticosti Island.

Justice Joe Kryczka Arena

**Southland Leisure Centre,
2000 Southland Drive S.W.**

Joe Kryczka (1935-91) was born in Coleman, Alberta and attended university in Edmonton, where he played hockey for the University of Alberta Golden Bears. He completed his law degree in 1958 and was appointed Justice of the Court of Queen's Bench in 1980. He served as president of both the Alberta Amateur Hockey Association and the Canadian Amateur Hockey Association. He was inducted into the AAHA's Hall of Fame in 1984 and the Alberta and Canadian Sports Halls of Fame in 1990. He was chairman of the committee which negotiated the first Canada-Soviet Hockey Series in 1972 and was on the board of directors of the Calgary Olympic Development Association. The main rink at the Southland Leisure Centre was re-named in his honour in 1990.

K

Kananaskis Drive   **Kelvin Grove, S.W.**

Kananaskis is an adaptation of the name of a Cree Indian. According to the legend, Kananaskis received what should have been a fatal blow from an axe but which merely stunned him. The incident was reported by the Palliser expedition during their explorations.

Kananaskis Hall   **University of Calgary Residence, N.W.**

This student residence was named after the mountain in Banff National Park, which is an adaptation of the name of a Cree Indian. (See Kananaskis Drive.)

Keeler Elementary School   **4807 Forego Avenue S.E.**

Albert George Keeler (1906-67) served in the navy during World War I and came to Forest Lawn from England in 1919. He settled in Albert Park and was a town councillor and member of the Bow River School Board for many years. He retired from the school board when Forest Lawn was annexed by The City of Calgary in 1961. Keeler was a founding member of the Forest Lawn Community Association. The school was named after him in 1960.

Kelsey Place   **Kelvin Grove, S.W.**

Several Canadian towns and natural features carry this name, likely in recognition of the achievements of explorer Henry Kelsey. There is also a village of Kelsey in Lincolnshire, England.

Kendall Place   **Kingsland, S.E.**

Kendall Place may have been named for Sergeant Ralph S. Kendall, who served with the RNWMP from 1905 to 1910, and then on the Calgary police force from 1911 until his retirement in 1940. Born in England, Kendall became a well known local author. Until 1924 he was sergeant in charge of the mounted squad and met many visiting notables, including the Duke of Windsor and Canada's Governor General Lord Byng.

Kennedy Drive   Kelvin Grove, S.W.

Originally Calgary's downtown streets were named after people connected with the CPR. This changed in 1904 when city council made the change from named to numbered streets. Kennedy Avenue, named after John S. Kennedy, a CPR director and member of the CPR Syndicate, became 13 Avenue South. Kennedy's name appeared again in Kelvin Grove, possibly in recognition of the old street name.

Kerby Centre   1133 - 7 Avenue S.W.

The Rev. George Kerby (1860-1944) arrived in Calgary in 1902 as the new minister of the Calgary Methodist Church. He was a dynamic and popular preacher who oversaw the construction of Central Methodist Church (later Central United), then the largest building in the city. He saw the need for more educational facilities and when a university was granted to Edmonton instead of Calgary, he pushed for a college to be established here. He was named principal of Mount Royal College in 1910 before the Provincial Government had even granted its charter. The college opened in 1911. Kerby remained as principal until his retirement in 1942 and then served as principal emeritus from 1942 to 1944. He also served on the college's board of governors from 1910 to 1944. He was very active in community life serving, among other duties, on the Calgary hospital board and as a school trustee. Mount Royal College relocated to the southwest area of the city in 1972 and the Kerby Centre for senior citizens, which opened in 1973, used the former Mount Royal College buildings. It was named after the man whose vision had brought higher education to Calgary. Kerby Hall at Mount Royal College is also named after him.

Kerfoot Crescent   Kelvin Grove, S.W.

Kerfoot Crescent may have been named for William Duncan Kerfoot (1852-1908), who came to the Calgary area from Virginia in 1880. He worked as manager of the British American Ranche Company until 1884, when he settled near Grand Valley Creek, northwest of Calgary, becoming the first rancher in the Cochrane district. His son, Duncan Irving Kerfoot (1886-1946), was said to be the first white child born in the rural area surrounding Calgary.

Ketchen Avenue   Harvey Barracks, S.W.

This street is named for Huntley D.B. Ketchen, who was born in India and began his army career as a second-lieutenant in the Imperial army from 1890 to 1893. He then served in the NWMP from 1894 to 1900 and with the Strathcona's Horse Regiment in South Africa from 1900 to 1901 before transferring to the Royal Canadian Dragoons. He was appointed commander of the 6th Canadian Infantry Brigade in February 1915 and retired as a major-general in 1928.

King Edward Elementary/Junior High School   **120 - 30 Avenue S.W.**

King Edward School was one of 19 sandstone schools erected by the board of education between 1894 and 1913. It was opened in 1913, along with King George School, and named after King Edward VII, who reigned from 1901 to 1910. Another school, now Alexandra Centre, was named for his wife, Queen Alexandra. King Edward School's first principal was William Aberhart (see William Aberhart Senior High School).

King George Elementary School   **2108 - 10 Street N.W.**

This school, built in 1912, was opened in September 1913. It was named in honour of King George V, who reigned as King of Great Britain and the Commonwealth from 1911 to 1936.

Kirby Place   **Kingsland, S.W.**

Kirby Place may have been named for Calgary-born William John Cameron (Cam) Kirby, who was an MLA for Red Deer from 1954 to 1959, leader of the Conservative Party of Alberta from 1958 to 1959 and was appointed as a Justice of the Alberta Supreme Court in 1960.

Klamath Place   **Kingsland, S.W.**

This street was likely named after the Klamath Indians, a tribe in Oregon, U.S.A..

Kootenay Street   **Kelvin Grove, S.W.**

Kootenay Street likely takes its name from Kootenay National Park, British Columbia, which is located southwest of Banff and southeast of Yoho National Parks. The park includes the headwaters of the Kootenay River, which eventually widens to become Kootenay Lake before entering the Columbia River. The name Kootenay is an Anglicization of Kutenai, the name of a B.C. Band.

Lacombe Centre   **14540 Bannister Rd. S.E.**

See Father Lacombe Senior High School.

Lacombe Way   **Lakeview, S.W.**

See Father Lacombe Senior High School.

Laird Court   **Lakeview, S.W.**

The name Laird may have been used in recognition of the Honourable David Laird (1833-1914) who became the first lieutenant-governor of the newly formed North-West Territories in 1876. He served in that position for one term until 1881, when he retired from public life. He once again became a public servant in 1898, when he was appointed Indian Commissioner, a position he held at the time of his death.

Lake Cameron Drive   **Lake Bonavista, S.E.**

There is a Cameron Lake located just south of Waterton Park. It was named in 1916 for Captain Donald R. Cameron, British Commissioner on the International Boundary Commission from 1872 to 1876.

Lake Fraser Drive, etc.   **Lake Bonavista, S.E.**

There is a Fraser Lake in British Columbia which is named after Simon Fraser. (See Simon Fraser Junior High School.)

Lake Louise Way, etc.   **Lake Bonavista, S.E.**

Lake Louise is located in Banff National Park. It is named for Princess Louise Caroline Alberta, fourth daughter of Queen Victoria.

Lambert Avenue   **Renfrew (St. George's Heights), N.E.**

Lambert Avenue may have been named for James Smith Lambert, a pioneer member of the NWMP, who served in Alberta from 1898 until 1902 and later lived in Calgary. A building contractor by trade, he built the NWMP detachment buildings in Macleod and Boundary Creek.

Lancaster Building   **304 - 8 Avenue S.W.**

Originally planned for construction in 1913, this building was not completed until after World War I. Its owner, J.S. Mackie, had an avid interest in history and named it after the House of Lancaster, one of the sides that fought in the Wars of the Roses in Britain (1454-85). Mackie came to Calgary in 1866 and was a successful businessman who served both as an alderman from 1894 to 1899 and as mayor from 1900 to 1901. The Lancaster Building was the first 10-storey structure built in downtown Calgary.

Lancaster Way   **Lakeview, S.W.**

George Cullis Lancaster was a city alderman from 1937 to 1948. He was very active in community life from the time of his arrival in the city in 1906 and this service was recognized when he was named the Calgary Junior Chamber of Commerce citizen of the year in 1957. He served on the boards of the Calgary General Hospital, YMCA, and Calgary zoological society and after his retirement was chairman of the Calgary Transit Commission. Lancaster died in Calgary in 1978 at the age of 91. Lancaster Way may have been named in his honour.

Lane Crescent   **Lakeview, S.W.**

Lane Crescent was probably named after George Lane, one of Calgary's "Big Four." (See Big Four Building.)

Langevin Bridge   **Bow River at 4 Street and 5 Street N.E.**

Sir Hector L. Langevin, federal Minister of Public Works and one of the Fathers of Confederation, visited Calgary in 1885 and at the request of the town council, petitioned the North-West Territories government for funds to build a bridge at 4 St. E. (then known as Dewdney St.). The wooden structure was finished in 1888 and was replaced by a steel structure in 1910. The new northbound Langevin Bridge opened in 1972.

Lansdowne Avenue   **Elboya, S.W.**

Henry Petty-Fitzmaurice, the 5th Marquis of Lansdowne, was governor general of Canada from 1883 to 1888 and made an official visit to Calgary in 1885. This street may be named in his honour.

Lassiter Court   **Lakeview, S.W.**

Lassiter Court may have been named for Oscar B. Lassiter (1885-1977), who began his farming career with 50 borrowed dollars and a borrowed tent, and rose to become the largest individual farmer in the British Empire. He arrived in Alberta from California in

1931, farmed at Chin and later at Bassano. In the 1940s, his cornfield at Chin was the largest in Canada. He gained international recognition after World War II when he undertook the supervision of what was named the World's Greatest Clearing project near Wanham in the Peace River district. He and his crew cleared 100,000 acres of land for veterans returning from the war.

Lathom Crescent   Lakeview, S.W.
Lathom Crescent may have been named for Edward George Bootle Wilbraham, 2nd Earl of Lathom, who was a director of the Oxley Ranch Company, northwest of Fort Macleod, and a shareholder in the CPR. There is also an Alberta village by this name.

Laurier Court   Lakeview, S.W.
The street is likely named for Sir Wilfrid Laurier, prime minister of Canada from 1896 to 1911. (See Sir Wilfrid Laurier Junior High School.)

Laval Avenue   Mount Royal, S.W.
Francois Xavier de Montmorency Laval (1623-1708) was the first Roman Catholic bishop of the city of Quebec from 1659 to 1688. He founded the Seminary of Quebec, now Laval University, and played a major role in the religious and civil affairs of the colony of New France.

Law Drive   Lakeview, S.W.
Law Drive may have been named for the Canadian-born statesman, Andrew Bonar Law, who was prime minister of Britain from 1922 to 1923, or for John Steele Law, who lived in Calgary for 50 years until his death in 1942. He was brewmaster for the Calgary Brewing Company until his retirement in 1934.

Lawrence Court   North Glenmore Park, S.W.
There were a number of Lawrences associated with early Alberta. The most notable was Sheridan Lawrence (1870-1952) who settled in Fort Vermilion, Alberta in 1888. He brought considerable fame to the province for the most northerly development of agriculture on the continent. Locally, one of Calgary's famous characters during the early part of the century was Joseph (Long Joe) Lawrence, who worked as a railway policeman from 1909 to 1912. At 6 feet 11 inches tall he towered over the railway platform and was a familiar sight to travellers. He was the tallest man in the Canadian army during World War I.

Lawrey Gardens   Bow River below Spruce Cliff, S.W.
John Lawrey was an Englishman who came to Calgary by way of the gold fields in California and the Cariboo. He was a squatter on land along the south side of the Bow River west of Shaganappi Point and ran a market garden there which supplied produce to both Fort Calgary and the early town of Calgary for many years. The CPR railway line was built through his land which isolated his gardens. He was allowed to build a road on the railroad right of way, which was his only access to town. Lawrey homesteaded on the top of the escarpment in the area which is now Spruce Cliff and hiked down the hill

to tend his garden. There is some confusion in civic and other records as to the spelling of Lawrey (Lowery and Lowry), but Ron Linden, who has done extensive research on John Lawrey, says that old records indicate the correct spelling is Lawrey.

Lawson Place   Lakeview, S.W.

This street may have been named for Mount Lawson in Kananaskis Country, which was named after Maj. W.E. Lawson, a topographer with the Geological Survey. It may also recognize Peter Lawson, who came to Calgary in 1927. He was one of the pioneers in the travel industry and the firm that he began in 1930, P. Lawson Travel became the largest travel agency in Canada. Lawson died in 1979 at the age of 73.

Laycock Park   64 Avenue and 4 Street N.E.

Thomas and Martha Laycock arrived in Calgary from Windermere, England in 1886. They farmed the land where Laycock Park is located. After their deaths, the farm was inherited by their youngest son, Thomas Hayes Laycock, who was born there in 1899. The land was eventually sold to Galleli and Sons cement company. When the park was named, approval for the name was given by Thomas Laycock. Laycock Drive in Thorncliffe is likely also named for the family.

Layzell Road   North Glenmore Park, S.W.

Arthur Layzell came to Calgary from England in 1901, working as a machinery salesman, hotelier and livestock commission agent. Until his death in 1939 he was considered to be the best auctioneer in volume of sales in Western Canada. He was a race horse expert who raised and ran his own horses and was the leading thoroughbred breeder in Western Canada in 1932. His son, Arthur G. Layzell, was a competitor in the first Calgary Stampede in 1912, and his grandson, Denny Layzell, was a well-known columnist for the Calgary Herald from 1939 until his death in 1971.

Leduc Crescent   Lakeview, S.W.

Rev. Hippolyte Leduc (1842-1918) was an Oblate priest ordained in 1864. He served in St. Albert, Edmonton and Calgary. As vicar-general he was a superior to Father Lacombe. The name Leduc is best known to Albertans as the site where the Alberta oil boom began in 1947. The town was named after Father Leduc.

Leeson Court   North Glenmore Park, S.W.

George Kidd Leeson came west in 1880. In 1886 he arrived in Morley where he opened a store. He was a partner with James Scott in the Royal Mail Line on north-south stage-coach routes in the North-West Territories before the railway built north-south lines. Leeson was well-known, not only in Calgary, but throughout the west. He died in Calgary in 1910 at the age of 68. It is likely that Leeson Court was named after this early Albertan.

Lefroy Court   Lakeview, S.W.

The name Lefroy may come from Mount Lefroy in the Canadian Rockies. It was named after General Sir John Henry Lefroy, head of the magnetic observatory in Toronto from

1842 to 1853. He conducted a series of magnetic observations in various Alberta locations during the winter of 1843-44.

Legare Drive   **Lakeview, S.W.**

At the suggestion of then alderman Grant MacEwan, Legare Drive replaced the original suggested name of Lenore Drive. The street name honours John Louis Legare who was instrumental in encouraging Sioux chief Sitting Bull to return to the United States after he fled to Canada in 1876 following the battle at Little Big Horn.

Len Werry Building (AGT)   **622 - 1 Street S.W.**

Len Werry was Alberta's minister of telephones when he died in an automobile accident in 1973 at age 45. He had been an MLA for the Calgary Foothills constituency for more than five years. The building was named in his memory when it was completed in 1974. The name was suggested by Calgary's mayor at the time, Rod Sykes.

Lepine Court   **Lakeview, S.W.**

Lepine Court may have been named for Ambroise-Dydime Lépine, adjutant-general in the provisional government of Louis Riel in 1869. After the Rebellion of 1869-70, Lépine fled to the United States. When he returned to Canada in 1873 he was sentenced to death for his part in the rebellion, but this was commuted to two years in prison and the loss of his civil rights. Those rights were restored some years before his death in 1923. Lépine is recognized as a hero by the Metis people.

Le Roi Daniels Elementary School   **47 Fyffe Road S.E.**

Born and educated in Calgary, Le Roi Daniels (1906-63) began teaching in rural Alberta and moved to Calgary in 1929. He became principal of Glengarry School in 1940, was appointed supervisor of elementary instruction in 1942 and director ten years later. In 1955 he became assistant superintendent of Calgary elementary public schools. He was also active in the Alberta Teachers' Association at local, district and provincial levels. Le Roi Daniels School opened in 1963, closed in 1984 and reopened in 1994.

Lester B. Pearson High School   **3020 - 52 Street N.E.**

Lester Bowles Pearson (1897-1972) was prime minister of Canada from 1963 to 1967. Before becoming leader of the Liberal Party in 1958, Pearson gained international fame as a statesman. As secretary of state for external affairs, he had helped create the North Atlantic Treaty Organization (NATO). He also served on the UN commission that drew up cease-fire plans to end the Korean War, was president of the UN General Assembly, and in 1957 became the first Canadian to win the Nobel Peace Prize after helping end a war in Egypt over control of the Suez Canal. In 1968 Pearson resigned as prime minister to become head of the World Bank Commission and remained active until he retired due to ill health in 1970.

Lethbridge Crescent   Lakeview, S.W.

This street takes its name from the city of Lethbridge which was originally known as Coalbanks. In 1885, it was re-named for William Lethbridge (1824-1901), first president of the North Western Coal and Navigation Company.

Levis Avenue   Mount Royal, S.W.

Most of the streets in Mount Royal were given names which reflect the history of Quebec. Francois-Gaston de Levis (1719-87) was a French army officer, second in command of the French army in Canada during the Seven Years' War. He aided in the defense of Quebec until leaving to protect Montreal from a British attack. When Montcalm died and Quebec fell, Levis assumed command of the army, but was unsuccessful in attempting to regain Quebec. He was compelled to capitulate in September of 1760 and returned to France where he was created Duc de Levis in 1784.

Lewis Drive   Lakeview, S.W.

There are a number of Lewises associated with Calgary after whom this street might be named. Margaret A. Lewis arrived in Calgary in 1912 and was active in organizing a suffrage society. She became a charter member of the Women's Institute in 1913, was the first female representative on the hospital board, was president of the Calgary Business and Professional Women's Club, and served many other organizations. She died in 1941. Clement Sherwood Lewis was a resident of Turner Valley and Bowness from 1929 to 1956. He was one of the first of the Yukon prospectors before the gold rush of 1898 and a friend of poet Robert Service and other legends of Canada's north. Joseph Henry Lewis, who began farming in the Beddington area in 1889, was one of the first settlers north of the Bow River. Another possibility is Lloyd Paris Lewis, one of the founders and first competitors in the Calgary Stampede's chuckwagon races. He came to Alberta from Indiana in 1904 and resided in Calgary briefly before his death in 1954.

Liddell Court   Lakeview, S.W.

Liddell Court may have been named for William Liddell, a prominent pioneer builder. He supervised construction of the Banff Springs Hotel, the University of Alberta medical building and other large construction projects throughout western Canada. He lived in Calgary from 1903 until his death in 1941. Another possibility is that it was named for Ken Liddell (1912-75), a columnist for the Calgary Herald from his arrival in Calgary in 1950 until his death. His column, which dealt with the people he met on his travels throughout Alberta, was one of the oldest continuous columns of its kind in a Canadian daily newspaper. He helped found the Calgary Tourist and Convention Association and was a director of the Calgary Historical Society. He received the White Hatter of the Year award in 1963 for his work in promoting tourism in Calgary and southern Alberta.

Lincoln Park   S.W.

Royal Canadian Air Force Station Lincoln Park was a 460-acre site between Crowchild Trail and 37th Street S.W., and Glenmore Trail and Currie Barracks. Prior to 1939, the site of Lincoln Park was a flying field with an unpaved landing strip. It was built up and used as a training and repair depot during World War II and for pilot refresher training programs between 1945 and 1951. It was then used as a ferry flight base until 1964, when the federal government closed the base and sold the site to The City of Calgary. During the war it was known as Number Ten Repair Depot and the name changed sometime between 1945 and 1952. The only Lincoln associated with the air force was Major A.G. Lincoln who helped organize the 12th Canadian Mounted Rifles in Calgary at the beginning of World War I. He was transferred to the Princess Patricia's Canadian Light Infantry in 1914 and from that regiment, went to the air force. During the last year of the war, Lincoln was a member of a British flying squadron that worked with the Italian forces and he was awarded the Mons medal. He was well known in Calgary where he practiced law prior to leaving for California in 1920. He paid numerous visits back to Calgary before his death in 1930. Lincoln Park may have been named in his honour. Lincoln Drive, Manor and Way are all located on what was once airfield land.

Linden Drive   Lakeview, S.W.

The name originally suggested for this street in Lakeview was Lorraine Drive. At the suggestion of then alderman Grant MacEwan, the name was changed to Linden to honour a pioneer Alberta family.

Lindsay Park Sports Centre   2225 Macleod Trail S.

This athletic facility is named after Dr. Neville James Lindsay (1845-1925), who arrived in Calgary in 1883 aboard the first CPR passenger train. He practiced medicine in the city until 1908, with a short break in 1898 to travel to the Yukon, where he prospected for gold and copper. Lindsay was also an alderman on Calgary's first town council, serving from 1884 to 1887. He served on City council from 1896 to 1897. When he retired from medicine he took up real estate, acquiring the subdivision which was known as Park Hill, land on which Lindsay Park now stands. In 1913, Lindsay began construction of his dream home, built of sandstone and brick. The house was never completed, possibly because the land on which he chose to build was unstable and possibly because of financial difficulties. The ruins, by the river in Rideau Park, have been known as "Lindsay's Folly," Lindsay's Castle" and "Deadman's Castle."

Lindstrom Drive   Lakeview, S.W.

Lindstrom Drive may have been named for Calgary artist Matt Lindstrom (1888-1975). Lindstrom came to Canada from Finland in 1929 and moved to Calgary in the early 1930s. He worked as a signpainter until 1943 when at age 55, he decided to become a full-time artist. He received scholarships to the Banff School of Fine Arts and also studied at the Provincial School of Fine Arts. Lindstrom's focus as an artist was on western and wildlife art.

Lismer Green   University of Calgary Family Housing, N.W.

The streets of the family housing units at the University of Calgary were named by the U of C Board of Governors to honour Canada's Group of Seven artists. While they wanted to honour many famous Canadians, they felt that using names from one particular group would promote a sense of unity to the project. Lismer was one of the seven original members of the group, which after their formation in 1920, worked primarily as landscape artists until they disbanded in 1933.

Livingstone Drive   Lakeview, S.W.

The street is named after a landowner in the Woodlands area. Originally Woodlands was to be called Livingstone, but as there was already a subdivision using street names beginning with "L," the name was changed.

Lloyd Crescent   Lakeview, S.W.

This street may be named for Benjamin S. Lloyd and his family, who came to the Calgary area in 1882 with the Shaw family of Midnapore. The Lloyd family moved further west to settle at Red Deer Lake. John Edric R. Lloyd was the first white child born in that area. He was a well-known farmer and rancher and retired to Calgary in 1942. Another possiblilty is the Rev. George Exton Lloyd (1861-1940) for whom Lloydminster is named. Lloyd was chaplain of the Barr colonists (see Barr Road) and was responsible for the success of the British immigration scheme. He later became Bishop of Saskatchewan.

Locke Court   Lakeview, S.W.

Locke Court may have been named in recognition of the community achievements of Ernie Locke. During his 15 years as district sales manager of Air Canada in Calgary, Locke served, among other roles, as president of the Calgary Tourist and Convention Association and as head of the United Appeal. After a transfer to Halifax, he returned to Calgary with his wife when he retired a short time later and lived here until his death in 1985. This street could also be named after another Locke who was one of Calgary's early ministers. Rev. Frederick William Locke came to Calgary in 1886. He served in the ministry of the Methodist and United churches for 40 years. He died at Calgary in 1944 at the age of 79.

Lodge Crescent   Lakeview, S.W.

This street may be named after a former CNR station in southwest Alberta. It was named for Sir Oliver Lodge (1850-1940), a British physicist, who, in 1894, was the first to suggest that the sun was a source of radio waves, a theory which was confirmed in 1942.

Logan Crescent   Lakeview, S.W.

Logan Crescent may have been named for the Logan Ridge west of Calgary. It was named in 1939 after one of the area's earliest settlers.

Lord Beaverbrook High School   9019 Fairmount Drive S.E.

William Maxwell Aitken (1879-1964) was born in Ontario. He followed his friend, R.B. Bennett to Calgary in 1897 at age 17 and stayed for a year, just long enough to open what was probably Calgary's first bowling alley. He campaigned for Bennett's successful bid for a seat in the Territories Legislature and then left for Edmonton and the East. He later moved to England where he entered politics and was one of only two people to serve in the British cabinet during both world wars, along with Winston Churchill. He was knighted in 1911 and elevated to a peerage in 1917. As Lord Beaverbrook he was known in Canada primarily as a publisher and philanthropist. He donated funds to many interests in New Brunswick, particularly the University of New Brunswick, of which he was chancellor, and helped finance the Calgary Power and Transmission Company in 1906.

Lorne Place   **North Glenmore Park, S.W.**

This street is named for Sir John Doughal Sutherland Campbell (1845-1914), Marquis of Lorne, later named 9th Duke of Argyll, and Canada's governor-general from 1878 to 1883. (See Marquis of Lorne Trail.)

Lougheed Building   **604- 1 Street S.W.**

One of Calgary's first lawyers, James Lougheed (1854-1925) came to Calgary from Brampton, Ontario in 1883. He was appointed to the Canadian Senate in 1889 and at age 35, was its youngest member and the last senator appointed by Sir John A. Macdonald. He sat as a senator for 36 years and served in the cabinets of prime ministers Robert Borden and Arthur Meighen. He was knighted in 1916. Lougheed was very involved in Calgary real estate and constructed a number of buildings (see Clarence Block and Norman Block). The Lougheed Building was built in 1911. (See also Lougheed Residence and Sir James Lougheed Elementary School.) Lougheed Drive in Lakeview was also likely named after him.

Lougheed Residence   **707 - 13 Avenue S.W.**

Now owned by the Alberta Government and designated a provincial historic site in 1977, the Lougheed residence was built by Sir James Lougheed for his family in 1891. He called his home "Beaulieu." It was owned by the Canadian Red Cross from 1947 until 1977 when the provincial government purchased it. (See Lougheed Building and Sir James Lougheed Elementary School.)

Louis Riel Elementary/Junior High School   **9632 Oakfield Drive S.W.**

The name chosen for this southwest junior high school, which opened in 1972, was a controversial one. Four hundred Calgary Metis signed a petition requesting that a school be named after Louis "David" Riel, who in 1869 and 1885 led Metis uprisings against the Canadian government. He was elected to Parliament in 1873, but because he was a fugitive, never claimed his seat. Considered a hero to the Metis and the father of the province of Manitoba, Riel sought sanctuary in Montana but returned to Canada in 1884 to resume his fight. As a result of his part in the rebellion of 1885, he was found guilty of treason and hanged in Regina in November 1885. Reil called himself "David" after the biblical King David.

Louise Bridge   **Bow River at 10 Street N.W.**

See Hillhurst (Louise) Bridge.

Louise Dean School   120 - 23 Street N.W.

Louise Dean (1895-1987) moved to Calgary with her husband in 1921. Throughout her life she was active in numerous volunteer organizations. She was one of the founders of the Calgary Birth Control Society, worked with the Community Chest (now the United Way), the YWCA, the Women's Canadian Club, the Calgary 1967 Centennial Committee, and a host of other organizations. She was a life-time member of the Volunteer Bureau and served a term as a school board trustee in 1938. She was named Citizen of the Year in 1976 by the Calgary Jaycees and was presented with The City's Pioneer Award in 1984. However, her most treasured honour was having a school, which provides secondary education to pregnant teens, named after her in 1981.

Louise Riley Branch Library   1904 - 14 Avenue N.W.

Louise Riley, daughter of Calgary pioneer E.H. Riley (see Riley Park, Hillhurst), joined the Calgary Public Library staff in 1930 and worked for 19 years to develop the children's section. She was appointed assistant librarian in 1949. Riley was popular on a weekly radio program telling children's stories, and worked to establish a close link between schools and libraries. She was the author of two children's books, The Mystery Horse and Train for Tiger Lily, and an adult novel, One Happy Moment. She died in Edmonton in 1957.

Louise Road   Lakeview, S.W.

This street was probably named for Princess Louise, daughter of Queen Victoria. (See Hillhurst (Louise) Bridge and Lorne Place.)

Lowes Court   Lakeview, S.W.

Fred Charles "Freddie" Lowes (1880-1950), was Calgary's first millionaire, making and losing a fortune during Calgary's real estate boom of 1910-13. Lowes came to Calgary from Ontario in 1902 and by 1906 he had his own business; F.C. Lowes and Company, real estate, insurance and financial brokers. The company, which also included his two brothers, opened up much of Calgary's south side - Glencoe, Elbow Park, Britannia, Rideau Park and Roxboro. Unfortunately, the company did not survive World War I and by 1916 was only a part of Calgary's history. Lowes lived his remaining years in reduced circumstances and poor health. It is likely in recognition of this early Calgarian that this street was named.

Lyle Avenue   North Glenmore Park, S.W.

Lyle Avenue may have been named in recognition of the community contributions of two Lyle brothers. Kennett I. Lyle served as a city alderman from 1954 to 1956. A real-estate broker in Calgary from 1929 to 1966, he helped found the Alberta Real Estate Association and was its first president from 1946 to 1948. He was on the executive council of the Calgary Chamber of Commerce, founded the Calgary Tourist and Convention Association and was elected founding president in 1958. He was later named Calgary's White Hatter of the Year. Kennett lived in Calgary for almost 60 years and died in 1987. His brother, Elmer Bowling "Pete" Lyle, was also an alderman, serving from 1952 to 1954.

He was a member of the Metro Calgary and Rural General Hospital Board and on the board of governors of Mount Royal College.

Lynch Crescent   **Lakeview, S.W.**

This street may have taken its name from Lynch Lake, southwest of Lethbridge. It is named after James S. Lynch, who farmed near the lake from 1909 until about 1919.

Lysander Crescent, etc.   **Lynnwood Ridge, S.E.**

The streets with the name Lysander likely take their name from the commander of the Spartan fleet which defeated the Athenians in 407 B.C. Two years later he captured Athens and ended the Peloponnesian War.

Macdonald Avenue   **Ramsay, S.E.**

Macdonald Avenue may have been named for Sir John A. Macdonald, first prime minister of Canada, who visited Calgary in 1886 aboard the first train to travel from Montreal to the Pacific Coast. However, there were a number of Macdonalds in early Calgary after whom the street might have been named. Angus MacDonald lived in Calgary for more that 36 years and died in 1929 at age 84. He was well-known in the city as a member of the survey party which marked the route of the Canadian Pacific Railway through Calgary. Alexander Donald MacDonald was a minister who came to Calgary in 1910. He took charge of the Children's Aid Society (later The City of Calgary Children's Aid Department), a position which he held for 14 years. He was also active in a number of charities until his retirement from active social work. A.B. Macdonald arrived in Calgary in 1883 and opened the Langdon-Shepard Supply Company. In 1886 he helped organize the Glengarry Ranch Company, which later became part of Pat Burns' holdings.

MacDonnell Avenue   **Harvey Barracks, S.W.**

Archibald Cameron Macdonell (1864-1941) (note spelling difference) was born into a military family and continued the tradition through a long and distinguished career. He entered the Royal Military College at Kingston, Ontario in 1883 and upon graduation joined the Canadian Militia. He became a lieutenant in the Canadian Mounted Infantry of the Permanent Corps of Canada in 1888 and a year later transferred into the North West Mounted Police (NWMP). He remained with the NWMP until 1907, with two of these years spent in voluntary service in the Boer War. In 1907 he was appointed major and second in command of the Royal Canadian Mounted Rifles, now the Lord Strathcona's Horse (Royal Canadians). In June 1917 he became a major-general in command of the 1st Canadian Division, leading them on their march into Germany. Macdonell became commandant of the Royal Military College in 1919 and served there until his retirement from the army in 1925. He then lived in Calgary for a short time where he worked with the Ranchmen's Club before retiring to Kingston.

MacEwan   N.W.

Carma Developers chose to name this subdivision to honour J.S. Grant MacEwan, Calgary historian, alderman and mayor, and Alberta lieutenant-governor. (See Grant MacEwan Elementary School.)

MacEwan Student Centre   University of Calgary, N.W.

The University of Calgary's students' centre, built in 1967 after years of work by student representatives, was dedicated as MacEwan Hall on November 17, 1967. The dedication reads: "This building is named in honour of John Walter Grant MacEwan, BSA, MS, LLD, DUC, Lieutenant Governor of Alberta, because of his many contributions to the city, the province, the history of the area and his interest in youth." The present MacEwan Student Centre, officially opened in 1987, is an outgrowth of the original MacEwan Hall. (See Grant MacEwan Elementary School.)

MacKay Drive   Meadowlark Park, S.W.

Donald Hugh Mackay (1914-79) was a Calgary alderman from 1945 to 1949 and mayor from 1949 to 1959. He was the first native Albertan to hold the position of mayor and made the white stetson the city's symbol, known world-wide. Mackay was also at the forefront in creating the annual Grey Cup festival. In 1948 he helped organize a parade and celebration in Toronto when Calgarians went there to watch the Stampeders win the Cup. Before 1948 the Grey Cup game had held little national interest, but from then on, it became an annual national event. The name MacKay Drive may have been chosen to honour this man who contributed so much to Calgary's national and international reputation. However, note the difference in spelling between the street name and the name of the man.

Mackay Road   Montgomery, N.W.

Mackay Road may be named for Alfred McKay, although the spelling is different. The street runs down the hill to the area near McKay's original homestead. (See Point McKay.)

MacKid Road, etc.   Mayland Heights, N.E.

These streets may have been named for Doctor Harry Goodsir Mackid who practiced medicine in Calgary from 1889 until his death in 1917. He was chief surgeon for the western division of the CPR and performed the first appendectomy in Calgary. Among his friends were Will and Charles Mayo of the Mayo Clinic, Rochester, Minnesota, and Professor Emil Shemk, medical advisor to the Czar of Russia. The first microscope used in Calgary was a gift to Dr. Mackid from Prof. Shemk after he was exiled to Vienna by the czar.

MacKimmie Library   University of Calgary, N.W.

Ross Anderson MacKimmie (1916-1992), a prominent Calgary lawyer who appeared frequently before the Supreme Court, was a native of Nova Scotia. After moving to Calgary he was called to the Alberta Bar in 1950 and was created Queen's Council in 1955.

MacKimmie served as chairman of the University of Calgary board of governors from 1975 to 1984. He was made an officer of the Order of Canada in 1985.

MacLeay Road   Mayland Heights, N.E.

This street may be named for Roderick MacLeay, a prominent rancher who settled in the High River area in 1899.

Macleod Trail   S.W.

Macleod Trail was named Blue Trail by pioneer motorists who assigned colours to principal roads. In 1924 it was called the Sunshine Trail, part of a north-south route designed to link Mexico and Alaska. However, the street's first official name was Drinkwater Street. For a time the portion which runs alongside Stampede Park was called Stampede Way. The street was given its present name because Macleod Trail runs south from Calgary to Fort Macleod which was named after Col. James Macleod, commissioner of the North West Mounted Police from 1876 to 1880. (See Colonel Macleod Elementary/Junior High School.)

Maddock Crescent, etc.   Marlborough Park, N.E.

These streets may have been named in recognition of Lillie Maddock Woodhall, one of early Calgary's prominent women. She and her husband came to Calgary in 1902 where she quickly became involved in numerous women's associations. She was the first president of the Calgary branch of the Women's Christian Temperance Union, served as president of the Local Council of Women and was a school board trustee in 1921 and 1922.

Madeleine d'Houet Bilingual Junior High School   108 - 22 Street N.W.

Madeleine d'Houet was born in France in 1781. After being widowed, she devoted her life to prayer, fasting and penance, eventually founding a religious order, the Society of Sisters, Faithful Companions of Jesus (FCJ). The FCJs closely followed the basic rule of their male counterparts, the Jesuits (Society of Jesus). FCJ sisters were among the first missionaries in Calgary and established St. Mary's, the first Catholic School in Calgary.

Maggie Street   Ramsay, S.E.

Maggie Street was named for Maggie Beattie, one of the daughters of Wesley Fletcher Orr, original owner of the land on which the street is situated. Before coming to Calgary, Orr purchased a large parcel of land on the east side of the Elbow River along with partner, Mrs. Wilfred C. Schreiber. He moved here from Barrie, Ontario in 1883 and became very active in the town's affairs. He worked as both the editor and manager of the Calgary Herald and served as an alderman from 1884 to 1891 and 1892 to 1894. He drafted the application for the incorporation of Calgary as a city and designed the new city's seal with the motto, "Onward Calgary." He was elected first mayor of the city of Calgary in 1894 and was re-elected again in 1895 and 1897. He helped convince the CPR to build their repair shops in Calgary and donated land to the CPR to encourage development in the city's east end. While Orr admitted that he worked to develop his own interests, he also worked zealously to promote Calgary, often putting the city's needs above his own, and encouraging every scheme that would advance the community. He died in 1898 at the age of 56.

Maitland Crescent, etc.   **Marlborough Park, N.W**

The nine streets in Marlborough Park with the name Maitland may take their name from Maitland Park in north London, England. Its name comes from William Maitland (1528-73), a Scottish patriot who abolished papal authority and became an advisor to Mary Stuart, the queen regent.

Manning Close, etc.   **Mayland Heights, N.W.**

These streets were probably named for Ernest Manning (see Ernest Manning High School), though the name may have been in recognition of Fred C. Manning, a city alderman from 1926 to 1929 and 1945 to 1947. Fred Manning came to Calgary in 1909 as an employee of the Revelstoke Sawmills Company. He left the company in 1922 to establish the Manning-Egleston Lumber Company.

Margaret Avenue   **Ramsay, S.E.**

See Alberta Avenue.

Marion Carson Elementary School   **5225 Varsity Drive N.W.**

Marion Carson school is named in recognition of the outstanding contribution made by one woman in the fields of public health, welfare and education. Marion Carson came to Calgary in 1893 and was instrumental in establishing the first tuberculosis sanitarium in Alberta in 1910. She served on the Calgary school board from 1920 to 1924 and as a member of the Calgary Library Board, helped to establish a central library. She was among the first to help feed the unemployed in Calgary during the Depression and worked toward the construction of free clinics for school children. She received the King's Medal in 1938 for her work with tuberculosis and was named Calgary's Citizen of the Year in 1946.

Markerville Road   **Mayland Heights, N.E.**

This street is likely named after a small Icelandic community west of Red Deer. Formed in 1902, it was famous for its cheese factory and was named after C.P. Marker, Alberta's Dairy Commissioner.

Marlborough   **N.E.**

The subdivision of Marlborough may be named for John Churchill, first Duke of Marlborough (1650 -1722), an English military commander and political figure. It may also take its name from the town of Marlborough (meaning "Marl's Hill"), England, which is situated 75 miles west of London.

Marquette Street   **Mount Royal, S.W.**

Most of the streets in Mount Royal are named after people who played a prominent role in French-Canadian history. Jacques Marquette (1637-75) entered the priesthood in France in 1654. He was sent to New France as a missionary in 1666 and worked among the Huron and Ottawa Aboriginals. He moved to the area around northern Lake Michigan in 1669 and founded the St. Ignace Mission there in 1671. He was sent by the Governor of New France to be the interpreter for Louis Jolliet on his voyage down the Mississippi in 1673. They were hoping to find a trade route to the Far East. In 1674 he went to Illinois country to found a new mission but was forced by ill health to abandon the attempt. He died while returning to the St. Ignace Mission.

Marquis of Lorne Trail — Highway 22X S.E.

This short stretch of Highway 22X on the southeast edge of Calgary is named after Sir John Doughal Sutherland Campbell, Marquis of Lorne. Campbell named the Provisional District of Alberta in 1882 after his wife, Princess Louise Caroline Alberta, fourth daughter of Queen Victoria. This name was given to the province in 1905. Campbell founded the Royal Society of Canada and helped to establish the National Gallery and the Royal Canadian Academy of Art. He visited Calgary during a trip to the Canadian West in 1881. (See Lorne Place.)

Marsh Road — Crescent Heights, N.E.

Daniel Webster Marsh was mayor of Calgary in 1889 and a prominent businessman in the city. A transplanted American, he was elected in 1896 as first president of the Western Stockgrowers' Association. Marsh Road may have been named in his honour.

Marshall Road — Marlborough, N.E.

There were at least two prominent Marshalls in Calgary. Robert Colin Marshall (1884-1962) was a city alderman from 1915 to 1919, mayor from 1919 to 1920 and a member of the Alberta Legislature from 1921 to 1926. He came to Calgary in 1902 and resided in the city until 1928, when the paving company for which he worked transferred him to Edmonton. Frank J. Marshall served as an alderman from 1917 to 1918. Little else is known about him.

Martha Cohen Theatre — Calgary Centre for Performing Arts, 205 - 8 Avenue S.E.

Dr. Martha R. Cohen is the founding president of the Calgary Centre for Performing Arts. She is a native Calgarian who has seen more than 40 years of volunteer work in a wide range of organizations. She received the Order of Canada in 1975 and an honourary doctorate from the University of Calgary in 1982. In October 1983, she and her husband, Dr. Harry Cohen, donated $1 million to the Centre, the last of three endowments for performance spaces.

Massey Place — Mayfair, S.W.

Charles Vincent Massey (1887-1967) was Canada's first native-born governor general. He was a history lecturer and worked in the family business, Massey-Harris Company, manufacturers of farm machinery, before beginning his diplomatic career in 1926. He served as Canada's first minister to the United States, as High Commissioner for Canada in Britain and as chairman of the Royal Commission on National Development in Arts,

Letters and Sciences. He served as governor general from 1952 to 1959 and travelled extensively throughout the country promoting national identity and unity. In 1961 he founded Massey College, a graduate college at the University of Toronto.

Maunsell Close   **Mayland Heights, N.E.**

This street may be named for the Maunsell brothers, early southern Alberta pioneers. Edward Maunsell (1854-1923), was a member of the first NWMP troop which arrived in Fort Macleod in 1874. He left the police force in 1877 to become a rancher in partnership with his brothers, Harry and George. By 1886 the Maunsell Brothers Ranch near Fort Macleod was running over 10,000 head of cattle. Harry Maunsell and his wife Mary retired to Calgary in 1935 and for the next 12 years Harry became a familiar figure at the Calgary Exhibition and Stampede.

Max Bell Centre   **1001 Barlow Trail S.E.**

Formerly called the Max Bell Arena, this facility was one of the beneficiaries of philanthropist George Maxwell Bell. (See Max Bell Theatre.)

Max Bell Theatre   **Calgary Centre for Performing Arts,**
                                                        205 - 8 Avenue S.E.

Born in Regina, George Maxwell Bell (1912-72) began his career supplying railway ties to the CPR. He invested his profits in the Turner Valley oilfield and came to Calgary in 1935 to work for his father at the family-owned newspaper, the Calgary Albertan. When his father died, Bell took over the newspaper. He invested in both the newspaper and petroleum industries. He was a philanthropist whose beneficiaries include the Max Bell Arena, now called the Max Bell Centre, and the Vancouver Aquarium. In his memory, the Max Bell Foundation donated $1 million to the Calgary Centre for Performing Arts to build the section which houses Theatre Calgary.

Mayfair   **S.W.**

The land for this subdivision was bought from Betty Mayland, daughter of Henry Mayland, after whom Mayland Heights is named. The developer chose the name in her honour. (See Mayland Heights.)

Mayland Heights   **N.E.**

Albert Henry Mayland was born in Minnesota in 1874 and came west to be a cowboy. He eventually became a horse-trader and after frequent sales trips to Alberta, decided that this was where he wanted to settle. When he came to Calgary, he purchased the Farmer's Abbattoir and re-named it Union Packing Company. His oil company was also one of the first producers when oil was discovered at Turner Valley in 1914.

Maynard Road
Mayland Heights, N.E.

Maynard Road may have been named for Lucien Maynard, one of the original Social Credit MLAs in Alberta. He sat in the legislature from 1935 to 1955 and was Alberta's attorney-general from 1943 to 1955.

McCall Drive
Calgary International Airport, N.E.

Freddie McCall was a World War I flying ace who shot down 37 German aircraft (five in one day) and two balloons. He returned to Calgary after the war to become a barnstormer and stunt flier. In 1919, when taking a sightseeing flight over the race track at the Calgary Exhibition, he lost speed and crash landed on the top of a merry-go-round to avoid hitting the crowd. No one was hurt. In 1927 McCall founded the Calgary Aero Club, later to become the Calgary Flying Club. He played a large part in the development of commercial aviation in western Canada. The original Calgary International Airport, to the south of the present airport, was named McCall Field in his honour.

McCall Way
Calgary International Airport, N.E.

The main service road at the Calgary International Airport is aptly named after Freddie McCall. The original name of the road was Aviation Boulevard but in 1987 it was changed as an alternative to re-naming the airport after McCall. The original airport was named McCall Field but was re-named the Calgary International Airport (McCall Field) in 1962. (See McCall Drive.)

McDougall Place
808 - 4 Avenue S.W.

Methodist missionary Rev. George McDougall, his wife and eight children, were the first white family to settle in what was to become the province of Alberta. In 1863 McDougall brought his family from their mission at Norway House on Lake Winnipeg to join their eldest son, John, who was already working at a mission near Fort Edmonton. Two other children joined the family a year later after finishing their education in the east. McDougall worked among the Aboriginal people for 16 years, laying the foundation for the Methodist church in the West and paving the way for agricultural settlement. He and his son John built the mission at Morley in 1873. Three years later, George died after becoming lost in a blizzard just north of Calgary. McDougall Place was built by the provincial government in 1906 as the first normal school for teacher training in Alberta. It was bought by the Calgary school board in 1922 and named in honour of the McDougall family. The school closed in 1981 and was sold to the provincial government to house the premier's southern office and other government offices. McDougall Court and McDougall Road in Riverside may also have been named for the McDougall family.

McHugh Bluff
North of the Bow River between Centre Street and 10 Street N.W.

McHugh Bluff was named in 1990 after Felix Alexander McHugh (1851-1912), one of the first settlers in the Calgary area. McHugh came to Alberta from Ottawa in 1883, arriving before the railway, and crossing the Bow River on the first ferry boat built in Calgary. He homesteaded below the escarpment in Sunnyside and contracted to supply wood to the NWMP. In 1884 he built the first building in downtown Calgary at 8 Avenue and 1 Street S.E. McHugh's daughter, Florence McHugh, was a well-known actress on the British stage during the 1920s. McHugh Court, Place and Road in Mayland Heights may also have been named for Felix McHugh.

McKenzie   S.E.

James S. McKenzie was among the first settlers in the area southeast of the town of Calgary. He came west from Montreal in 1882 and filed for a homestead in the area of the subdivision which now bears his name. The street names in the subdivision were chosen solely for their "Mc" prefix, and not to recognize any particular people.

McKinnon Crescent, etc.   Mayland Heights, N.E.

This group of streets is likely named for Laughlan McKinnon (1865-1948), a pioneer farmer in the Calgary area. He came west from Ontario in 1886 at age 21 to work as a ranch choreboy. He soon became a full-fledged ranch hand and in 1894 bought his own ranch at Dalemead, about 12 miles southeast of Calgary. By 1921 the ranch had become a family company operation called the LK Ranch and Farming Company. Since that time it has expanded to ranches throughout southern Alberta and one in British Columbia. McKinnon and his wife left the ranch in 1921 to reside in Calgary.

McKnight Boulevard   N.W. - N.E.

Flying Officer William Lindstone McKnight (1919-41) was one of Canada's top air aces during World War II. He shot down 23 German planes before he was killed while flying over France in 1941. Born in Edmonton, McKnight came to Calgary at age one and was raised in the city. He attended Stanley Jones Elementary School and Crescent Heights High School. He received the Distinguished Flying Cross in 1940 for shooting down four planes in two days and added a bar to the cross for destroying another six planes during the Battle of Britain. The street bearing his name was originally called John Laurie Boulevard, but in 1970 the section east of 14th Street N.W. was named McKnight Boulevard in his honour.

McMahon Stadium   1817 Crowchild Trail N.W.

The stadium is named after oilmen and brothers Frank and George McMahon who, in 1960, donated $300,000 to see work on the stadium begin, and later underwrote another $400,000 so that it could be finished. The stadium was started in the spring of 1960. The contractor was Burns and Dutton, whose president, former NHL president Merv "Red" Dutton, bet the McMahons $1,500 that it would be impossible to build the stadium before the start of the 1960 football season. When the stadium was finished in a record 103 working days, Dutton dutifully paid his debt — by presenting George McMahon with 1,500 one-dollar bills!

McNeill Road   Mayland Heights, N.E.

McNeill Road may have been named for Edward Peele McNeill, who served as a judge of the Calgary District Court from 1913 until his retirement in 1941. Born in Ireland in 1863, he came to Canada in 1873 and to Alberta in 1898. He practiced law in Fort Macleod and was named King's Counsel in 1913. McNeill remained in Calgary until his death in 1954. Another possibility is that it was named for John C. McNeill, or his son, Leishman. A pioneer builder who came to Calgary in 1886, John McNeill constructed many of the city's first permanent buildings. He later went into the paving business as Calgary's first paving contractor. He retired from the contracting business in 1916 and died in Calgary in 1941. Leishman McNeill (1896-1964) grew up in Calgary and wrote a book and many articles on Calgary's early days. He was honourary secretary of the Alberta Old Timer's Association, an associate director of the Calgary Exhibition and Stampede board and in 1955 he was made an honourary chief of the Sarcee Indian tribe.

McPherson Road   Riverside, N.W.

There were two McPherson families of note in this area and this street could be named after one of them. Addison McPherson (1846-1929) was an interesting early Albertan who arrived in Edmonton in 1868. He was a prospector and freighter who travelled throughout the West. McPherson's Coulee, west of Airdrie, was named for him. McPherson later ranched in the High River area and became wealthy through the oil fields in Turner Valley. When he died in Calgary in 1929, he was one of Alberta's oldest pioneers. The Joseph McPherson family came to Alberta in 1883 and settled southwest of Calgary. They later moved to Springbank and became well known as livestock breeders. Their Clydesdale horses won many top awards at Calgary stock shows. The McPherson sons, John, Robert and Hugh, all worked at the sawmills of Col. James Walker, in the Kananaskis area and in Calgary.

McTavish Road, etc.   Calgary International Airport, N.E.

David Franz McTavish began his flying career in the late 1930s, barnstorming in southern Ontario. He came to Calgary with the British Commonwealth Air Training Plan for pilots at the beginning of World War II. In 1945 he began Chinook Flying Service, one of the first companies operating out of the Calgary airport after the war. The firm was unique because it covered all aspects of flying, including: training, charter service, maintenance, air ambulance service, crop spraying and aerial advertising. It received the first "Class A" flying school license in Canada, allowing training of international students with government funding. When the roads at the airport were being named, his students requested that his be used for the road leading to Hangar No. 5 - Chinook Flying Service's hangar. McTavish died from carbon monoxide poisoning in a light helicopter crash on February 8, 1963 at age 46.

Middleton Drive   Mayland Heights, N.E.

Middleton Drive may have been named for Samuel H. Middleton (1886-1964), Anglican archdeacon of Lethbridge from 1943 to 1949. He was well known in southern Alberta for over 40 years of service to the Peigan Indians at Brocket from 1906 to 1909 and the Blood Indians at Standoff from 1909 to 1949. In recognition of his service, he received many awards, including the King's Jubilee Medal in 1935 and the Canadian Efficiency Decoration in 1936. He was named Commander of the Order of St. John of Jerusalem in 1937. He was also instrumental in the creation of the Waterton-Glacier International Peace Park.

Another possibility is that the drive was named for Sir Frederick Middleton (1825-1898) who was commander of the Canadian Militia during the Riel Rebellion of 1885.

Millar Road   **Mayland Heights, N.E.**

There were two prominent Millars in early Alberta. Malcolm Tanner Millar came west with the North West Mounted Police in 1880 and was a pioneer rancher who founded the town of Millarville, southwest of Calgary. He died in Calgary in 1937 at the age of 76. William Archer Millar (1898-1983) came to the city from Scotland in 1919 and worked in the dairy business for 42 years. He was a familiar figure at the Stampede as made deliveries there for Union Dairies for 30 years.

Miller Avenue   **SAIT Campus, N.W.**

When the streets of SAIT were re-named in 1985, most were given the name of one of the institution's early principals. Dr. James C. Miller was SAIT's first president from 1916 to 1917.

Millican Estates   **S.E.**

When Calgary became the home of the CPR repair shops, real estate in the area became valuable. In 1912, landowner J.C. Wilson agreed to sell 154 acres to Calgary lawyer and land developer W.J. Millican, who named his subdivision Millican Estates. The boom did not last, however, and Millican never got title to the land. In 1920 Wilson was finally able to repossess the land through the courts, but the name remained.

Mills Estates   **S.E.**

Adam Francis Hirsh Mills was the original owner of all of the land from 17th Avenue to 24 Avenue S.E. between Spiller Road on the west and 11th Street on the east. He also owned property north of 9th Avenue S.E. in Inglewood. This subdivision is named for him.

Millward Place, etc.   **Mayland Heights, N.E.**

These streets were likely named for Joseph Henry Millward, one of the town of Calgary's first four councillors. He was elected shortly after the Town of Calgary was incorporated on November 17, 1884. Millward was Calgary's first painter, operating a business located on Stephen Avenue (now 8th Avenue). He served as a councillor for several years.

Milton Williams Junior High School   **92 Malibou Road S.W.**

Thomas Milton Williams served during the Riel Rebellion as one of Colonel Sam Steele's scouts. He arrived in Calgary by ox-cart in the early 1880s after a six-month journey from Winnipeg. He lived in the Glenmore district, where he was secretary of schools for 30 years. When he retired in 1929 he moved to Sylvan Lake where he died in 1947 at age 83. He is buried in Union Cemetery.

Monsignor E.L. Doyle Elementary School   8887 Scurfield Drive N.W.

Edwin Lawrence Doyle (1890-1959) came to Calgary as a teacher in 1917. He studied theology privately and was ordained as a priest in 1919. He taught at St. Mary's Boys' School from 1919 to 1938, became parish priest of St. Anne's in 1938 and was elevated to monsignor in 1956. Father Doyle was the first elected president of the Calgary Separate School Local of the Alberta Teachers' Association. He died enroute to visit his family in Prince Edward Island.

Monsignor Neville Anderson Elementary School   327 Sandarac Drive N.W.

As a young child, Neville Ramsay Anderson (1898-1988) emigrated with his family from Ireland. He was ordained as a Catholic priest and came to the Diocese of Calgary in 1925. He laboured as a priest in the Calgary diocese for 63 years, frequently visiting schools and encouraging both teachers and students.

Montcalm Crescent   Mount Royal, S.W.

Most of the streets in Mount Royal were given names which reflect the history of Quebec. Louis-Joseph de Montcalm, Marquis de Montcalm (1712-59) was commander of French troops in North America from 1756 until his death at the Battle of the Plains of Abraham in 1759. This battle led to the fall of Quebec and the eventual fall of New France.

Montgomery   N.W.

Originally this area was called Shouldice Terrace, the name James Shouldice had given to his family home located here. (See Shouldice Park.) Another Alberta town, Shouldice, south of Gleichen was also named after this man. This created some postal confusion, so during World War II the Shouldice family was asked to re-name one or the other. They changed the name of the Calgary community to Montgomery, after Field Marshall Montgomery of Alamein. The town of Montgomery was annexed at its request by The City of Calgary in 1963. One source claimed that the post office in the area from 1947 to 1959, was named after Hugh J. Montgomery, the area's MLA from 1930 to 1935.

Moodie Road   Mayland Heights, N.E.

There were two distinguished Moodies in Calgary. J.F.M. "Frank" Moodie (1878-1943) was a Calgary geologist who came west from Ontario at the turn of the century and helped develop the coal industry around Drumheller. He became manager of the Sentinel Oil company near Black Diamond in 1927 and was prominent in the Turner Valley oil fields during the boom years of 1928 and 1929. The other possibility is Marion Elizabeth Moodie, the first nursing graduate in Alberta. She came to Calgary in 1891 and entered the Calgary General Hospital as a nursing student in 1895. She was the only graduate when she finished her course in 1898. She then nursed for 30 years and later retired in Calgary where she died in 1958 at the age of 91.

Morley Trail, etc.   **Banff Trail, Charleswood, Dalhousie, N.W.**

These three sections of road are the remnants of the original Morley Trail, which angled northwest from just west of the zoo through Riverside, Bridgeland, Rosedale and west along the approximate route of Crowchild Trail to Morley. Morley was originally called Morleyville by Rev. John McDougall who established a mission there. He is said to have named it after Rev. Dr. Morley Punshon, president of the Canada Conference of the Methodist church who endorsed the establishment of the mission.

Morrison Street   **Mount Royal, S.W.**

Joseph Wanton Morrison (1783-1826) was a career officer in the British army, even though he was born in New York. He served in Canada during the War of 1812 and was British commander during the Battle of Chrysler's Farm, which helped save Montreal from attack.

Mother Mary Greene Elementary School   **115 Edenwold Drive N.W.**

Born in 1843 in County Tipperary, Ireland, Mary Greene became a Sister in the Faithful Companion of Jesus (FCJ). On the invitation of Bishop Grandin, she and 12 companions arrived in Canada in 1883 to establish convents and schools in Brandon, St. Albert and St. Laurent. When the Riel Rebellion broke out, Mother Greene and three companions moved further west to Calgary. As superior of the mission and principal of the Order's first school, she worked closely with both the Oblate Missionaries and her personal friend and advisor, Judge Rouleau (see Rouleauville Square), to secure government recognition for Catholic Schools. In 1885, the Lacombe Roman Catholic Separate School District No. 1 was formally established; the district later became the Calgary Roman Catholic Separate School District No. 1. Mother Greene was the first superintendent of the fledgling school board and had established a high school by 1888. In 1913 she was transferred to a position in Australia. Eight years later, in poor health, she returned to Calgary where she remained until her death in 1933 at age 90.

Mother Teresa Elementary School   **121 Midlake Boulevard S.E.**

The daughter of an Albanian grocer, Mother Teresa was born Agnes Gonxha Bojaxui in Macedonia (now Yugoslavia) in 1910. She joined a religious order in Ireland in 1928 and was immediately sent to India. In 1948, the year she became an Indian citizen, she began her work among the poor by founding a religious order called Missionaries of Charity. It is dedicated to working with the poor and especially the destitute. Sanctioned by Rome in 1950, the order has branches in 50 Indian cities and 30 countries. In 1979, Mother Teresa received the Nobel Peace Prize for her work.

Motherwell Road   **Mayland Heights, N.E.**

Motherwell Road may have been named for William Motherwell, an early Calgary contractor who built many of the older homes along the Elbow River. Motherwell came to Calgary in 1912 and served with the 103rd Calgary Regiment during World War I. He returned to Calgary after the war and became the founding manager of Union Tractor and Harvester

Company. He died in Calgary in 1982. Another possibility is that it was named for the Hon. W.R. Motherwell, federal minister of agriculture from 1921 to 1930, who was well known throughout the prairies. In 1901 he helped found the Territorial Grain Growers Association, one of the first co-operative movements in the West.

Mount Norquay Gate, etc.   **Mountain Park, S.E.**

These streets take their names from Mount Norquay in Banff National Park. It was named for the Hon. John Norquay, who was premier of Manitoba from 1878 to 1887, and who climbed the mountain in 1887 or 1888.

Mount Robson Circle, etc.   **Mountain Park, S.E.**

These streets may take their names from Mount Robson, in Jasper National Park, highest mountain in the Canadian Rockies. The origin of the name has never been officially documented. However, it has been suggested that it was named for Colin Robertson (1783-1842), who worked for both the North West Company and the Hudson's Bay Company. In 1820 he sent a group of Iroquois fur hunters into the area where the mountain is located, and they may have named it after him. The name Robson's Peak was in common use as early as 1863.

Mount Victoria Place   **Mountain Park, S.E.**

Mount Victoria was named in 1897 by J.J. McArthur, a Dominion Land Surveyor, in honour of Queen Victoria.

Munro Drive   **Mayland Heights, N.E.**

This street may have been named for Lieutenant Campbell Stuart Munro, MID, a Calgarian who died in World War II. MID means Mentioned in Despatches and is a special notation highlighting action above the call of duty. The street may also be named for Alex Munro (see Alex Munro Elementary School).

Munro Park   **Edmonton Trail and 17 Avenue N.E.**

Originally called Mount View Park, this area was a city-operated recreational park which included hockey rinks and a speed skating oval in winter and baseball fields in summer. A smaller area was made into a decorative park and re-named Munro Park in 1960 upon the retirement of Alex Munro, superintendent of the parks department for 21 years (see Alex Munro Elementary School). A baseball diamond is still located at the east end of the park.

Murdoch Manor   **808 - 5 Street S.E.**

George Murdoch (1850-1910) was a harness maker who arrived in Calgary from New Brunswick in 1883. He was an enthusiastic participant in community life. In 1884 he was elected to a committee of six citizens chosen to oversee the affairs of the community until it could be incorporated. In November 1884 the Town of Calgary was incorporated and on December 3 Murdoch was elected its first mayor. When his wife and family joined him after the election, his wife brought Calgary's first piano with her. Murdoch was mayor for two years and then served for many years as justice of the peace. Murdoch Manor, a senior citizens' housing project, opened in 1973.

Murphy Road   **Mayland Heights, N.E.**

Murphy Road may have been named for Emily Murphy, a prominent Alberta author and feminist. Murphy was responsible for the passage of the Dower Act which gave women a share in their husband's farmlands. She served for 17 years as a magistrate of the Alberta courts and worked with Nellie McClung and others to have women recognized as persons by the British North America Act. A second, more remote possibility is that it was named for a prominent Calgary sportsman, Harold "Spud" Murphy who came to Calgary in 1912. He played hockey for the Calgary Broncs during the 1920s and became involved in thoroughbred racing during the 1930s. He died at the Victoria Park race track in 1967 at age 62.

Murray Place   **Mayland Heights, N.E.**

There were several Murrays associated with early Alberta and this street may be named for one of them. Murray Lake, southwest of Medicine Hat, was named for George Murray, a pioneer who arrived in the area in 1897 and whose family ranched there until 1947. Another George Murray was one of Calgary's last blacksmiths. He began working when he arrived in Calgary from Scotland in 1910 and was still busy at his trade in 1958 at the age of 68. A third possibility is Dr. Thomas F. Murray, a well-known Calgary doctor who served as Indian agent and medical superintendent of the Sarcee Reserve from 1921 until his retirement in 1947. He died in Calgary in 1952 at the age of 59.

Muttart Art Gallery   **2nd Floor, 1221 - 2 Street S.W.**

Situated on the second floor of the Memorial Park Library, the art gallery opened in 1977 and is named for Gladys and Merrill Muttart, founders of the Muttart Foundation in Edmonton. The gallery was funded through a $100,000 donation from the foundation, which was started in 1953 with funds from the Muttarts' lumber companies located throughout Alberta. The Muttart Art Gallery exhibits contemporary western Canadian art and teaches art programs to city school children.

Nanton Road   **North Haven, N.W.**

Nanton is a southern Alberta town named after Sir Augustus Meredith Nanton (1860-1925). He was a partner in the Winnipeg financial firm of Olser, Hammond and Nanton, agents for the CPR in planning and selling townsites on the railway line. Nanton directed the Western Patriotic Fund and Victory Loan Campaigns during World War I, for which he was knighted in 1917. Nanton Road likely takes its name from the town.

Nat Christie Park   **14 Street and Bow Trail S.W.**

Nathaniel John "Nat" Christie (1873-1954) came to Calgary in 1901 to establish a clothing store. He later switched to the laundry business, opening the Ontario and Premier Laundries with his two brothers as partners. He was active in the Alberta Horse Breeders Association, became a stockholder of the Calgary Exhibition in 1915 and served as president from 1926 to 1933. In 1981 Christie's sister, Dr. Clara Christie-Might, set up a foundation in Christie's memory to re-invest money into the community where he had lived for 53 years. Funded primarily by the proceeds from the sale of land that Christie owned near the city limits, the foundation is interested in projects that will have a lasting effect on the city. Such projects have included the University of Calgary Faculty of Medicine's Christie Unit for Reproductive Medicine, an annual philharmonic concert, and redevelopment of facilities at the Boy Scouts' Camp Gardner near Bragg Creek. Nat Christie Park was built in 1984. The Park was funded by the Nat Christie Foundation and the Calgary Beautification Foundation. (See Christie Park.)

Nellie Breen Park   **14 Street and St. Monica Avenue S.E.**

The park was established in the early 1970s, but little development was done until 1989 when it was given its name. It honours Nellie Breen, then 85, the first of four generations of Inglewood residents who have lived in Inglewood since 1921. She has been an active member of the Inglewood Community Association for over 60 years and was instrumental in having the City build its first community swimming pool. She participated, in costume, in the Stampede parade for 60 years and as of 1994, was still active.

Nellie McClung Centre   **SAIT Campus, N.W.**

Nellie McClung (1873-1951) began her teaching career in Manitoba in 1889 when she was 16 years old. She became an author and a temperance leader, but is best known for fighting for social reform and women's rights. Largely as a result of her actions, women in Manitoba won the right to vote in 1916. McClung was elected to the Alberta Legislature in 1921 and after her defeat in 1926, the McClung family moved to Calgary where they lived until 1934. She and four other women began a court battle in 1927 to determine whether, under the British North America Act, women were "persons" and could be appointed to the senate. Britain's Privy Council ruled in their favour in 1929. McClung's long career included many firsts, including being the first woman on the Canadian delegation to the League of Nations. She was also the first woman on the board of governors of the Canadian Broadcasting Corporation, and the first woman elder of the United Church of Canada. The McClung home stands at 15 Avenue and 7 Street S.W. The Nellie McClung Centre is home of the Alberta College of Art and Design.

Nellie McClung Elementary School   **2315 Palliser Drive S.W.**

See Nellie McClung Centre.

Nelson Road   **North Haven, N.W.**

Nelson Road likely takes its name from the city of Nelson, B.C.. There is also a Fort Nelson in B.C. and English hamlet of Nelson in Lancashire, all of which were named for Lord Nelson, a British admiral who died at the Battle of Trafalgar.

Nesbitt Road   **North Haven, N.W.**

Nesbitt Road may have been named for Leonard D. Nesbitt, a veteran southern Alberta newspaperman. Nesbitt came to Canada from Ireland at the turn of the century. He arrived in Calgary in 1910 to be sports editor of the Albertan. He later moved to the Herald as a senior reporter before buying the Bassano News and Brooks Bulletin. He became superintendent of publicity for the Alberta Wheat Pool in 1926 and retired in 1955. In 1960 he was commissioned by the Wheat Pool to write its history, which was published in 1962 as Tides in the West. During his years in Calgary he was very active in community work. Nesbitt died in Calgary in 1969 at the age of 81.

Newcombe Place   **North Haven, N.W.**

It is possible that Newcombe Place was named for Percy Lynn Newcombe, one of Calgary's earliest musicians. He came to Calgary in 1904 and within a few months became choir leader at Central Methodist Church. He served as a choir director until his death in 1952. He was also well known in western Canada as an adjudicator of music festivals and was principal of Mount Royal Conservatory of Music from 1923 until his retirement in 1935.

Nickle Arts Museum   University of Calgary, N.W.

Samuel Clarence Nickle (1889-1971) was the son of a shoemaker who eventually owned his own store, The Slipper Shop, on 8th Avenue where the Bay store now stands. He lost his shop during the Depression and survived by selling pea soup. He made his fortune in the oil business beginning as a speculator in the mid-1920s. He eventually consolidated all his business ventures into Canadian Gridoil Limited. The Nickel Arts Museum was made possible thanks to Nickle's generous $1 million donation given to the University of Calgary in 1970. The museum was completed in 1979. Many other donations have been made to the community through the Nickle Foundation. Shortly before his death, Nickle received an honourary doctorate from the University of Calgary in recognition of his years of community service.

Nickle Junior High School   2525 Bonavista Drive S.E.

This school was named after oilman and philanthropist Sam Nickle (see Nickle Arts Museum) and his son, Carl. A publisher in the oil industry, Carl Nickle (1914-90) was founder and president of the Nickle Foundation, which awards grants and bursaries to high school students. He was active in community life in Calgary, serving as a director of the Boy Scouts, YMCA, and the Calgary Exhibition and Stampede. To commemorate Canada's centennial in 1967, Carl Nickle donated part of his valuable collection of 10,000 coins to the Glenbow Foundation and other parts to the Provincial Museum and the University of Alberta. His coins form a special numismatic section at the Nickle Arts Museum. Nickle Junior High School opened in 1972.

Nickle Road   North Haven, N.W.

Nickle Road in North Haven is likely named after Sam and Carl Nickle. (See Nickle Arts Museum and Nickle Junior High School.)

Nickle Theatre   Mount Royal College, 4825 Richard Road S.W.

The renovations of the Nickle Theatre, formerly the Ford Theatre, were made possible in part by grants from the Nickle Foundation. The theatre was named in memory of Sam C. Nickle (see Nickle Arts Museum) and Carl O. Nickle (see Nickle Junior High School).

Nimmons Park   19 Avenue S.W. between 17 and 17A Streets

Irish-born William Nimmons (1830-1919) was a rancher. In 1882 while still in Britain, he bought all of what is now Bankview from the Hudson's Bay Company, paying $8 an acre. His home stands at 1827-14 Street S.W. The park was a project of the members of the Bankview community, who were concerned with the lack of green space in their community. It was funded by a grant from the Alberta 75th Anniversary Commission and opened in 1984.

Niven Place   North Haven, N.W.

Niven Place may have been named in honour of Robert Henry Niven, the first Calgarian to be decorated during World War II. Educated in Calgary, Niven joined the Royal Air

Force in 1935 and received the Distinguished Flying Cross in 1940 for "gallantry and devotion to duty in the execution of air operations." He died in 1942 when his plane was shot down over the North Sea. His son, Robert Niven, was president of the Calgary Olympic Development Association.

Noble Road   North Haven, N.W.

Noble Road may take its name from Charles Sherwood Noble (1873-1957), who homesteaded near Claresholm in 1902 and later farmed near Lethbridge. Noble was famous for inventing the Noble cultivator, a machine which made dry-land farming possible. Noble Farms still operate near Nobleford, Alberta, named in his honour.

Nolan Road   North Haven, N.W.

Nolan Road is probably named for Patrick J. "Paddy" Nolan, a criminal lawyer in early Calgary. A witty Irishman born on St. Patrick's Day, he practiced law in Calgary from 1889 until his death at age 49 in 1913. He took cases that interested him regardless of the guilt or innocence of the defendant or their ability to pay. In 1907 Nolan was appointed King's Counsel, one of the first to be appointed in Alberta. He was a much sought after speaker and one of the original members of the senate of the University of Alberta.

Nordegg Crescent   North Haven, N.W.

Nordegg Crescent takes its name from the Alberta town of Nordegg. Martin Nordegg (1868-1948) arrived in Canada from his native Germany in 1906. Funded by German capital, he quickly established the Canadian Northern Western Railway, Brazeau Colleries (a coal mining company of which he was director and vice-president) and the town in west-central Alberta that bears his name. During World War I, his holdings were confiscated because of his German nationality but they were later returned to him.

Norma Bush Arena   2424 University Drive N.W.

Norma Pauline Bush (1930-74) was a Calgary nurse who was active in both sports and community activities. She was involved with the Calalta Figure Skating Club, Canadian Figure Skating Association and numerous community and home and school associations. She also coached fastball, basketball and hockey, and helped organize the District Three Hockey School (now the Northwest Hockey School). Bush was a two-time recipient of the Bridgeland-Riverside Community Association's sportsman of the year award.

Norman Block   126 - 132 - 8 Avenue S.W.

The land on which the Norman Block stands was originally the site of Sir James Lougheed's first Calgary home. When he moved his family to a larger home in 1890, he built the Norman Block on the site and named it after one of his sons. The building once housed a theatre and the stage was sometimes used for boxing matches. Tommy Burns, the only Canadian to become the world heavyweight boxing champion, fought there occasionally between 1911 and 1913. The historic plaque on the building was unveiled in 1986 by Lougheed's grandson, Alberta's premier, Peter Lougheed.

Unfortunately, much of the original character of the building has been hidden by modern renovations.

Norquay Court, etc.   **North Haven, N.W.**

See Mount Norquay Gate.

Norquay Hall   **University of Calgary Residence, N.W.**

See Mount Norquay Gate.

Norris Road   **North Haven, N.W.**

This street may have been named for John Norris, an Edmonton pioneer, who worked for the Hudson's Bay Company and later was a partner in the firm of Norris and Carey. In the 1890s he ran cattle west of Calgary.

Northcote Road   **North Haven, N.W.**

Northcote Avenue was the original name of both 5 Avenue S., from 4 Street W. to Riverfront Avenue S.E., and Centre Avenue E., from 6 Street to 11 A Street. These names disappeared when The City changed from named to numbered streets in 1904. In its early years, Calgary streets were named after CPR officials and others with ties to the CPR. Sir Stafford Northcote was the governor of the Hudson's Bay Company who arranged to sell its fur-trading rights in the West to Canada in 1869, thus opening the way for the building of the CPR. The name Northcote appears again in North Haven, perhaps in recognition of the earlier street.

O.S. Geiger Elementary School   **100 Castlebrook Drive N.E.**

Orwill St. Clair "Pelk" Geiger was born in Didsbury and lived in Alberta all his life. He was a resident of Calgary from 1929 until his death in 1987 at age 80. He taught in the public school system from his arrival in Calgary until he was appointed supervisor of division II (grades 4 - 6) in 1961. He became superintendent of elementary schools in 1964 during which time he encouraged the upgrading of elementary reading and arithmetic programs, introduced French instruction at the elementary level and was instrumental in the expansion of elementary libraries and the development of outdoor education. He retired in 1971. His nickname "Pelk" was given to him when he began taking boxing lessons at age seven after seeing a match in Calgary between two boxers named Pelkey and McCarty.

Ogden   **S.E.**

Isaac Gouverneur Ogden (1844-1928) was a senior official of the CPR. He began his railway career in 1871 after leaving the banking profession. He joined the CPR in 1881, became comptroller in 1887 and a vice-president in 1901. In 1910 he became vice-president of finance and accounting. At that time, Ogden was the last of the original officers of the CPR and he was still serving the company at the time of his death. His name was given to the railroad shops, located in Ogden, when they were completed in 1913. At the time, this was the only CPR repair depot between Winnipeg and Vancouver.

Osborne Crescent   **Richmond (Knob Hill), S.W.**

This crescent was probably named for Fred E. Osborne a city alderman from 1918 to 1920 and 1922 to 1924, and mayor of Calgary from 1927 to 1929 (see F.E. Osborne Junior High School).

Our Lady of Peace Elementary/Junior High School   14826 Millrise Hill S.W.

Dating from the early days of the Church, Our Lady of Peace is another title for Mary, the Mother of Jesus. Mary is honoured for her perfect accord with her Son, Jesus who brought peace to the world — peace the world cannot understand. The first Catholic Church and mission in Southern Alberta was named Our Lady of Peace.

CALGARY

P

Palliser   **S.W.**

Formerly called Pump Hill and Belvedere, this subdivision was finally named after Captain John Palliser (see Captain John Palliser Elementary School). Many of the street names in Palliser were chosen by the developer only to adhere to The City rules regarding the naming of subdivision streets. The only one named after another geographical location is Palermo (Italy, Maine, New Jersey, North Dakota).

Palliser Hotel   **133 - 9 Avenue S.W.**

In 1857 Captain John Palliser was sponsored by the Royal Geographical Society and the British government to assess the country west of the Red River and report on its physical features, the quality of its natural resources and possibilities for settlement. The hotel, which opened in 1914, was built and named by the CPR. (See also Captain John Palliser Elementary School.)

Palmer Bridge   **McKnight Boulevard at Nose Creek, N.E.**

John "Jock" Ender Palmer was one of western Canada's aviation pioneers. He flew during World War I with the Royal Flying Corps and won a Military Cross for bravery. After the war he became a barnstormer and flying instructor. In June 1922 he attempted Canada's first official airmail flight from Lethbridge to Ottawa, but it was unsuccessful due to engine problems and a landing accident. He continued his flying career through World War II. Palmer died in Calgary in 1964.

Palmer Road   **Calgary International Airport, N.E.**

See Palmer Bridge.

Patrick Airlie Elementary School   1520 - 39 Street S.E.

Born in Ireland in 1889, Patrick Airlie was a carpenter by trade. He came to Albert Park, then an independent village, in 1911. He served on the Bow River School District Board for 37 years and was instrumental in organizing the first community association and the first library in the Forest Lawn area. Airlie resided in the Albert Park district until his death in 1955. The school bearing his name is built on the site of the old Bow River School.

Patterson Heights   S.W.

This subdivision is named after a family who were long-time residents of the area.

Pattison Bridge   Elbow River at 1 St. S.E.

A native of England, Private John George Pattison (1875 - 1917) was the only Calgary resident to be decorated with the Victoria Cross in World War I. He won the honour on April 10, 1917 at Vimy Ridge where he single-handedly eliminated a German machine gun and crew which was holding up an advance of Canadian troops. He was wounded but returned to combat shortly thereafter. However, he was killed by an enemy shell on June 3, 1917.

Patton Court, etc.   Pump Hill, S.W.

Thomas and Ella Patton came to Alberta in 1903 and settled near Midnapore. They moved to the area where Pump Hill is located, then called the Glenmore district, about ten years later. Thomas Patton was a landscape artist, naturalist and conservationist, and made his living as a market gardener. The street adjacent to their former residence was named Patton Road in recognition of the family's contribution to the development of the community.

Pearce Estates   1440 - 17 A Street S.E.

William Pearce, Dominion Superintendent of Lands and Mines, was a strong supporter of irrigation in Alberta. He believed that only an irrigation business could get the financial backing to make it a viable proposition. When he was unable to persuade others to form an irrigation company, he took on the job himself, creating the Calgary Irrigation Company in 1894. However, because he was a federal employee, he was eventually ordered to disassociate himself from any ties with the firm. After 1897, a number of wet years and new dry-farming techniques used by farmers made local irrigation no longer necessary and the company eventually went bankrupt. However Pearce had shown that a government-backed corporation was a necessity if irrigation was to be used in the future.

Peigan Trail   S.E.

Peigan Trail is named in recognition of the Peigan Indian tribe, part of the Blackfoot nation. They have a reserve in southern Alberta and another in northern Montana.

Pennsylvania Road   Penbrooke Meadows, S.E.

The American state of Pennsylvania was named after its founder, William Penn (1644-1718). An English Quaker, Penn sailed to America in 1682 to seek freedom from religious persecution.

Peter Lougheed Hospital   3500 - 26 Avenue N.E.

Grandson of Senator Sir James Lougheed, Edgar Peter Lougheed was born in Calgary in 1928. During his high school and university years he was an outstanding athlete and he played football professionally with the Edmonton Eskimos. Lougheed graduated with a law degree from the University of Alberta in 1952 and went on to complete a business administration degree from Harvard in 1954. He practiced law in Calgary, was elected leader of the provincial Conservatives in 1965, elected MLA for Calgary West in 1967, and in 1971, at age 43, became premier of Alberta. He led the province through its most prosperous years during the oil boom and retired from provincial politics in 1985. Lougheed Provincial Park, in Kananaskis Country, is also named for him.

Point McKay   N.W.

Alfred McKay came west from Ontario and in his early years worked as a ferryman at the site of the first ferry-crossing on the Bow River. It was located where the Centre Street Bridge now stands. McKay later homesteaded at the point on the Bow River which now bears his name. His sandstone home still stands in the southeast corner of the Point McKay townhouse complex.

Pop Davies Athletic Park   Ogden Road at 66 Avenue S.E.

Jack Trevor "Pop" Davies was an active volunteer in the Millican-Ogden community for 28 years until his death in 1979. He was also active with the Boy Scouts and other youth organizations and worked with the Rehabilitation Society for the Handicapped which, in 1976, gave him a lifetime membership in recognition of his 27 years of volunteer work. He was also involved with the Ogden Branch of the Royal Canadian Legion and with other community groups.

Prince of Wales Elementary School   253 Parkland Way S.E.

H.R.H. Prince of Wales, Charles Phillip Arthur George, is the eldest son of Queen Elizabeth II and heir to the British throne. He was invested as Prince of Wales at Caernarvon Castle, Wales, on July 1, 1969 at age 21. The school named in his honour opened in December 1977 after his visit to Calgary that year. Permission to name the school was granted by the Queen's representative in Canada, Governor General Jules Leger in April 1977.

Prince's Island Park   **Bow River, between Centre Street and 6th Street W.**

Peter Anthony Prince (1836-1925) was manager of the Eau Claire Sawmills from 1886, when the company was established, until he retired in 1916. The sawmills processed timber for the Eau Claire and Bow River Lumber Company. The company dredged a channel on the south side of the Bow River so logs could be floated down to their mill on 2 Street S.W., thus creating the island. In 1889 Prince formed the Calgary Water Power Company, forerunner of Calgary Power Limited (now Transalta Utilities Corporation). Thanks to Prince, Calgary became the fifth Canadian community to have street lighting. Prince was also one of the founders of the Calgary Iron Works and built what was once a familiar sight on Calgary's skyline, the Robin Hood Flour Mills, on the site now occupied by Gulf Canada Square.

Princess Obolensky Park   **4 Street and 36 Avenue S.W.**

Princess Tanya Obolensky (1906-1991) escaped from her native Russia during the revolution. She was educated in Rome and Vienna, married an Austrian count, and immigrated to Canada in 1931. She lived on the Bow River Ranch for a number of years. In the 1950s she opened Calgary's first boutique, which she named La Boutique. It was a huge success and eventually evolved into both a social centre and meeting place for immigrants. She retired and sold La Boutique in the early 1970s spending her later years on Rideau Place, close to the small park that bears her name. The park was funded by friends who wished to honour her.

CALGARY

Q

Queen Alexandra Close, etc.   **Queensland Downs, S.E.**

These streets are likely named for Queen Alexandra (1844-1925), consort of King Edward VII of Great Britain (see Alexandra Centre).

Queen Anne Road, etc.   **Queensland Downs, S.E.**

There are five streets in Queensland Downs with the name Anne. They were likely named for Queen Anne of Great Britain and Ireland (1665-1714) who reigned from 1702 to 1714.

Queen Charlotte Drive, etc.   **Queensland Downs, S.E.**

The five streets in Queensland Downs with the name Charlotte are likely named for Queen Charlotte of Mecklenburg-Strelitz, wife of King George III of Great Britain.

Queen Elizabeth Elementary/Jr./Sr. High School   **512 - 18 Street N.W.**

Queen Elizabeth High School was built in 1953, the year after the coronation of Queen Elizabeth II. It was named in her honour.

Queen Elizabeth Park   **73 Avenue and 44 Street N.W.**

This park, dedicated in 1953, was named to commemorate the coronation of Queen Elizabeth II in 1952. Developed in 1951, it was called Tuininga Park for two years before being rededicated. The original name was to honour Dave Tuininga, a part-owner of the land on which the park is situated and an ardent supporter of sports in Bowness. The park is maintained by The City's parks department with volunteer help from the Bowness Branch of the Royal Canadian Legion.

Queen Isabella Close   **Queensland Downs, S.E.**

Queen Isabella Close is likely named for Isabella, queen of Castile and Leon (1451-1504). Her major contribution to history was the financing of the voyage of Christopher Columbus to the new world.

Queen Tamara Place, etc.   **Queensland Downs, S.E.**

Of all the street names in Queensland Downs, only Queen Tamara cannot be identified with an actual ruler. The origin of the name is uncertain.

CALGARY

R.B. Bennett Elementary School   **6305 - 33 Avenue N.W.**

Richard Bedford Bennett (1890-1947) was the first prime minister of Canada to come from the West and the only one to date from Calgary. He came to Calgary from New Brunswick in 1897 to work in James Lougheed's law office. He entered federal politics in 1911, became leader of the Progressive Conservative Party in 1927 and was elected Prime Minister in 1930. Unfortunately, he began his term at the beginning of the Great Depression and many of the problems he inherited were blamed on the government. The Conservatives were defeated by the Liberals in 1935 and Bennett retired from Canadian politics two years later. (See also Viscount Bennett Centre.) The school originally opened as Viscount Bennett School in 1942 before Bowness was annexed to The City of Calgary. However when Bowness joined the city, the name was changed as there was already a Viscount Bennett High School in Calgary.

R.T. Alderman Junior High School   **725 Mapleton Drive S.E**

Robert Thomas Alderman (1894-1969) came to Canada from England in 1910 and arrived in Calgary two years later. He worked as a carpenter at the CPR Ogden shops until his retirement in 1949. He was an active member of the Calgary labour council, served as a Calgary school board trustee from 1932 to 1940 and was elected chairman in 1939. He introduced the concept of junior high schools to the Calgary school system in 1933. He served as an alderman from 1940 to 1952. In 1956 he helped establish Calgary's Golden Age Club and became a lifetime member. He was also a lifetime member of the Royal Canadian Legion.

Radisson Heights   **S.E.**

Pierre Esprit Radisson (c1636 - c1710) was a French explorer and fur trader. He and his brother-in-law, Médard Chouart, Sieur de Groseilliers, were the first white men to explore the area north and west of the Great Lakes. Born in France, Radisson came to Canada in 1651, was captured by the Iroquois in 1652 and escaped about two years later. Radisson and Groseilliers explored around Lake Superior, and after quarreling with the French over fur trading rights, worked for the English. Their reports on the wealth to be had from furs led to the founding of the Hudson's Bay Company in 1670. Radisson worked for the company from 1670 to 1675 and 1684 to 1687. He settled in England in 1687. There is also a community called Radisson in central Saskatchewan.

Radnor Avenue   Renfrew, N.E.

This street may have taken its name from a CPR station northwest of Calgary. It was established in 1884 and was named after Wilma Radnor, daughter of the 5th Earl of Radnor. Radnor is also a county in Wales.

Rae Crescent   Radisson Heights, S.E.

This street may have taken its name from Mount Rae, southwest of Calgary. It was named for Dr. John Rae (1813-93) who took part in a number of expeditions searching for the Franklin Expedition between 1848 and 1854. (See Sir John Franklin Junior High School.)

Ramsay   S.E.

Prior to 1956, the area which comprises Ramsay was known as Burnsland, Mills Estate, Brewery Flats and Grandview. The community association applied for a charter under the name Grandview Community Association in 1956. However, a charter could not be granted under that name because a Grandview Association already existed in Edmonton. The community then chose Ramsay after Silas Alexander Ramsay (1850-1942) who had been a Calgary alderman from 1894 to 1898, 1901 to 1903 and 1904 to 1906, and was mayor of Calgary from 1904 to 1905. Ramsay came west from Ontario in 1870 and served during both the Red River Rebellion of 1870 and the Riel Rebellion. He settled in Calgary in the early 1880s and established a successful machinery business.

Ramsay Elementary School   2223 Spiller Road S.E.

Although the subdivision and school have the same name, they may not be named after the same person. While the subdivision honours Silas A. Ramsay, mayor of Calgary from 1904 to 1905, the school, erected in 1912, may have been named after William Thomson Ramsay, who sold the school board the property on which the school stands. (See Ramsay Street.)

Ramsay Street   Ramsay, S.E.

Ramsay Street was probably named after William Thomson Ramsay who came to Calgary about 1884 as an agent for the Northwest Land Company. He was the major landowner in the area around 1890. (See Ramsay Elementary School.)

Reader Crescent   Renfrew, N.W.

Reader Crescent may have been named after William R. Reader. (See Reader Rock Gardens.)

Reader Rock Gardens   **Macleod Trail and 25 Avenue S.E.**

William R. Reader was superintendent of the Calgary parks department from 1913 to 1942. He had been a school teacher in his native England but his interest in horticulture brought him to Calgary as gardener for Pat Burns, whose mansion and gardens were on the present site of the Colonel Belcher Hospital. One of Reader's projects was a rock garden on the hillside behind the home of parks superintendent Richard Iverson. Eventually a 10-room home also occupied the spot. The gardens which surrounded Reader's home were at one time world-famous. It took seven years (from 1922 to 1929) just to lay out the rockery. In earlier years, when gardening was a more popular pastime, up to 850 varieties of seeds were collected from Reader Rock Gardens to be exchanged with other famous gardens worldwide.

Reeve Theatre   **University of Calgary, N.W.**

In 1977 the Francis F. Reeve Foundation approached the University of Calgary concerning a $1 million donation for construction of a new theatre. The university received approval from the provincial government for a matching grant and plans were made public in 1978. The theatre is an experimental theatre labouratory. The Francis F. Reeve Foundation was established jointly by Reeve and his wife Winnifred in 1954. Winnifred (Eaton) Reeve (1887-1954) had her first story published at age 14. She was a prolific writer, reporter, novelist and playwright, who wrote under the pseudonym Onoto Watana. She was an early member of the Calgary Women's Press Club and founding member, along with Mark Twain, of the Authors' League of America. Francis Reeve (1879-1956) began his career in New York working on a tugboat. He eventually became vice-president of Red Star Towing and Transportation Company and moved to Alberta in 1917 to a ranch called Bowview, now the site of the Ghost Reservoir. He moved to Calgary in 1925 and founded the brokerage firm of F.F. Reeve and Company. At this time he began his long association with the oil industry, eventually founding Dominion Oilfield Supply and the Canadian Exploration Company.

Richard Road   **Mount Royal College, S.W.**

This area was originally planned as a subdivision called Richmond Park. When the major streets were being named, The City's planning department was looking for something different than the standard English-sounding names, and decided to name a street after a prominent French Canadian. They chose Maurice "Rocket" Richard (pronounced "Ree-shard"), who played hockey for the Montreal Canadians from 1942 to 1960. When Richard retired from hockey in 1960 he held the record for the most goals scored in regular season play.

Richardson Street   **Harvey Barracks, S.W.**

Arthur Herbert Lindsay Richardson won the first Victoria Cross awarded to a Canadian during the Boer War. On July 5, 1900 he and 30 comrades, members of the Strathcona's Horse Regiment, were led into an ambush. During the retreat, Richardson went back to rescue Corporal McArthur, who had been wounded and fallen from his horse. Both men returned safely to camp.

Richardson Way, etc.   **Mount Royal College, S.W.**

Ernest L. "Ernie" Richardson came to Calgary in 1903 as assistant to the secretary of the Board of Trade and Inter-Western Pacific Exhibition. He became manager of the Calgary Exhibition four years later and remained in that position for 33 years, until his retirement in 1940. In 1923 the rodeo element of the exhibition became an annual event and the name changed to the Calgary Exhibition and Stampede. The area around Mount Royal College was originally called Richmond Park and the street names were chosen to fit the subdivision name.

Richmond   **S.W.**

The community of Richmond likely takes its name from the English towns of Richmond, Yorkshire and Richmond, Surrey. Both towns take their names from the Earl of Richmond. The first earl of Richmond, Alan Rufus of Penthèivre in Brittany, built the castle in Richmond, Yorkshire, in 1071. Richmond, Surrey was originally called Sheen. Its name was changed in 1500 by order of King Henry VII, who was earl of Richmond in Yorkshire. The word Richmond was taken from the French "Richemont." which means "strong hill."

Riel Place   **Raddison Heights, S.E.**

Riel Place was likely named for Metis leader Louis Riel. (See Louis Riel Elementary/Junior High School).

Riley Park   **800 - 12 Street N.W.**

The 20 acres on which the park stands was donated to The City of Calgary in 1910 by Ezra Hounsfield Riley with the stipulation that it be used for park purposes only. City council decided to name the park after Riley and development began in 1912. Some sources say that Riley stipulated that the only team sport to be played there would be cricket, however no documentation has been found to support this. Riley was one of the ten children (seven sons and three daughters) of Thomas Riley, who arrived in Calgary in 1887 and homesteaded what is now the areas of Upper Hillhurst and Hounsfield Heights. Ezra Riley was twice elected to the Alberta Legislature for the riding of Gleichen. When he resigned in 1910 to protest the make-up of the new provincial cabinet, his younger brother, Harold, replaced him. (See Harold W. Riley Elementary School.)

Robert Warren Junior High School   **12424 Elbow Drive S.W.**

Robert Warren was born in England and came to Canada as a child. He came to Calgary from Fort Macleod in 1925 to attend normal school, then taught in a number of small towns before receiving his B.A. from the University of British Columbia in 1931. After becoming a principal and school inspector, he then took his M.Ed. at Harvard in 1940. Warren returned to Calgary in 1945 as an inspector of high schools and was appointed assistant superintendent in 1950 and superintendent in 1951. Warren was superintendent of schools for 19 years until his retirement in 1972. During his tenure, Calgary's public school population grew from 18,000 to 80,000 students.

Robson Crescent Radisson Heights, S.E.

See Mount Robson Circle.

Roland Michener Elementary School 5958 - 4 Avenue N.E.

Daniel Roland Michener (1900-91) was born in Lacombe, Alberta, the son of a Canadian senator. He attended Oxford University as a Rhodes Scholar, served with the Royal Air Force during World War I and was called to the Ontario bar in 1924. A Conservative, he served in the Ontario legislature from 1945 to 1948, in the Canadian House of Commons from 1953 to 1962 and was Speaker of the House from 1957 to 1962. He was appointed high commissioner to India and Canada's first ambassador to Nepal in 1964 and returned to Canada in 1967 to accept the post as 20th governor general of Canada, a position he held until 1974.

Rose Kohn Memorial Arena 502 Heritage Drive S.W.

Rose Kohn (1900-67) was originally from England and came to Calgary in 1941. She immediately became involved in community life, as founder of both the Victoria and Bridgeland-Riverside Community Associations. She was the originator of community association hockey leagues, through the Calgary Community Recreation Association, which later became the Calgary Community Sports Association. She also started baseball and basketball leagues. In 1954 the Booster Club named her Calgary's Sportswoman of the Year. Today countless children benefit from the thousands of volunteer hours given by Kohn during her lifetime.

Ross Road SAIT Campus, N.W.

The streets at SAIT were re-named in 1985 and most were given the names of the institution's early principals. Joe H. Ross served as principal from 1919 to 1924.

Rouleau Crescent Radisson Heights, S.E.

This street may have been named for Calgary pioneers Charles and Hector Rouleau. (See Rouleauville Square.)

Rouleauville Square 17 Avenue and 1 Street S.W.

Rouleauville was a small village south of Calgary which was built on what is now the site of Holy Cross Hospital. Originally this area was home to a Catholic mission, founded in 1875. Rouleauville was named for Charles Barromée Rouleau, and his brother, Edward Hector Rouleau. Charles became a chief justice of the Supreme Court of the North-West Territories and his brother was chief surgeon to the North West Mounted Police. By 1907 Rouleauville had been annexed by The City of Calgary and although the area was originally planned as a French-Canadian Roman Catholic stronghold, the many English-speaking settlers changed the nature of the community. By World War I, the name of the area had been changed to "Mission" after the original mission established there.

Rundle   **N.E.**

Three of the four subdivisions originally known collectively as The Properties were named after mountains in the Canadian Rockies - Rundle, Temple and Whitehorn. The fourth, Pineridge, is named after a ridge in the Canadian Rockies. Mount Rundle, a well known landmark east of the town of Banff, was named after Methodist missionary Robert T. Rundle (1811-96). He was the first Protestant missionary in Alberta serving the Stoney and Cree Indians from 1840 to 1848. He returned to England in 1849 due to ill health caused by the hardships in the frontier West.

Rundle Hall   **University of Calgary, N.W.**

See Rundle subdivision.

Rundle Lodge   **632 - 13 Avenue S.E.**

Calgary's first public hospital, built in 1894 and later used by the militia and as an isolation hospital, bore the name Rundle Lodge after Robert T. Rundle (see Rundle subdivision). From 1956 to 1971 it was used as a senior citizens' lodge. The building was demolished in 1973, two years after the opening of a new building. Portions of the original walls now stand as a historic site on 12 Avenue between 5 and 6 Streets S.E.

Rupert Road   **Renfrew, N.E.**

Rupert Road may take its name from Rupert's Land. In 1670, King Charles II granted a charter to the Hudson's Bay Company which included all the area whose rivers drain into Hudson Bay, one of which is the Bow River. The area was called Rupert's Land after Prince Rupert, nephew of Charles II, and first governor of the Hudson's Bay Company. Rupert's Land became part of Canada in 1870.

Russell Road   **Renfrew, N.E.**

Russell Road may have been named after John W. Russell, who came to Calgary in 1910 and served as a city alderman for ten years from 1922 to 1928 and 1929 to 1934. A second possibility is that it was named for Charles M. "Charlie" Russell, famous cowboy artist and sculptor from Montana. Russell spent several months in the High River area in 1888 painting Alberta scenes, including pictures of the North West Mounted Police. He also attended the first Calgary Stampedes in 1912 and 1919.

Sackville Drive   **Southwood, S.W.**

Sackville Drive may have been named for John Percy Sackville, a prominent agricultural-ist who retired to Calgary from the University of Alberta in 1947. He was serving as an associate director of the Calgary Exhibition and Stampede at the time of his death in 1971. It may also have been named for Sackville, Nova Scotia.

St. Alphonsus Elementary/Junior High School   **928 Radnor Avenue N.E.**

Originally a lawyer, Alphonsus Liguori (1696-1787) was ordained a priest in 1726 minis-tering in and around Naples. In 1732 he founded the Congregation of the Holy Redeemer, an order of priests dedicated to preaching to the poor in rural areas. A pro-lific writer, Alphonsus wrote popular books on Mary, the Rosary, and the Eucharist which are still available today. His most important written work is <u>Moral</u> <u>Theology</u>. He was canonized (declared a saint) in 1839.

St. Andrew Elementary School   **4331 - 41 Avenue S.W.**

One of the twelve apostles and brother of Simon Peter, Andrew was a disciple of John the Baptist before meeting Jesus. One of the first disciples chosen by Jesus, Andrew in turn brought his brother Peter to meet him. Although it is known that Andrew was mar-tyred in 60 A.D., the place of his death is uncertain. Andrew is patron saint of both Russia and Scotland and the saltire cross, or St. Andrew's cross, is the emblem of Scotland.

St. Angela Elementary School   **231 - 6 Street N.E.**

Angela Merici (1474-1540) founded the Ursuline nuns. Orphaned early in life, she and several companions dedicated themselves to teaching poor girls. They placed themselves under the patronage of St. Ursula and companions, fourth century virgins and martyrs. The church authorities at that time were unwilling to recognize the new concept of nuns being uncloistered and mobile, so the sisterhood was not formalized by the Church until

1565. The Ursuline order is the oldest teaching order of women in the Roman Catholic Church. Calgary's St. Angela's School had its beginnings in 1913 as the Bridgeland Separate School. It operated in a former Lutheran church purchased by the Separate School Board. It was re-named in 1923 when it moved down the street to larger quarters.

St. Anne Francophone Elementary/Jr./Sr. High School   1010 - 21 Avenue S.E.

Although very little factual knowledge exists concerning St. Anne, tradition holds that she was the mother of the Virgin Mary. Despite the lack of historical data, devotion to St. Anne has always been popular, especially among the French, who credit her with intervening on their behalf in several important historical events. St. Anne school began operating in the basement of East End Church in 1909 and moved into the present building in 1911.

St. Anthony (Further Education)   4811 - 6 Street S.W.

St. Anthony of Padua (1195 -1231) was born in Lisbon, Portugal. He originally entered the priesthood with the Order of the Holy Cross, but was so drawn to the life of St. Francis of Assisi that he obtained permission to join the Franciscan Order. He was a gifted preacher and known for his holiness. Stories concerning his sanctity and many miracles attributed to him were prevalent even before his death and led to a popular devotion to St. Anthony as patron of lost articles.

St. Augustine Elementary/Junior High School   7112 - 7 Street S.W.

Augustine (340-430) was the son of a Roman father and a Christian mother. As a young man he abandoned Christianity and lived with his mistress for 15 years. He later returned to his Christian faith and was baptized in 387. Augustine is one of the Roman Catholic church's greatest intellectuals and his writings form the foundation of the beliefs of the Christian church.

St. Bede Elementary School   333 Bermuda Drive N.W.

Bede the Venerable (672-735) was an English monk who was considered one of the most learned men of his age. His best-known work, Historia Ecclesiastica, an account of Christianity in England, is a major source of early English history. The title "the Venerable" was given to acknowledge his wisdom and learning. He was the first to date events A.D., Anno Domini, after the birth of Christ.

St. Benedict Elementary School   10340 -19 Street S.W.

St. Benedict was born into a noble Roman family in 480. His love for God and desire to live a holy life eventually led him to leave society and live in a cave. Within a few years, many young men asked to join him. St. Benedict's motto was "pray and work." His writings, which specified the way of life for the monks, are still in use today in various Christian communities. Pope Paul VI in 1964 bestowed five particular titles on St. Benedict, among them "Messenger of Peace," "Architect of Unity," and "Herald of the Christian Faith."

St. Bernadette Elementary School   **55 Lynndale Crescent S.E.**

Marie-Bernarde Soubirous was born to a peasant family in 1844 in the small village of Lourdes, France. As a child, Bernadette, as she came to be called, suffered from asthma, a disability which impeded her education. At age 14, as she was praying in a small grotto, Bernadette had a vision of a "beautiful lady," who later identified herself as the Immaculate Conception (a title for the Virgin Mary). She appeared to Bernadette on 18 separate occasions. During one appearance, Bernadette began to dig in the ground, saying that the Lady had told her to "drink of the fountain". Shortly thereafter, a spring bubbled up. Many miraculous healings have been attributed to these waters and the shrine built at Lourdes continues to draw thousands of pilgrims who pray and bathe in the waters in hope of healing or of deepening their faith in God. Bernadette later became a nun and after suffering through a long illness, died in 1879.

St. Bonaventure Junior High School   **1710 Acadia Drive S.E.**

Giovanni di Fidanza (1221-1274) was born in Bagnorea, Italy. According to one legend he received the name Bonaventure from Francis of Assisi who cured him of an illness during childhood. He became a Franciscan monk in 1238 and was a leading figure at the 14th General Council at Lyons in 1274. Bonaventure was a great philosopher and theologian and a prolific writer.

St. Boniface Elementary School   **927 Lake Sylvan Drive S.E.**

St. Boniface was born in England in 680. He was educated in a Benedictine monastery from the age of 13 and later became a monk. With the pope's blessing, Boniface went to Germany to evangelize and convert the people there. Despite many dangers, he eventually was ordained Bishop of Germany. Patron saint of Germany, St. Boniface was killed in Holland in 755.

St. Catherine Elementary School   **11 Canata Close S.E.**

Catherine Benincasa (1347-1380) was born in Siena, Italy, the youngest of 23 children. She demonstrated a great love for God and devotion to prayer at a very young age. She became known for charity to the poor and sick and for many mystical experiences including visions of Christ. Although unable to read or write, Catherine was declared a Doctor of the Church in 1970. The title indicates that her wisdom and insights were so great that they have been of fundamental importance in Church learning.

St. Cecilia Bilingual Elementary School   **610 Agate Crescent S.E.**

Although there is little historical data on St. Cecilia, it is known that she was a Roman of noble birth in the early days of Christianity. According to legend, she had made vows of virginity to God but her father forced her to marry Valerian, a Roman nobleman. He, along with his brother, Tiburtius, were soon converted to Christianity. The three served God by caring for the sick and burying the dead. Valerian and his brother were martyred for refusing to sacrifice to the Roman gods. Cecilia was herself brought to trial for her faith, but so persuasively defended her cause that her accusers were themselves converted. Later, she too was martyred. St. Cecilia is the patron saint of musicians.

St. Charles Congregated Elementary/ Junior High School   2445 - 23 Avenue S.W.

Charles Borromeo (1538-1584) was archbishop of Milan. When his uncle, Cardinal de Medici, became pope (Pius IV) he heaped honours on his nephew and brought him to Rome. But Charles' real desire was to work with his own people and in 1565 he received permission from the new pope, Pius V, to live in his diocese, the first resident bishop in 80 years. He immediately began reform and worked diligently with the people. But his hard work took its toll and he died in Milan at the age of 46. St. Charles Congregated School serves children from throughout the city in Grades 4 to 9 who have special learning needs.

St. Clement Elementary School   1140 Mayland Drive N.E.

St. Clement was the third successor of St. Peter as pope in the year 91. He was exiled to the Crimea by Emperor Trajan, condemned to death, and died a martyr in 100. Little else is known about St. Clement except that he knew St. Peter and St. Paul, and that he was the author of a famous letter to the Corinthians concerning a schism which had shaken the Church.

St. Cyril Elementary/Junior High School   2990 Cedarbrae Drive S.W.

St. Cyril was born in 315 and educated in Jerusalem. He became a priest and for several years educated those being initiated into the Church. His battles against heresies resulted in his being expelled from Jerusalem three times. His sermons on the Nicene Creed and the sacraments are still in existence and he is remembered for being able to teach the mysteries of the faith so simply and profoundly that everyone could understand.

St. Dominic Elementary School   4820 Dalhart Road N.W.

Dominic Savio was born in Italy in 1842. Very early, he devoted his life to prayer. At the age of 12, he entered the school administered by St. John Bosco (see Don Bosco Elementary/Junior High School) and lived in the Home for Boys. Dominic was noted for his love and concern for his fellow students, as well as his great desire for the salvation of their souls. He died of an illness at the age of 15.

St. Francis High School   877 Northmount Drive N.W.

St. Francis High School opened in 1961 with a section for girls and boys and a separate principal for each. It is named after Francis of Assisi (1181-1226), the son of a prosperous textile merchant in the city of Assissi, Italy. As a young man he was active in the social life of the city. Captured in a war with nearby Perugia, he spent almost two years in prison. The suffering he saw there made him re-think the purpose of his life. In 1205, after having a vision of Christ, he rejected his material life and devoted himself to serving the poor. He founded the Franciscan religious order in 1209 and although many

Franciscans became priests, Francis himself remained a layman. He was canonized (declared a saint) in 1228.

St. George's Heights   N.E.

Lots in St. George's Heights were offered for sale in 1912 and were advertised as "the last piece of close inside property in this city unsold." It was given its name because it was connected to St. George's Park (St. George's Island) by a steel bridge offering residents easy access to a recreational area.

St. George's Island   Bow River between 6 Street and 15 Street S.E.

Originally the three island group was named after the three British patron saints - St. Andrew (Scotland), St. George (England) and St. Patrick (Ireland). Although better known now as part of St. George's Island, the island to the west is still officially known as St. Patrick's Island. The other two, where the zoo is located, are known collectively as St. George's Island. The islands were named in 1890 and established as Calgary's first civic park in 1907. The islands had been donated to the Town of Calgary by the Dominion Government with the condition that they be developed as a park. The zoo on the island began in 1918 with a pen housing two mule deer. (For more information on the zoo, see Baines Bridge.)

St. Gerard Bilingual Elementary School   1204 - 96 Avenue S.W.

St. Gerard Majella was born in Italy in 1726. At the age of 23, he joined the newly-formed Redemptorist order and became known for his humility, piety and diligence. Upon taking final vows to the priesthood in 1752, he added the additional pledge of always doing that which was most pleasing to God. Many supernatural gifts were attributed to St. Gerard, but it is for his goodness, charity and devotion to God that his is considered a saint. He died in 1755. St. Gerard is the patron saint of mothers and expectant mothers.

St. Gregory Junior High School   5340 - 26 Avenue S.W.

Pope St. Gregory the Great (540-604) was born in Rome to a wealthy patrician family. Known as an honest and successful public servant, Gregory became prefect of Rome but later gave up his prominent position to devote his life entirely to God. In 575 he converted his home into a monastery, became a monk himself and eventually established six more monasteries in Sicily. He was ordained and sent to Constantinople as papal ambassador in 579 and was elected pope in 590. Gregory was responsible for the spread of Christianity to England and wrote the Gregorian Chant, still in use in the Church today.

St. Helena Junior High School   320 - 64 Avenue N.W.

Helena (250-330) was the daughter of an innkeeper in Drepanum, Bithynia, now northwest Turkey (not the daughter of an English prince as some sources claimed). She was the mother of Constantine, who became emperor of the Roman Empire in 306. Shortly after Constantine and fellow emperor Licinius declared Christianity legal in the empire,

Helena was converted. At an advanced age, she journeyed to Jerusalem and is credited with finding the remains of the cross used to crucify Jesus. She was a zealous supporter of Christianity, building churches on the Mount of Olives and at Bethlehem.

St. Henry Elementary School   7423 - 10 Street N.W.

The son of a wealthy duke, St. Henry (973-1024) was born in Bavaria. After his father's death, Henry became Duke of Bavaria and in 1002, after the death of a cousin, became Emperor of Bavaria. In 1014, he was crowned Holy Roman Emperor by Pope Benedict VIII. St. Henry was a consummate politician and a man of faith, known for dealing with issues of government from the perspective of God's law and of his own responsibilities to the Church. He did much to consolidate the power of the German monarchy and to reform and unify the Church within his realm.

St. Hubert Elementary School   310 - 72 Avenue N.E.

Following the death of his wife, Hubert became a priest after seeing a cross between the horns of a stag while he was hunting. Thus, he is the patron saint of hunters. He became bishop of Liege in 705 and died in 727.

St. James Elementary/Junior High School   2227 - 58 Avenue S.W.

Also known as St. James the Greater, James was an apostle of Jesus and the brother of St. John the Apostle. A fisherman by trade, he was born in Bethsaida in Galilee. Tradition says that James travelled as far as Spain to preach the Gospel. The first of the apostles to die for Christ, James was beheaded in Palestine in 42 by King Agrippa I.

St. John (Fine Arts) Elementary   15 - 12 Street N.W.

St. John was an apostle of Jesus and is often known as St. John the Evangelist. Along with his brother, St. James the Greater, John was one of the disciples closest to Jesus. It was to John that Jesus committed the care of His mother Mary as He was dying on the cross. He was a founder of the Church at Jerusalem and after some years, went to Ephesus in Asia Minor. He authored the gospel which bears his name and is also credited with writing the Book of Revelation, thought to be written when he was imprisoned on the Island of Patmos for his teachings. He died in Ephesus at approximately age 94.

St. Joseph Elementary School   2512 - 5 Street N.W.

Mentioned only in the Gospels of Matthew and Luke, St. Joseph was the husband of the Virgin Mary and foster father to Jesus. In Scripture, Joseph is a carpenter, "a righteous man," a descendant of David. He accepted marriage to Mary after a dream, fled to Egypt to protect his family following another dream, and spent his life protecting and caring for Jesus and Mary. The Catholic Church has long honoured Joseph for his holiness, humility and obedience to and love of God, witnessed by the fact that God trusted him with the care of His own Son.

St. Jude Elementary School   **730 Woodbine Boulevard S.W.**

Jude was one of the apostles listed in Luke and Acts. In Matthew and Mark the name Thaddeus appears and scholars believe that he and Jude are the same person. He may also be the author of the Epistle of Jude, though scholars disagree on this point. Jude was possibly martyred in Persia. Devotion to St. Jude has been very popular; he is known as the patron saint of hopeless or desperate causes.

St. Luke Bilingual Elementary School   **1232 Northmount Drive N.W.**

Luke was the author of the third gospel and of the Acts of the Apostles, the fifth book of the New Testament. He was a Gentile physician who accompanied Paul on two of his missionary journeys. Legend says he painted several portraits of Mary and thus he is the patron saint of painters and physicians.

St. Margaret Elementary/Junior High School   **3320 Carol Drive N.W.**

Born in the Burgundy region of France, Margaret Mary Alacoque (1647-90) entered the convent of the Visitation nuns in 1671. For nearly two years, she was granted visions of Christ in which He called her to reveal the love of His Sacred Heart to the world. Through her efforts and prayer, devotion to the Sacred Heart of Jesus grew in popularity, resulting in a special feast day in the Catholic Church calendar, October 16.

St. Maria Goretti Elementary School   **375 Hawkstone Drive N.W.**

Born in 1890 to a poor peasant family in Corinaldo, Italy, Maria Goretti showed particular devotion to and faith in God from an early age. After her father's death in 1900, Maria took over many of the household duties so that her mother could support the family as a field labourer. They shared living quarters with the Serenelli family and many difficulties arose in this arrangement. On July 5, 1902, as Maria cared for her younger sister, the Serenelli's 18 year old son, Alessandro, began to harass her. He threatened her and, after her continued resistance, stabbed her. From her deathbed, Maria not only forgave him, but promised to pray for him continually in order that his soul be saved. She died the following day. After eight years in prison, Alessandro Serenelli repented and begged forgiveness, returning to his Catholic faith. He spent the rest of his life as a gardener and labourer. Alessandro himself testified on Maria's behalf in the process of her beatification. St. Maria Goretti is honoured for her practice of heroic virtue, for the forgiveness and love she demonstrated, and for her willingness to stand firm in her beliefs, even when threatened with death.

St. Mark Elementary School   **4589 Marbank Drive N.E.**

Mark, author of the second gospel, was the companion of Paul, Peter and Barnabas. He travelled with Paul and Barnabas on the first missionary journey, but returned to Jerusalem from Pamphylia. He later travelled with Barnabas and was with Paul during his imprisonment in Rome. Tradition says that his gospel represents the teachings and memoirs of Peter. Mark was martyred during the reign of Nero in 74 A.D. and his body was brought to Venice in the 9th century. He is the patron saint of Venice.

St. Martha Elementary/Junior High School   6020 - 4 Avenue N.E.

Biblical references to Martha, a sister of Mary and Lazarus, can be found in Luke 10:38-42 and John 10:1-46. She lived in Bethany, in Israel. Scripture says that Jesus loved her, her sister and her brother, and that she welcomed Jesus into her home. She was present when Jesus raised Lazarus from the dead four days after he was buried. Martha is patron saint of homemakers and lay sisters.

St. Mary's Senior High School   111 - 18 Avenue S.W.

As the Mother of Jesus, Mary is pre-eminent among Catholic saints. There are 11 feast days dedicated to her during the year. She is reported to have appeared numerous times during the last century-and-a-half, most notably at Lourdes, France (see St. Bernadette) and Fatima, Portugal. St. Mary's was the first Catholic school established in Calgary. It opened in 1909 as St. Mary's Girls' School. St. Mary's Boys' School opened in 1928.

St. Matthew Elementary and   416 - 83 Avenue S.E.
Bilingual Junior High School

One of the twelve apostles and author of the first gospel, Matthew was a Jewish tax collector who left all behind to follow Christ. He is called Levi in the gospels of Mark and Luke. Traditions differ concerning the method and place of his martyrdom.

St. Michael Elementary/Junior High School   4511 - 9 Avenue S.W.

St. Michael the Archangel is one of three archangels mentioned in Scripture. An archangel is generally referred to as a "lead, chief or ruling angel." St. Michael the Archangel is mentioned in Daniel 10:13, Jude 9 and Revelation 12:7, where he defeats the dragon (commonly regarded as the devil).

St. Monica Avenue   Inglewood, S.E.

Monica (331-387) was mother of St. Augustine. She was married to Patricius, a pagan, who was known for his immoral lifestyle and violent temper. Because of her persistent prayers, Patricius, his mother, and later Augustine himself were converted to Christianity. Monica is the patron saint of married women.

St. Monica Elementary/Junior High School   235 - 18 Avenue S.W.

See St. Monica Avenue.

St. Patrick Elementary School   6006 Rundlehorn Drive N.E.

The patron saint of Ireland, Patrick (389-461) was born in Britain. He was captured by pirates as a youth and was taken to Ireland where he was a slave for six years. He was then either released or escaped and fled to Britain. He returned to pagan Ireland as an adult and was instrumental in converting much of the island to Christianity. Legend says he drove a plague of snakes out of Ireland and explained the Holy Trinity by using the shamrock with three leaves on one stalk , to represent the Three Persons in One God. March 17 has become known as St. Patrick's Day.

St. Paul School (Ecole Ste. Anne Annex)　　　　**124 - 24 Avenue N.E.**

Educated as a Pharisee, Saul of Tarsus spent his early adult life as a persecutor of Christians and took part in the stoning of Stephen, the first Christian martyr. After meeting Christ in a vision on the road to Damascus, he changed his name to Paul and became an apostle to the Gentiles. He spent the rest of his life preaching and ministering to the Gentiles throughout the Middle East and southern Europe. Thirteen of the New Testament epistles were written by him.

St. Peter Elementary School　　　　**720 - 58 Street S.E.**

Peter was one of Jesus' twelve apostles. He was introduced to Jesus by his brother, Andrew. He was called Cephas (Aramaic for rock) by Jesus. He became leader of the disciples in Jerusalem after the Ascension. Tradition says that he was the first bishop (pope) of Rome and was martyred in that city in 67 A.D.

St. Philip Elementary School　　　　**13825 Parkside Drive S.E.**

According to the Gospel of John, Philip was the fourth apostle to follow Jesus. Born in Bethsaida, he met Jesus in Galilee and committed his life to him. Philip was present at the "miracle of the loaves and fishes," and in the upper room at Pentecost. He preached the Gospel in Samaria and was responsible for baptizing many. Philip eventually preached in Asia Minor and was martyred at Hierapolis by soldiers loyal to Emperor Domitian.

St. Pius Elementary Bilingual School　　　　**2312 - 18 Street N.W.**

The first pope to be canonized (declared a saint) in 342 years, Pius X (1835-1914) was born Guiseppe Sarto in Riese, Italy. At the age of ten he expressed his desire for the priesthood. Having been born into a very poor family, this would have been impossible except for the generosity of the parish priest which enabled him to attend school. He was ordained in 1858 and from the start of his priesthood became known for his love for and service to the poor. Ordained as a bishop in 1884, he became Cardinal Patriarch of Venice in 1893 and was elected pope in 1903, taking the name of Pius X. He was canonized in 1954.

St. Rita Elementary School　　　　**7811 Ranchview Drive N.W.**

Rita of Cascia (1381-1457) was born near Spoleto, Italy and became a nun after the death of her husband and two sons. In 1441 she suffered a thorn-shaped wound on her forehead after hearing a sermon on the crown of thorns. It remained unhealed for 15 years. She was canonized in 1900 and is the patron saint of desperate causes.

St. Rose of Lima Elementary/Junior High School   **2419 - 50 Street N.E.**

Isabel de Santa Maria de Flores (1586-1617) was born in Lima, Peru. Known for her beauty, she resisted her parents' efforts to have her marry and joined the Third Order of St. Dominic. She lived as a recluse in a garden shack and had many mystical visions which priests and doctors decided were supernatural. The garden became the spiritual centre of Lima. She was canonized in 1671 and became the first saint of the Americas. She is the patron saint of South America and of the Philippine Islands.

St. Rupert Elementary School   **111 Rundlehill Drive N.E.**

Rupert was bishop of Worms and Salzburg, preaching the gospel in the area of the Danube and Regensburg in Bavaria. One source states that he was the son of St. Bertha, who, after a visit to Rome with his mother, joined her in giving away all his possessions and became a hermit near Bingen (Rupertsburg), Germany. He died in 710 A.D.

St. Stephen Elementary/Junior High School   **10910 Elbow Drive S.W.**

St. Stephen was the first known martyr for the Christian faith. All that is known about him can be found in The Acts of the Apostles, Chapters VI and VII. It is thought that Stephen was a Greek-speaking Jew and thus was chosen as one of the seven men assigned to look after the needs of Greek-speaking widows. He was a zealous preacher who accused the Jews of continued disobedience to God. His words so enraged the Jewish Sanhedrin that the members stoned him to death. In imitation of Christ, Stephen forgave his killers even as they threw stones, offered himself to God, and had a vision of heaven before dying. The name "Stephen" means "victorious one," signifying his victory over death.

St. Sylvester Elementary School   **7318 Silver Springs Boulevard N.W.**

A Roman by birth, Sylvester became pope in 314 A.D., presiding over the Roman Church for 21 years. Although there is not an abundance of historical data, tradition indicates that Sylvester worked closely with the Emperor Constantine and was prominent in the governing of the early Christians. St. Peter's Basilica in Rome was built by Constantine during his reign. Sylvester died in 355 A.D.

St. Thomas Aquinas Elementary School   **4540 - 26 Avenue S.W.**

St. Thomas (1225-1274) was born near Aquino, Italy and educated at a Benedictine monastery. However, in 1244 he became a Dominican monk, a move which his family so strongly opposed, that they kidnapped him and held him at Rocasecca Castle for 15 months. Thomas was a great intellectual and a prolific writer. He was canonized in 1323 and is the patron saint of universities, colleges and schools.

St. Thomas More Elementary School   **6110 Temple Drive N.E.**

A lawyer, author and member of parliament, Thomas More (1478-1535) was a friend of King Henry VIII of England and eventually became his Lord Chancellor. When the king wanted to declare his marriage to Catherine of Aragon invalid, Thomas fell out of favour by supporting church teaching and by upholding the marriage contract. Upon his further refusal to recognize the validity of Henry's marriage to Anne Boelyn, he was imprisoned in the tower of London. He was subsequently tried and beheaded on July 6, 1535. He was canonized in 1935.

St. Vincent de Paul Elementary/Junior High School　　4525 - 49 Street N.W.

Vincent de Paul (1580-1660) was born at Pouy, France. He is known for his work with the poor and for the founding of the Sisters of Charity in 1633. He was canonized in 1737 and is the patron saint of all charitable groups.

St. Wilfrid Elementary School　　4225 - 44 Avenue N.E.

St. Wilfrid (633-709) was born in Northumbria, England. He studied in Rome and upon returning to England was instrumental in introducing Roman practices (such as the method of calculating Easter) to replace Celtic customs. He also founded numerous monasteries.

St. William Elementary School　　11020 Fairmount Drive S.E.

Born into a wealthy French family, from an early age St. William showed great devotion to God. Though he spent much time in prayer, practiced penance and was deeply humble, he was always joyful and inspirational to others. A Cistercian monk, he eventually became abbot of his community and was later chosen Archbishop of Bourges. He served his diocese by travelling widely to preach, minister to the poor and sick and spread the message of Christ to all he met. At his death in 1209, he was buried in ashes at his own request. He was canonized in 1218.

Sam Livingston Building　　4 Street and 12 Avenue S.W.

Built to house federal government offices, the Sam Livingston Building sits on a former piece of Sam Livingston's ranch. Livingston (1828-97) was an Irish adventurer who travelled the American and Canadian west from California to the Cariboo in search of gold. He settled in the Calgary area in 1874 as a trader and farmer. His homestead now lies under the Glenmore Reservoir. Livingston planted the first fruit trees to survive a Calgary winter, owned the first herd of milk cows in the area and was the first to sell milk on Calgary streets. He was the first farmer in the area to use machinery for mowing, raking and threshing and his success helped to promote southern Alberta as good farming land. Mary Dowler, one of Livingston's 14 children, assisted at the ribbon cutting ceremony when the building opened in December 1966.

Sam Livingston Elementary School　　10211 Bonaventure Drive S.E.

See Sam Livingston Building.

Samis Road   Crescent Heights, N.E.

Adoniram Judson Samis came west from Ohio in 1893 to live in the Olds area and later in Morley. He moved to Calgary in 1904 where he was successful in real estate. He was elected to city council in 1906 and served until 1912. He was City commissioner in 1913, returned to City council in 1915, and served as City commissioner again from 1917 to 1922. He then moved to Los Angeles where he resided until his death in 1942.

Sarcee Trail   N.W. - S.W.

Sarcee Trail honours the Sarcee Indian tribe (now called the Tsuu T'ina Nation), who have a reserve on the western outskirts of the city. The Sarcees were originally part of the Beaver tribe in the north but broke away and became part of the Blackfoot confederacy.

Scotchman's Hill   6 Street S.E. between Alexander Avenue
                              and Salisbury Street

The bluff on the northeast side of the old Stampede grandstand provided a free panoramic view of the Stampede chuckwagon races and infield events and was nick-named "The Scotsman's Grandstand" by early Calgarians. The name, which is unofficial, has since been revised to Scotchman's Hill. It is also referred to as Scotsman's Hill. The hill may have been named after Angus Fraser, a Scot who was the second manager of the Hudson's Bay Company in Calgary. The hill was originally named Fraser's Hill or Frazer's Hill.

Scurfield Drive   Scenic Acres, N.W.

In August 1985 the Calgary Planning Commission approved the re-naming of Scenic View Drive N.W. as Scurfield Drive N.W. in memory of Ralph Scurfield, a major land-holder in Scenic Acres. (See Scurfield Hall.)

Scurfield Hall   University of Calgary, N.W.

Ralph Thomas Scurfield, a Winnipeg teacher, moved to Calgary in 1952 and began his career in the construction business. He served as general manager and president of the Nu-West Group of companies and its predecessors from 1957 to 1981 when he became chairman of the board. During Scurfield's years with the company it developed from a small, home construction company to an international development company worth $1.5 billion in 1980. He was also part-owner of the Calgary Flames. In 1980, the family of Ralph Scurfield donated $8 million to build a new school of business at the University of Calgary and funds were matched by the province. Scurfield Hall opened in the fall of 1985, seven months after Scurfield was killed in an avalanche while helicopter skiing in British Columbia.

Seattle Drive   Southwood, S.W.

Seattle Drive is likely named for the largest city in the state of Washington. Founded in 1852, the city of Seattle was named for a chief of the Duwamish Indian tribe, who was friendly towards the city's founders. Chief Seattle died in 1866.

Selkirk Drive   Southwood, S.W.

This street may have been named for Thomas Douglas, 5th Earl of Selkirk, who was the first to colonize western Canada when he brought Irish and Scottish settlers to Red River, Manitoba in 1811.

Senator Burns Building   SAIT Campus, N.W.

The buildings at SAIT were re-named in 1985. The new names were chosen to reflect Calgary's heritage and the former Tower Building was renamed to honour one of Calgary's earliest businessmen, Patrick Burns. (See Big Four Building.)

Senator Patrick Burns Junior High School   2155 Chilcotin Road N.W.

See Big Four Building.

Senator Patrick Burns Memorial Gardens   10 Street and 10 Avenue N.W.

This hillside rock garden is a memorial to Patrick Burns, one of Calgary's "Big Four" (see Big Four Building). His legacy to the city has lived on through the Burns Memorial Foundation.

Seymour Avenue   Southwood, S.W.

This street may have been named for Frederick Seymour (1820-1869), governor of the Colony of British Columbia. He opposed the colony's union with Canada and died while on a peace mission to northern coastal Indians. Another Seymour was Joseph B. Seymour who was elected to city council in 1933 and served as an alderman until 1935. Although he only served one term in public office, he took an active interest in city politics throughout his 30 years' residence in the city, until his death at age 49 in 1941.

Shannon Avenue   Shawnessy, S.W.

Shannon Avenue and the 12 other streets in Shannon Village in the subdivision of Shawnessy may have been named after a pioneer resident of the area, Joseph Shannon. He came to the Calgary district in 1882 and homesteaded a section of land south of Fish Creek and west of where Macleod Trail crosses the creek. Shortly after his arrival he obtained a government contract to supply rations to the Sarcee Indians. He became their close friend and advisor. Shannon died at Calgary in 1933.

Shaughnessy High School   2336 - 53 Avenue S.W.

This school opened in 1968 and is named after Thomas George Shaughnessy (1853-1923), who was president of the Canadian Pacific Railway from 1899 to 1918. Shaughnessy began his railway career in his hometown of Milwaukee at age 16. He joined the CPR in 1882 as general purchasing agent and helped save the firm from bankruptcy during 1884 and 1885 by placating creditors at a time when the CPR's credit was strained to the limit. Shaughnessy was appointed vice president in 1891 and president in 1899 and served as president during the period of the greatest expansion in the railway's history. Although he retired as president in 1918, he remained chairman until his death. He was knighted in 1901 and created First Baron of Shaughnessy, Montreal and Ashford in 1916.

Shaw Road   Midnapore, S.E.

One of the original streets registered in 1913 by the town of Midnapore is named after one of the town's early citizens. Samuel and Helen Shaw and their nine children immigrated to the Calgary area from Kent, England in 1882. They travelled by rail to Swift Current and from there by wagon train. They stored 30 tons of machinery for a woollen mill in Winnipeg until the railroad reached Calgary in 1883. The family operated a woollen mill in Midnapore for many years. Shawnee Slopes Golf Course, built on Shaw's original homestead land, was developed in 1965 and operated by William Shaw, Samuel Shaw's grandson.

Shawnee   S.W.

The land on which this development was built was originally owned by the Samuel William Shaw family. (See Shaw Road.)

Shawnessy   S.W.

The area was settled by two pioneer families, the Shaws (see Shaw Road) and the McInneses. The McInnes' barn, which was built in 1908 and renovated by the subdivision's developer, Genstar, is now the Shawnessy Community Centre.

Shepard Road   S.E.

Shepard Road heads south towards the hamlet of Shepard, southeast of Calgary. A CPR station built here in 1884 was named after D.C. Shepard of Minneapolis. He was one of the partners of Shepard and Langdon, railway contractors who had an agreement with the CPR to build the section of railway from Flat Creek, Manitoba (near Brandon) to Fort Calgary. This length of track was 672 miles long and was the largest contract awarded by the CPR.

Sheriff King Home   Address unlisted

Peter Willoughby King was a bachelor who came to the city in 1866 when he was appointed sheriff of Calgary. When Alberta became a province in 1905 he gave up his position and retired to his ranch just outside the city. When King died in 1920 at age 87, his will stipulated that his whole estate, worth over $250,000, be used to build and maintain a home for needy women and their children. The first home was completed in the community of Rosedale in 1922.

Sherman Avenue   Southwood, S.W.

Sherman Avenue may have been named for Most Rev. Louis Ralph Sherman who served as Anglican Bishop of Calgary from 1927 to 1943. He was consecrated Bishop of Calgary at age 41, one of the youngest bishops in Canada. W.B. Sherman was another important figure in Calgary. He opened Sherman's Opera House in 1905 and Sherman's Rink in 1907, the latter being destroyed in a fire in 1915. Sherman went on to become a major theatre owner in Calgary, and his most impressive house was the Sherman Grand which featured movies and live performances.

Shillington Crescent   Southwood, S.W.

Shillington Crescent may have been named for Dr. Richard N.W. Shillington, who came to Calgary in 1910 and served as the medical officer in charge of the Veterans' Convalescent Hospital in Calgary from 1932 to 1948.

Shouldice Bridge   Bow River - Bowness Road N.W.

Completed in 1912 as part of an agreement between The City and developer John Hextall, this bridge opened Bowness for development. (See John Hextall Bridge.) The original bridge, which was named after James Shouldice (see Shouldice Park and Montgomery subdivision) is now a foot and bicycle bridge called the Hextall Bridge. The new Shouldice Bridge, adjacent to the old, was opened in 1987.

Shouldice Lodge   4730 - 19 Avenue N.W.

This senior citizen's home is named after James Shouldice who donated the land on which it stands. (See Shouldice Park and Montgomery subdivision.)

Shouldice Park   Bowness Road and 56 Street N.W.

James Shouldice came west in 1901 with his wife Margaret, and family. Around 1910, he and neighbour, Alfred S. MacKay, donated about 100 acres of land to The City of Calgary for a park. No time limit was set as to when the park had to be developed. When the Trans-Canada Highway was built, the federal government paid The City $43,000 for a right-of-way through the land. In 1952 Fred L. Shouldice, one of James' sons, bequeathed $17,000 to The City of Calgary to build a swimming pool on the park property. However, The City was so slow in developing the site that the Shouldice family sponsored a fundraising drive themselves to finance it. The pool was finally built in 1967. (See Montgomery subdivision.)

Sifton Boulevard   Elbow Park, S.W.

Arthur Lewis Sifton (1858-1921) was born in Ontario and came to Calgary in 1889. He was town solicitor and wrote the charter which enabled Calgary to become a city in 1894. He served as Commissioner of Public Works in the North-West Territories government and was Chief Justice of the Superior Court in both the North-West Territories and in Alberta after its creation in 1905. He was premier of Alberta from 1910 to 1917 and served federally as minister of customs, secretary of state and privy councillor. He was one of the two Canadian signatories on the Treaty of Versailles which ended World War I in 1917.

Simon Fraser Junior High School   **5215 - 33 Street N.W.**

Simon Fraser (1776 -1862) began working for the North West Company in 1792 and became a partner in 1801. He is famous for his activities during the years 1805 to 1808, when he expanded the activities of the company into the interior of British Columbia. He established the first trading posts there and explored the river now named in his honour. He later moved to Athabasca and the Red River. He retired from the North West Company around 1819. He then entered into private business ventures, most of which failed, and died in poverty on the same day as his wife.

Simons Crescent, etc.   **Thorncliffe, N.E.**

Simons Crescent and Simons Road were likely named after W.E. Simons (see Simons Valley Road), as the road originally ran further west and connected with Simons Valley Road. However, it may have been named for Percy W. Simons, a veteran of the North West Mounted Police who lived in Calgary for 56 years. He joined the force in 1882 and served through the Riel Rebellion. He was stationed at Fort Calgary in its earliest days and made Calgary his home when he retired from the force after eight years of service.

Simons Valley Road   **Hidden Valley, N.W.**

Simons Valley received its name from the first postmaster of the area, W.E. Simons. A book on the history of the area, The Nose Creek Story notes that Simons won first prize at an exhibit of produce at the Public Market in Calgary in the early 1900s. He eventually moved back to Eastern Canada. There is some disagreement as to whether W.E. Simons spelled his name with an "i" or with a "y."

Sinclair Crescent   **Southwood, S.W.**

This street may be named for Robert Falconer Sinclair, who came to Calgary in 1884 and resided in the city until his death in 1985 at age 103. He was an avid sportsman and was still playing golf at the age of 100. He was one of the first students to attend a convent school in Calgary and upon graduating, became an employee of the CPR where he worked for 50 years.

Sir James Lougheed Elementary School   **3519 - 36 Avenue S.W.**

James Alexander Lougheed (1854-1925) was a lawyer from Ontario who followed the railway west and found fame and fortune in Calgary. He arrived in the town in 1883 and opened a law office, with one of his important clients being the CPR. His fortune was made in real estate and business ventures. He was appointed to the Senate in 1889 and became Senate leader of the Conservative Party in 1906, a post he held until his death. In 1916 he was given a knighthood in recognition of his work as president of the Military Hospitals Commission during World War I. (For further information on Sir James Lougheed, see Lougheed Building, Lougheed Residence, Clarence Block and Norman Block.)

Sir John A. Macdonald Junior High School 6600 - 4 Street N.W.

John Alexander Macdonald (1815-91) had a long career in Canadian politics which saw him serve as the Dominion of Canada's first prime minister from 1867 to 1873. He served a second term from 1878 until his death. He held office for 19 years, second in length only to W.L. Mackenzie King. Macdonald played a leading role in Canada achieving Confederation, and for his efforts, he was knighted. Macdonald also played a crucial role in the building of Canada's railway.

Sir John Franklin Junior High School 2215 - 8 Avenue N.E.

John Franklin was born in England in 1786. He served in the Royal Navy and between 1818 and 1822, made two Arctic expeditions. In 1825 he journeyed overland to the north and further explored the Arctic regions. He was knighted in 1829 in recognition of his achievements. In 1845 he led an expedition in search of a North-West Passage. His ships and the men aboard were last seen in Lancaster Sound on July 26, 1845. When Franklin failed to return, his wife sponsored numerous expeditions to search for him, resulting in extensive exploration of the Arctic.

Sir Wilfrid Laurier Junior High School 819 - 32 Street S.E.

Wilfrid Laurier (1841-1919) began his political career in 1871 as a Liberal member of the Quebec legislature. He was elected to Parliament in 1874, became leader of the Liberal party in 1887, prime minister in 1896 and was knighted in 1897. During the time that Laurier was prime minister, Canada sent troops to fight in the Boer War in South Africa, Alberta and Saskatchewan became provinces, and the Naval Services Bill, which saw the creation of a Canadian navy, was passed. The Liberals were defeated in 1911, but Laurier remained leader of the party and a member of Parliament until his death.

Sir Winston Churchill High School 5220 Northland Drive N.W.

Winston Spencer Churchill (1874-1965) is considered by many to be one of the greatest statesmen in the world's history. He served as prime minister of Britain during World War II and his courage, oratory and faith in victory inspired his countrymen to fight on at a time when they stood alone against Nazi Germany. Churchill was not only a states-man and politician, but also an author. In 1953, the same year he was knighted, he won the Nobel Prize for literature. Churchill's career began as an army lieutenant in 1895 and ended in 1964. He served his country for 69 years under six monarchs.

Slater Park 2015 - 26 Street S.E.

The land on which Slater Park stands is adjacent to an irrigation canal that was leased to The City of Calgary in 1973 for $1 a year by the Western Irrigation District (WID). It was named after P.W. Slater, who was the WID's general manager and who had been with the company for more than 50 years. The park is a natural area with an equestrian-hiking trail and also houses the headquarters of the Forest Lawn Canoe Club.

Snowdon Crescent   Southwood, S.W.

Snowdon Crescent may have been named for prominent Calgary businessman, C.C. Snowdon, who came to Calgary in 1908 and founded a wholesale oil business, which eventually spread throughout western Canada. Snowdon was a keen gardener and his garden was a noted beauty spot in the city. The crescent may also have been named for Herbert H. Snowdon (1915-85), a native Calgarian who was a prominent sportsman in the city. He played football for the Calgary Broncs and the Calgary Stampeders. A third possibility is that it was named for Mount Snowdon, meaning "snow hill," the highest peak in Wales.

Spiller Road   Manchester, S.E.

Edward Vincent "Ted" Spiller (1878-1970) devoted much of his life to the Boy Scout movement in Calgary. Spiller was involved from the beginning in 1910, when the concept of the scouting movement reached Calgary. He was one of the organizers of the 1920 Scout Jamboree when 5,000 scouts welcomed Lord Baden-Powell, founder of the scouting movement.

Spokane Street   Southwood, S.W.

This street takes its name from Spokane, Washington, which is named after the Spokane Indians, native to Washington state.

Stampede Park   13 Avenue and 6 Street S.E.

Stampede Park was set aside as an exhibition ground as far back as 1889. The property was transferred to The City and the Exhibition Association with the explicit agreement that if The City tried to subdivide the land, it would revert to the Federal Government. The parks department headquarters were there for a time, however it was never recognized as a city park. The land was officially named Victoria Park in 1901, after Queen Victoria, when the city limits were extended to include the area. Some of the facilities that were available over the years at Victoria Park were a race track, picnic area, rifle range, baseball diamond, soccer and rugby fields, various exhibition halls, electric generating station and a sunken garden. The name was changed to Stampede Park in 1975.

Stanley Jones Elementary School   950 - 6 Street N.E.

Stanley Livingston Jones, a Calgary lawyer, was a member of the law firm Lent, Jones and Mackay. He left Calgary along with his wife in the first month of World War I to join Britain's war effort. Jones was commissioned a lieutenant with the Princess Patricia's Canadian Light Infantry and his wife served as a nurse. Lieutenant Jones was wounded in battle twice before he gained the rank of major. In 1916 he was wounded again, captured by Germans and died in a prison camp. Mrs. Jones was commissioned as a lieutenant by the French army for her work as a nurse in the war zone, the first western Canadian, and perhaps the first Canadian woman, to be so honoured. She died in 1955. Stanley Jones School was originally called Bridgeland School but was renamed in 1916.

Stanley Park 4011 - 1A Street S.W.
S.W.

Stanley Park was set aside as a park and named by 1924, but there was little or no development of the area until the 1960s when landscaping began. The significance of the name Stanley is unknown. One possibility is that it was named to honour Frederick Arthur Stanley, Baron Stanley of Preston, governor-general of Canada from 1888 to 1893, who donated a trophy for amateur hockey in 1893 called the Stanley Cup. It may also have been named for the famous newspaper reporter, Sir Henry Stanley, who located the African missionary, David Livingstone, or for a village in Yorkshire, England. The name Stanley means "stoney Leah (meadow)."

 Steele Avenue **Harvey Barracks, S.W.**

Samuel Benfield Steele (1849-1919) was a sergeant major when the North West Mounted Police was created in 1873. He served on the force for 25 years, becoming superintendent in 1885. He was in command of the Strathcona's Horse Regiment in the Boer War and commanded the second Canadian contingent sent overseas during World War I. Steele was knighted in 1918 and retired from the army shortly thereafter. He died in England during the great influenza epidemic of 1918-19 while waiting to be repatriated to Canada.

 Stephen Avenue Mall **8 Avenue S.**

Originally the streets in downtown Calgary were named after officers or shareholders of the Canadian Pacific Railway. On March 17, 1904 City Council passed by-law no. 528 changing all street names to numbers. Stephen Avenue, named after the first CPR president Sir George Stephen became 8th Avenue. The 8th Avenue Mall, built in 1969-70, reverted to the original name in 1982 although for mailing purposes it is still 8th Avenue. Stephen Avenue is one of only three streets in the city with a dual name. The other two are Daqing Avenue (2nd Street S.W.) and Jerusalem Road (16 Street S.W.).

 Stew Hendry Arena **814 - 13 Avenue N.E.**

Born in Calgary, Stewart Alexander Hendry (1929-87) was signed by the Chicago Black Hawks in 1947 and sent to Oshawa to play in the junior league. He then served as back-up goalie for the Western Hockey League's Calgary Stampeders. Later, he was the liaison between Molson Breweries, his employer, and the Calgary Flames. He played an important part in the Flames' celebrity golf tournament and Progress Club dinners, earning thousands of dollars for Big Brothers, Uncles at Large and the Special Olympics. The Renfrew Arena was re-named in his honour in 1986.

 Stoney Trail **N.W.**

Stoney Trail honours the Stoney tribe, which is part of the plains Assiniboine nation. The closest Stoney reserve to Calgary is at Morley, Alberta.

Strathcona Park   S.W.

Strathcona is a name historically linked to the entire Strathcona Park-Coach Hill area. It is named after Lord Strathcona. Donald Alexander Smith (1820-1914) was a Scot who joined the Hudson's Bay Company in 1838 and by 1870 had become its chief commissioner. In 1869 he was appointed by the federal government as a special commissioner to arrange the transfer of Rupert's Land to Canada during the Red River Rebellion. He was elected to the House of Commons in 1871. Although for political reasons he was never a member of the syndicate formed to build the Canadian Pacific Railway, he risked his personal fortune to see it finished, and was given the honour of driving the last spike upon its completion in 1885. He was knighted in 1886 and raised to the peerage in 1887, becoming Baron Strathcona and Mount Royal.

Strathcona Street   Harvey Barracks, S.W.

This street is named in recogniton of Lord Strathcona who, during the Boer War, equipped the Strathcona's Horse Regiment, a unit of mounted rifles, which currently makes its headquarters in Calgary and is now known as the Lord Strathcona's Horse (Royal Canadians). (See Strathcona Park.)

Stu Peppard Arena   5300 - 19 Street S.W.

Stu Peppard (1905-1990) was involved with hockey for most of his life. He played junior hockey, coached and officiated, and eventually became involved at an administrative level. He came to Calgary in 1945 and founded the Calgary Junior Hockey League in 1948. He served on the Alberta Amateur Hockey Association board of directors and was Calgary Junior Hockey League president for 30 years. He was named Calgary Booster Club Sportsman of the Year in 1964 and elected to the Alberta Sports Hall of Fame in 1974. He was an uncle of actor George Peppard. Glenmore Arena, the first city rink built and the home of Junior "B" hockey in Calgary, was re-named after Peppard in 1984.

Swann Mall   University of Calgary, N.W.

Dr. Gordon C. Swann, a Calgary orthodontist, was appointed to the Board of Governors of the University of Calgary in 1968. He served as a board member for six years and as vice-chairman for three years. He was appointed chairman of the board in 1974 and retired in June 1975. Swann Mall was dedicated in September 1975. Board member and Students' Council president, David Wolf, described Dr. Swann as one who had "made a lot of effort with us" and dealt "honestly and conscientiously" with student concerns.

Sydenham Road   Mount Royal, S.W.

Most of the streets in Mount Royal were given names which reflect the history of Quebec. Charles Edward Poulett Thomson, 1st Baron Sydenham (1700-1841), was appointed governor general of British North America in 1839. He was influential in the union of Upper and Lower Canada and wrote the constitution of the new province. He was unpopular with the French minority because of his policy of Anglicization.

Tache Avenue   **Thorncliffe, N.W.**

Tache Avenue is likely named for Alexandre A. Taché (1823-1894), archbishop of St. Boniface who played a major role in the history of western Canada. Taché was born in Quebec and ordained as a priest in 1845 at the Red River Colony, in what is now Manitoba. He founded many new missions in the region of Saskatchewan and helped the many settlers coming to this area. He was instrumental in helping to restore order after the Red River Rebellion.

Talon Avenue   **Mount Royal, S.W.**

Jean Talon (1625-1694) was the first chief local intendant of New France from 1665 to 1668 and 1669 to 1672. He took the colony from a small outpost to a strong, well-populated province. He returned to France when he saw that his desire for a large empire conflicted with the French administration's desire of a small, easily defensible colony.

Taylor Crescent   **Thorncliffe Heights, N.E.**

Harry "Kamoose' Taylor was a prominent frontiersman who was associated with the early history of Calgary. He was a whiskey trader who quit the trade after an encounter with the NWMP. He later operated a billiard room on the flats close to Fort Calgary. This street may have been named for him.

Tecumseh Road   **Knob Hill, S.W.**

Tecumseh Road lies adjacent to the naval base HMCS Tecumseh. (See HMCS Tecumseh.)

Temple   **N.E.**

Three of the four subdivisions originally known collectively as The Properties were named after mountains in the Canadian Rockies - Temple, Rundle and Whitehorn. The fourth,

Pineridge, was named after a ridge in the Canadian Rockies. Temple Mountain was named after Sir Richard Temple, who was president of the Economic Science and Statistics Section of the British Association for the Advancement of Science in 1883. That year he led the British Association excursion to the Rocky Mountains.

Terry Fox Junior High School   139 Falshire Drive N.E.

It is fitting to have a school named after someone who has become a role model to many Canadian youth. An athlete with a desire to teach physical education, Terry Fox (1958-1981) saw his dreams shattered when he lost his right leg to cancer in 1977. He captured the hearts of Canadians when, after two years of training on an artificial leg, he attempted to run across Canada to raise money for cancer research. His Marathon of Hope began on April 20, 1980 in St. John's Newfoundland, and ended in Thunder Bay, Ontario 135 days later, when a recurrence of his cancer forced him to return to his home in Vancouver. But his spirit and courage live on, and he is remembered each September 13 when thousands of people across Canada participate in the Terry Fox Marathon of Hope Day.

Thacker Street   Harvey Barracks, S.W.

Percival Edward Thacker graduated from the Royal Military College in Kingston in 1894. It was the beginning of a long and distinguished army career. He served in South Africa and as adjutant general of the Canadian overseas forces during World War II. Most of his army career was spent in England.

Thomas B. Riley Junior High School   3915 - 69 Street N.W.

Thomas B. Riley, a native of England, came to Calgary in 1903 to work for the Canadian Pacific Railroad. He was a member of the public school board from 1921 to 1928 and served as chairman for three years. During his time on the school board he was instrumental in securing free textbooks for students. In 1930, after 27 years with the CPR, he resigned to become a metal work instructor at Western Canada High School. He was elected City commissioner in 1933 and held the post until 1936. He was then employed by The City in various capacities, including placement officer and housing registrar, a position he held until his retirement in 1947. A machinist by trade, when he died in 1968, Riley was the oldest living member of Local 357, International Association of Machinists. He had been a member for 65 years. It was at the suggestion of the machinist's union and the Calgary Labour Council that Thomas B. Riley Junior High School was named in his honour in 1967.

Thomas Riley Building   SAIT Campus, N.W.

When the buildings of SAIT were re-named in 1985, the Trades and Technology Building was given the name of Thomas Riley, who homesteaded in the Hillhurst area and farmed the land on which the SAIT campus stands. (For information on the Riley family, see Riley Park, Hounsfield Heights, Louise Riley Branch Library and Harold W. Riley Elementary School.)

Thomas Street   Thorncliffe Heights, N.W.

Thomas Street was likely named for Robert Cadogan Thomas, an early Calgary businessman and alderman. Thomas arrived in Calgary in 1884 and was a farmer, teamster and
owner of Calgary's first ice-making company. He later made his fortune in construction
and the hotel business and served as a city alderman in 1905 and from 1924 to 1927.

Thomson Avenue   Renfrew (St. George's Heights), N.E.

Thomson Avenue may have been named for Robert "Bobby" Thomson, livestock superintendent of the Calgary Exhibition and Stampede from 1926 to 1949. A well-known and
popular citizen, Thomson came to Calgary in 1910 as a horseman and show-ring driver.
He was a recognized authority on both light horses and dogs, and often served as senior
judge at horse and dog shows throughout Canada and the United States. He died in
Calgary in 1956 at the age of 71.

Thomson Bros. Block   110, 112 - 8 Avenue S.E.

This building was constructed in 1893 by M.P. Thomson to house the Thomson
Brothers' stationery and printing business. It was later home to drygoods, hardware and
banking establishments, among others. It was declared an historic site by the provincial
government in 1982.

Thornton Road   Thorncliffe, N.W.

This street may take its name from Mount Thornton in Jasper. It was named after Sir
Henry Thornton (1871-1933) who was president of the CNR from 1922 to 1932.

Tom Baker Cancer Centre   Foothills Hospital, N.W.

Thomas Baker was a teacher and administrator in Alberta for 43 years. For 30 years he
worked toward getting improved treatment centres for cancer patients. He was chairman
of the Alberta Cancer Board and a director of the Canadian Cancer Society. In 1974 Baker
received an honourary doctorate from the University of Alberta and in 1989 was awarded
the Sir Frederick Haultain Prize for Humanities by the Alberta government. Baker is
retired and lives in Evansburg, Alberta.

Tom Brook Athletic Park   19 Street and 98 Avenue S.W.

Tom Brook (1908-81) was a Calgary oilman who was a great supporter of sports in
Calgary. He was president of the Calgary Stampeders from 1948 to 1950 and was inducted into the Canadian Football Hall of Fame in 1975. He helped finance the development
of the park on land which he originally owned.

Tom Campbell's Hill   Northwest of the zoo's north parking lot, N.E.

The hill was named for a huge billboard advertising Tom Campbell's Smile Hats, which
were manufactured in Calgary. The Smile Hat Shop was a well-known store in the city
from 1912 to 1948. The "Smile Kewpie," with a silk hat and cane and the slogan "Wear a

Tom Campbell Hat and Smile" were very familiar to Albertans. Tom Campbell's Hill is now a natural park, planted with native grasses and wildflowers. It was used from approximately 1965 to 1985 to handle zoo expansion as home of the hoofed animals.

Tomkins Square   **17 Avenue S.W. between 8 and 9 Streets**

This slim, block-long strip of land was owned by Henry William Tomkins, a long-time resident of the city. Upon his death in December 1914, his wife Elinor complied with his wish that the land be given to The City of Calgary for use as a public park. She donated the land to The City in August 1915.

Townsend Street   **Bridgeland, N.E.**

Townsend Street was likely named for David T. Townsend, chief surveyor for the Canadian Pacific Railway in Calgary from 1912 to 1943. In the early years, he surveyed the districts of Sunalta, Mount Royal, South Mount Royal and Bridgeland.

Travis Crescent   **Thorncliffe Heights, N.W.**

Travis Crescent may have been named for Jeremiah Travis (1829-1911), a federal stipendiary magistrate in Calgary from 1885 to 1886. A prohibitionist, he tried to suppress the illegal liquor traffic in Calgary, but created such an uproar that he was removed from the bench. He then went into real estate and became one of Calgary's first millionaires.

Tregillus Street   **Thorncliffe, N.W.**

William John Tregillus (1858-1914) was born in Plymouth, England. Before coming to Canada he worked in the flour-milling industry in the West Country of England. Upon arriving in Calgary in 1902 he leased a farm southwest of the city and soon owned considerable real estate. He delivered Calgary's first pasteurized and bottled milk, produced Calgary's first directory and in 1912, opened a brick plant. He was one of a group of prominent Calgarians who worked to establish a university in the city and in 1909 donated 160 acres of land for its use. He was a member of the Board of Governors of the fledgling university which failed when it was unable to obtain degree-granting status. Tregillus was also instrumental in the formation of the Farmer's Union of Alberta (which became the United Farmers of Alberta) and served as a city alderman from 1912 to 1914.

Trelle Drive   **Thorncliffe Heights, N.E.**

Trelle Drive may have been named for Herman Trelle, a farmer from the Peace River district who brought world attention to Alberta as a grain producing province. Trelle won the world wheat championship in 1926. He was barred from competing from 1932 to 1935 because he had won too often but when he was able to return, he once again won. Trelle lived briefly in Calgary as a munitions inspector for the CPR during World War II and was murdered in California in 1947.

CALGARY

U

Underwood Place   **University Heights, N.W.**

Underwood Place was probably named for Thomas Underwood (1863-1948), a prominent contractor who was a city alderman from 1894 to 1895, 1896 to 1901 and 1903 to 1904. He was mayor of Calgary from 1902 to 1903. As an alderman, Underwood was largely responsible for the development of Central Park and was a strong supporter of the Chinese community. Originally from England, Underwood came to Calgary from Winnipeg in 1885 as a carpenter for the CPR. He became a self-employed contractor in 1887 and was later involved in coal mining as the owner of the Diamond Coal Company in 1906. The Underwood Block (1311 - 1 St. SW), built by Underwood in 1911, was destroyed by fire in 1989. He also built the three buildings which over the years have been home to First Baptist Church. Underwood's wife Margaret (Graves) was also a pioneer Calgarian, who came to the city with her family in 1884. She was the first president of the YWCA, which she helped establish in 1911, and served on its board until her death in 1934.

Usher Road   **University Heights, N.W.**

Usher Road may have been named for Thomas Usher, a well-known pioneer Alberta rancher. He and his brother, Charlie, arrived in Alberta from Scotland in 1902 as protégés of William Roper Hull. They worked on Hull's 25 Ranch, southwest of Calgary, for two years and took part in some of western Canada's last big cattle round-ups. They established their own ranch in the Big Valley district, east of Calgary, in 1903. Thomas Usher lived and worked on the ranch until the time of his death in 1972 at age 90.

CALGARY

V

Valois Avenue   **Mount Royal, S.W.**

Most of the streets of Mount Royal were given names which reflect the history of Quebec. Valois is the family name of a line of French kings who ruled from 1328 to 1589. In 1534 Francis I of the House of Valois sent Jacques Cartier to the New World. Cartier sailed into the Gulf of St. Lawrence, landed on the Gaspé Peninsula and claimed it for France. In addition, there was Michel-Francois Valois (1801-1869), a medical doctor from Point Claire, near Montreal, who was jailed for his prominent part in the 1837 Rebellion. After his release, he served in the Quebec assembly from 1851 to 1857.

Vancouver Crescent   **Varsity Acres, N.W.**

Vancouver Crescent likely takes its name from the city of Vancouver, B.C., which was named for British captain George Vancouver who sailed and explored in the area in the early 1790s.

Vandyke Place, etc.   **Varsity Acres, N.W.**

These streets may have taken their name from American author Henry Van Dyke (1852-1933), best known for his inspirational stories such as The Story of the Other Wise Man and The First Christmas Tree, or perhaps for Flemish artist Sir Anthony Van Dyck (1599-1641), whose name is pronounced "vandike" although it is spelled like "vandick."

Van Horne Crescent   **Vista Heights, N.E.**

William Cornelius Van Horne was born in Illinois in 1843 and employed as an office boy in a railway station at age 14. He worked his way up and within 12 years was the superintendent of the Chicago and Alton Railroad. In 1882 he became general manager of the Canadian Pacific Railway, supervised the construction of the line over the Rockies to the Pacific, and became chairman and president of the company in 1888. In 1894 he was made a knight commander of the Order of St. Michael and St. George. He died in 1915. Originally Calgary's downtown streets were named for people with ties to the CPR and

12th Avenue S. was named Van Horne Avenue. The name was abandoned in 1904 when City council voted to change from named to numbered streets. The name appears today in Vista Heights, perhaps in recognition of the former street name.

Van Horne High School   **3015 Utah Drive N.W.**

Van Horne Secondary School officially opened in May 1967, as Calgary's first public school designed specifically as a vocational school. (See Van Horne Crescent.)

Varley Drive   **University of Calgary Family Housing, N.W.**

When the University of Calgary Board of Governors named the streets of the U of C family housing units, they to chose to honour members of Canada's Group of Seven artists. They wanted to recognize famous Canadians and felt that choosing names from one group gave a sense of unity to the housing project. F.H. Varley was one of the original members of the group, which worked together from 1920 to 1933.

Vercheres Street   **Mount Royal, S.W.**

Marie-Madeline Jarrett de Vercheres (1678-1747) is famous for her defense of the family fort against the Iroquois in 1692. According to the story, at age 14 she took command and with the assistance of her two young brothers, two soldiers and an old man, defended the fort for a week until relief came from Montreal. The accuracy of the story, which has been handed down over the years, has been questioned. However, it is historically correct that the incident did indeed take place.

Victoria Community School   **411 - 11 Avenue S.E.**

Built in 1903, this school was named to honour Queen Victoria. The community itself did not become known as Victoria Park until after 1905.

Victoria Park   **S.W.**

One of the earliest residential sections of the city, Victoria Park was originally called East Ward. The name Victoria Park referred to the exhibition grounds, named after Queen Victoria in 1889. The residential area ceased to be known as East Ward when the ward system of government was dropped in 1905. Because the area was adjacent to the exhibition grounds, which had been annexed in 1901, it gradually became known as Victoria Park as well. The original Victoria Park exhibition grounds are now known as Stampede Park.

Vincent Massey Junior High School   **939 - 45 Street S.W.**

See Massey Place.

Virginia Drive   **Varsity Acres, N.W.**

Virginia Drive may take its name from the American seaboard state of Virginia. The state was probably named in honour of Queen Elizabeth I, known as the "Virgin Queen."

Viscount Bennett Centre (Continuing Ed.)   **2519 Richmond Road S.W.**

This school is named after R.B. Bennett, prime minister of Canada from 1930 to 1935. After he retired from Canadian politics in 1937, he moved to England and was active during World War II with the Ministry of Supply and the Red Cross. In 1941 he was given the title Viscount Bennett of Mickleham, Calgary and Hopewell, and took a seat in the British House of Lords. As a philanthropist, Viscount Bennett gave away millions of dollars, primarily for educational purposes. Viscount Bennett Centre for Continuing Education was formerly Viscount Bennett Junior/Senior High School. (See also R.B. Bennett Elementary School.)

CALGARY
W

W.O. Mitchell Elementary School   511 Silvergrove Drive N.W.

William Ormond Mitchell was born in Weyburn, Saskatchewan in 1914 and received his bachelor of arts degree from the University of Alberta in 1942. He wrote his first novel, Who Has Seen the Wind, in 1947. He is the author of numerous novels, short stories, articles and plays, primarily about prairie life. He was awarded the Leacock Medal for Humour in 1962 and has been a writer in residence of Massey College, University of Alberta, University of Windsor and University of Calgary. Mitchell resides in Calgary.

W. R. Castell Central Library   616 Macleod Trail S.E.

William Rentoul Castell was born in Ontario and achieved a master's degree in library science. He worked at the Fort William (now Thunder Bay) library before coming to Calgary as chief librarian in 1945. He spent 28 years in that capacity until his retirement in 1973. His initial task was to give the Calgary Public Library collections greater depth in a number of fields, but his greatest contribution was in expansion of library services. When Castell came to Calgary, the department consisted of the Carnegie Library in Central (now Memorial) Park, and a branch library in Crescent Heights. When he retired, the main library was housed in a six-storey building downtown, with 13 branches scattered throughout the city.

Wainwright Place, etc.   Willow Park, S.E.

These streets may take their name from the Alberta town of Wainwright. It was named after William Wainwright (1840-1914) who became second vice-president of the Grand Trunk Pacific Railway in 1911. An Eleanor Wainwright served as head nurse of the Calgary General Hospital from 1911 to 1925. In 1912 she founded the Calgary Community Nursing Bureau and was its registrar until her retirement in 1952. She died in Calgary in 1953.

Walrond Road   **Willow Park, S.E.**

Walrond Road may have been named after one of southern Alberta's first large ranches. The Walrond Ranch was formed in 1883 by dominion veterinary surgeon Dr. Duncan McEachern of Montreal. It was named after Sir John Walrond Walrond of London, England, who arranged for the company's financing with British capital and became its president. The ranch was sold in 1962 and ceased operations at that time.

Ward Block   **105 - 107 - 8 Avenue S.W.**

The Ward Block received its present name when it was purchased by Dudley Ward in 1911. It was built in 1898 by Sir James Lougheed and was originally known as the Granville Block.

Watson Road   **Willow Park, S.E.**

There are two interesting Watsons in Calgary's past after whom Watson Road might have been named. John G. Watson came to Calgary from Ontario in 1899. He served as an alderman from 1906 to 1909 and 1910 to 1912. During this time he became known as "Gravity" Watson, because of his promotion of a gravity water system with headwaters on the Elbow River southwest of the city. Watson was a stonemason and operated a quarry south of the Bow River. City hall, Carl Safran Centre and several other old public buildings are built of sandstone from his quarry. The other was James Cameron Watson (1891-1986) who came to Calgary in 1912 and worked for AGT for many years. He served as a city alderman from 1943 to 1945. Although he was not anxious to take on the position, he ran for mayor in 1946, only because he thought he would not win. He did, however, and found the job so interesting that he was elected for two more terms, until he was unseated by Don Mackay in 1950. Watson later retired to Lethbridge where he died in 1986.

Weaselhead Flats   **37 Street S.W. between 66 and 90 Avenues**

Weaselhead is a natural area on the southwest side of the Glenmore Reservoir and at the west end of Glenmore Park. It was named after a Sarcee Indian who made his camp in the river valley beginning in the late 1800s. He lived here for about 50 years. This area was once part of the Sarcee Indian Reserve but was sold to The City of Calgary in 1931, two years before the completion of the Glenmore Reservoir.

Wedgewood Drive   **Wildwood, S.W.**

Many of the streets in Wildwood have names that are English in origin. This may be why the name Wedgewood was chosen. Josiah Wedgwood (1730-1795) was the most famous of English potters. Wedgwood china is one of England's biggest exports. Note the difference in spelling between the name of the street and the potter.

Wellington Place   **Wildwood, S.W.**

Like many of the streets in Wildwood, Wellington Place has a name which is likely British in origin. Arthur Wellesly, 1st Duke of Wellington (1769-1852) was the English commander of the allied European forces which defeated French Emperor Napoleon I at the Battle of Waterloo in June 1815.

Wilcox Street   **Willow Park, S.E.**

This street may take its name from Mount Wilcox in Banff National Park. The mountain is named after Walter Dwight Wilcox, who travelled through the pass next to the mountain in 1896 and wrote a book named The Rockies of Canada, published in 1906.

Wilde Road   **Willow Park, S.E.**

Wilde Road may have been named for a NWMP officer, W.B. Wilde. In 1896 he was murdered by an Aboriginal fugitive named Charcoal, near Pincher Creek. The search for his killer became the largest manhunt in the Alberta area up to that time.

Wilkinson Place   **Willow Park, S.E.**

This street may have been named to honour Rose Wilkinson who was born in Ireland and came to Calgary in 1927. She served as an alderman from 1935 to 1955, and from 1944 to 1963 as the Social Credit MLA for Calgary North. In 1959 she defeated then Liberal leader Grant MacEwan. Known to many simply as "Rosie," she was a well loved and respected politician. When she retired from City Council she was given a civic reception, the first ever for a local politician. Wilkinson died in Edmonton in 1968 at the age of 83.

Willard Road   **Willow Park, S.E.**

Willard Road may have been named to honour Hank Willard of Vulcan who won five consecutive world chuckwagon championships at the Calgary Exhibition and Stampede between 1951 and 1955.

William Aberhart High School   **3009 Morley Trail N.W.**

William Aberhart (1878-1943) was appointed principal of Crescent Heights High School in 1915 and also became a radio evangelist, broadcasting the "Back to the Bible Hour" on CFCN radio beginning in 1925. In addition, he founded the Alberta Prophetic Bible Institute. During this time, he became interested in the economic theories of Social Credit and tried to have them adopted by the government in power, the United Farmers of Alberta. When he was rebuffed, Aberhart organized the Social Credit Party and won the provincial election by a landslide in 1935. He then became premier and led the first Social Credit government in the world, remaining in that position until his death in 1943.

William Reid Elementary School   **1216 - 36 Avenue S.W.**

Willliam Ferguson Reid (1902-52) and his parents came to Calgary from Scotland in 1913. He was active in community affairs, the Junior Chamber of Commerce of Canada and the Chartered Accountants Association of Alberta. A Calgary public school board trustee from 1945 to 1950, he was chairman from 1946 to 1950. He was also chairman of the Calgary University Committee which campaigned for five years to establish a Calgary branch of the University of Alberta, and was successful in 1952.

William Roper Hull Child & Family Services & School   2266 Woodpark Avenue S.W.

When William Roper Hull (see Hull Estates) died in 1925, one of the provisions of his will was that after the deaths of the personal beneficiaries - his wife, brother and sister- a trust fund be established with the residue of his estate to build a home for orphans. Mrs. Hull died in 1953, leaving a $4 million legacy. The William Roper Hull Home for Children was finally built in 1962 after much debate as to what kind of facility it should be. Originally it was to be a home for orphan boys, then for disturbed boys, but ended up being a home to boys aged 12 to 16 years in needy circumstances. It was an innovative, cottage-style home, with 12 boys and house parents sharing each cottage. Currently, William Roper Hull Child and Family Services is a treatment centre for emotionally and psychologically disturbed children and their families, and includes residences and a school.

William Street   Ramsay, S.E.

See Alberta Avenue.

Willingdon Boulevard   Willow Park, S.E.

This street may be named for Freeman Freeman-Thomas, 1st Marquis of Willingdon, who served as governor-general of Canada from 1931 to 1936. He made his first official visit to Calgary in 1927. There is also an Alberta town named for him.

Wilma Hansen Junior High School   963 Queensland Drive S.E.

Wilma Hansen received her B.Comm. from the University of Alberta in 1926. She was active for many years in the Home and School Association, was president of the Calgary Council and Alberta Federation of Home and School Associations and an executive member of the Canadian Federation of Home and Schools. She was made a life member of each. Hansen was elected to the Calgary public school board in 1961 and retired in 1967, at which time she was awarded a life membership in the Alberta School Trustees Association. She was a strong supporter of an autonomous University of Calgary and served as chairman of the Calgary University Committee from 1963 to 1966. She received an honourary doctorate from the University of Calgary in 1969. Wilma Hansen Junior High School opened in 1985.

Wilson Road   Willow Park, S.E.

Wilson Road may have been named for James Wilson, whose architectural firm, Child and Wilson, served as town engineers from 1890 to 1894. Wilson was City engineer in 1896. This street may also have been named after Mount Wilson in Banff National Park. This mountain honours Thomas Edmund Wilson (1859-1933), who served with the NWMP in 1880 and in 1881 joined Major A.B. Rogers in his search for a pass across the mountains for the CPR. In 1884 Wilson began a packing and guiding business at Banff and later operated a trading post on the North Saskatchewan River. He was the first white man to see Takakkaw Falls, Lake Louise and Emerald Lake. There is also a Wilson Range, east of Waterton Lakes and a Wilson Peak named by Lieutenant Blakiston of the Palliser

Expedition (see Blakiston Drive) after Lieutenant Charles William Wilson (1836-1903), who was secretary for the British Boundary Commission from 1858 to 1862.

Windsor Park   **S.W.**

Residential development in Windsor Park began in the 1940s and the area was annexed to The City of Calgary in 1951. The name reflects the British influence on early Calgary: Windsor has been the name of the British royal family since 1917, when King George V changed his name from the German Saxe-Coburg to the English Windsor to appease his British subjects during World War I. The area directly north of Windsor Park, Brittania, also reflects a British theme.

Wolfe Street   **Mount Royal, S.W.**

General James Wolfe (1727-1759) was commander of the British forces that defeated the French at the Battle of the Plains of Abraham. Although he was mortally wounded, Wolfe lived long enough to learn of the victory, which was the beginning of British rule in Canada.

Woodman Junior High School   **8706 Elbow Drive S.W.**

Frank Leslie Woodman, a native of Nova Scotia, taught school near Boston before coming to Calgary in 1915. He taught at Crescent Heights High School from 1915 to 1935, then became a physics teacher at Western Canada High School, the year that school became a composite high school, the first of its kind west of Winnipeg. He was principal of the school from 1938 until his retirement in 1954. Woodman served on the Calgary public school board from 1955 to 1958 and was also active athletically, both as a coach for school football and hockey teams, and as a timekeeper and referee for junior and professional football games. In 1959 he was named Calgary's Sportsman of the Year, the year the school bearing his name was built. Woodman died in 1967 at the age of 77.

Wood's Homes   **9400 - 48 Avenue N.W.**
                                               805 - 37 Street N.W.

George Wood came to Canada from Scotland as a Presbyterian minister in 1908. After the death of his first wife, he moved from Melfort, Saskatchewan to Innisfail. There, in 1915, he took in the motherless children of a soldier about to be shipped overseas. This was the beginning of Wood's Christian Home. Wood met his second wife, Annie Jarvis, while on a fundraising visit to Calgary. In 1926 John Hextall's mansion (see John Hextall Bridge) in Bowness became home to the Woods and 32 homeless children. George Wood died in 1928 but Annie continued their mission until her death in 1939. By 1962 other agencies were caring for neglected children so the mandate of the Wood's Home changed to caring for disturbed children. The original home closed in 1969 and re-opened in 1970, operating under the Provincial Department of Health. The agency has since expanded and now includes several locations in Calgary, Red Deer, Medicine Hat and Lethbridge. Wood's Homes continues to be a private agency with some public funding.

Woodsworth Road   **Willow Park, S.E.**

Woodsworth Road may have been named for former Methodist minister J.S. Woodsworth, who was one of the organizers of a meeting in Calgary on July 31, 1932 which saw the birth of the Co-operative Commonwealth Federation (CCF). He was chosen the following day to be the president of the first National Council of this new political party. The CCF was an active force in Canadian politics from 1932 until 1961 when it became known as the New Democratic Party.

Subject Listing

 Arts and Culture

Betty Mitchell Theatre
Jack Singer Concert Hall
John Dutton Theatre
Martha Cohen Theatre
Max Bell Theatre
Muttart Art Gallery
Nickle Arts Museum
Nickle Theatre
Reeve Theatre

 Bridges

Baines Bridge
Calf Robe Bridge
Cushing Bridge
Graves Bridge
H. Kroeger Bridge
Harry Boothman Bridge
Harvie Bridge
Hillhurst (Louise) Bridge
Ivor Strong Bridge
John Hextall Bridge
Langevin Bridge
Louise Bridge
Palmer Bridge
Pattison Bridge
Shouldice Bridge

Buildings

Alexander Calhoun Branch Library
Alexandra Centre
Alex Walker Tower
Anderson Apartments
Andrew Davison Building
Austin Nixon Manor
Baker House
Barron Building
Beveridge Block
Big Four Building
Birkenshaw Apartments
Bob Edwards Building
Brewster Hall
Burns Building
Carroll Place
Carter Place
Chief Crowfoot Centre
Clarence Block
Colonel Belcher Hospital
Colonel James Walker Building
Congregation House of Jacob Mikveh
    Israel Synagogue
Craigie Hall
Cross Bow Auxiliary Hospital
Cross House Garden Cafe
Deane House
Devenish Design Centre
Doll Block
Dr. Vernon Fanning Extended Care Centre

E.H. Crandell Building
Edwards Place Senior Citizens Apartments
Elveden Centre
Eugene Coste Building
Francis Klein Centre
General DeLalanne Lodge
George Boyak Nursing Home
George C. King Home
George Murdoch Building
Georgina Thomson Branch Library
Harry Hays Building
Hays Farm
Hull Estates
Hunt House
J.J. Bowlen Provincial Building
Jacques Lodge
John Ware Building
Kananaskis Hall
Kerby Centre
Lacombe Centre
Lancaster Building
Len Werry Building
Lougheed Building
Lougheed Residence
Louise Riley Branch Library
MacEwan Student Centre
MacKimmie Library
McDougall Place
Murdoch Manor
Nellie McClung Centre
Norman Block
Norquay Hall

Palliser Hotel
Peter Lougheed Hospital
Rundle Hall
Rundle Lodge
Sam Livingston Building
Scurfield Hall
Senator Burns Building
Sheriff King Home
Shouldice Lodge
Swann Mall
Thomas Riley Building
Thomson Bros. Block
Tom Baker Cancer Centre
Ward Block
W. R. Castell Central Library
Wood's Homes

 Parks

Buckmaster Park
Colonel James Walker Park
David Shelton Park
Ed Corbett Park
Edworthy Park
George Moss Park
George R. Gell Park
J.H. Woods Park
James Short Park
Lawrey Gardens
Laycock Park
McHugh Bluff
Munro Park
Nat Christie Park
Nellie Breen Park
Nimmons Park
Pop Davies Athletic Park
Prince's Island Park
Princess Obolensky Park
Queen Elizabeth Park
Reader Rock Gardens
Riley Park
St. George's Island
Scotchman's Hill
Senator Patrick Burns Memorial Gardens
Shouldice Park
Slater Park
Stanley Park
Tom Campbell's Hill

Tomkins Square
Weaselhead Flats

 **Schools
Calgary Board of
Education
(Public Schools)**

A.E. Cross Junior High School
Alex Ferguson Elementary School
Alex Munro Elementary School
Alice M. Curtis Elementary School
Andrew Davison Elementary School
Andrew Sibbald Elementary School
Annie Foote Elementary School
Annie Gale Junior High School
Banting and Best Elementary School
Bishop Pinkham Junior High School
Bob Edwards Junior High School
Branton Junior High School.
Buchanan Elementary School
Cappy Smart Elementary School
Captain John Palliser Elementary School
Catherine Nichols Gunn Elementary
    School
Cecil Swanson Elementary School
Chief Justice Milvain Elementary School
Chris Akkerman Elementary School
Christine Meikle School (Special Ed)
Clarence Sansom Community School
Clem Gardner Elementary School
Colonel Irvine Junior High School
Colonel J. Fred Scott Elementary School
Colonel Macleod Elementary/Junior High
    School
Colonel Sanders Elementary School
Colonel Walker Community School
Connaught Community School
David D. Oughton Elementary School
David Thompson Elementary School
Douglas Harkness Community School
Dr. Carl Safran Centre (Continuing Ed.)
Dr. E.P. Scarlett High School
Dr. E.W. Coffin Elementary School
Dr. Gladys McKelvie Egbert Community
    School
Dr. Gordon Higgins Junior High School
Dr. Gordon Townsend School

Dr. J.K. Mulloy Elementary School
Dr. Norman Bethune Elementary School
Dr. Oakley School
Earl Grey Elementary School
Emily Follensbee Centre
Ernest Manning High School
Ernest Morrow Junior High School
Ethel M. Johnson Elementary School
Eugene Coste Elementary School
F.E. Osborne Junior High School
Fred Parker Elementary School
Fred Seymour Elementary School
G.W. Skene Elementary School
Georges P. Vanier Junior High School
Grant MacEwan Elementary School
Guy Weadick Elementary School
H.D. Cartwright Junior High School
Harold Panabaker Junior High School
Harold W. Riley Elementary School
Haultain Memorial Elementary School
Henry Wise Wood High School
Ian Bazalgette Junior High School
Jack James High School
James Fowler High School
James Short Memorial Elementary School
Janet Johnstone Elementary School
Jennie Elliott Elementary School
Jerry Potts Elementary School
John G. Diefenbaker High School
John Ware Junior High School
Keeler Elementary School
King Edward Elementary/Junior High
    School
King George Elementary School
Le Roi Daniels Elementary School
Lester B. Pearson High School
Lord Beaverbrook High School
Louis Riel Elementary/Junior High School
Louise Dean School
Marion Carson Elementary School
Milton Williams Junior High School
Nellie McClung Elementary School
Nickle Junior High School
O.S. Geiger Elementary School
Patrick Airlie Elementary School
Prince of Wales Elementary School
Queen Elizabeth Elementary/ Jr./Sr.
    High School

R.B. Bennett Elementary School
R.T. Alderman Junior High School
Ramsay Elementary School
Robert Warren Junior High School
Roland Michener Elementary School
Sam Livingston Elementary School
Senator Patrick Burns Junior High School
Shaughnessy High School
Simon Fraser Junior High School
Sir James Lougheed Elementary School
Sir John A. Macdonald Junior High School
Sir John Franklin Junior High School
Sir Wilfrid Laurier Junior High School
Sir Winston Churchill High School
Stanley Jones Elementary School
Terry Fox Junior High School
Thomas B. Riley Junior High School
Van Horne High School
Victoria Community School
Vincent Massey Junior High School
Viscount Bennett Centre (Continuing Ed.)
W.O. Mitchell Elementary School
William Aberhart High School
William Reid Elementary School
William Roper Hull Child & Family
     Services & School
Wilma Hansen Junior High School
Woodman Junior High School

 **Schools
Calgary Catholic
Board of
Education**

Bishop Carroll High School
Bishop Grandin High School
Bishop Kidd Junior High School
Bishop McNally High School
Blessed Kateri Tekakwitha Elementary
     School
Brebeuf Elementary/Junior High School
Cardinal Newman Elementary/Junior
     High School
Don Bosco Elementary/Junior High
     School
Father Damien Elementary School
Father Doucet Elementary School

Father James Whelihan Elementary
     School
Father Lacombe Senior High School
Father Scollen Elementary/Junior High
     School
Holy Family Elementary School
Holy Redeemer Bilingual Elementary
     School
Holy Trinity Elementary School
John Paul II Elementary School
John XXIII Elementary/Junior High
     School
Madeleine d'Houet Bilingual Junior High
     School
Monsignor E.L. Doyle Elementary School
Monsignor Neville Anderson Elementary
     School
Mother Mary Greene Elementary School
Mother Teresa Elementary School
Our Lady of Peace Elementary/Junior
     High School
St. Alphonsus Elementary/ Junior High
     School
St. Andrew Elementary School
St. Angela Elementary School
St. Anne Francophone Elementary/Jr./Sr.
     High School
St. Anthony (Further Education)
St. Augustine Elementary/Junior High
     School
St. Bede Elementary School
St. Benedict Elementary School
St. Bernadette Elementary School
St. Bonaventure Junior High School
St. Boniface Elementary School
St. Catherine Elementary School
St. Cecilia Bilingual Elementary School
St. Charles Congregated Elementary/
     Junior High School
St. Clement Elementary School
St. Cyril Elementary/Junior High School
St. Dominic Elementary School
St. Francis High School
St. Gerard Bilingual Elementary School
St. Gregory Junior High School
St. Helena Junior High School
St. Henry Elementary School
St. Hubert Elementary School

St. James Elementary/Junior High School
St. John (Fine Arts) Elementary
St. Joseph Elementary School
St. Jude Elementary School
St. Luke Bilingual Elementary School
St. Margaret Elementary/ Junior High
     School
St. Maria Goretti Elementary School
St. Mark Elementary School
St. Martha Elementary/Junior High
     School
St. Mary's Senior High School
St. Matthew Elementary and Bilingual
     Junior High School
St. Michael Elementary/Junior High
     School
St. Monica Elementary/Junior High
     School
St. Patrick Elementary School
St. Paul School (Ecole Ste. Anne Annex)
St. Peter Elementary School
St. Philip Elementary School
St. Pius Elementary Bilingual School
St. Rita Elementary School
St. Rose of Lima Elementary/ Junior High
     School
St. Rupert Elementary School
St. Stephen Elementary/Junior High
     School
St. Sylvester Elementary School
St. Thomas Aquinas Elementary School
St. Thomas More Elementary School
St. Vincent de Paul Elementary/Junior
     High School
St. Wilfrid Elementary School
St. William Elementary School

 **Sports and
Leisure**

Archie Boyce Arena
Bob Bahan Pool and Fitness Centre
Burns Stadium
Copot Arena
Earl Grey Golf Club
Ernie Starr Arena
Father David Bauer Arena

Frank McCool Arena
George Blundun Arena
Henry Viney Arena
Jack Setters Arena
Jack Simpson Gymnasium
Jefferies Pond
Jimmie Condon Arena
Justice Joe Kryczka Arena
Lindsay Park Sports Centre
Max Bell Centre
McMahon Stadium
Norma Bush Arena
Pearce Estates
Rose Kohn Memorial Arena
Rouleauville Square
Stampede Park
Stew Hendry Arena
Stu Peppard Arena
Tom Brook Athletic Park

 Streets

Abbot Avenue
Abbott Place
Aberdeen Road
Adams Crescent
Addison Place
Adelaide Street
Albany Place
Alberta Avenue
Alcott Crescent, etc.
Alexander Crescent
Alexander Street
Allan Crescent
Amherst Street
Anderson Road
Anne Avenue
Armstrong Crescent
Assiniboine Road
Astoria Crescent
Athlone Road
Austin Road
Bagot Avenue
Baker Crescent
Baldwin Crescent
Bannerman Drive
Bannister Road
Barclay Mall

Barlow Trail
Barr Road
Barrett Drive
Batchelor Crescent
Baylor Crescent
Beaconsfield Crescent, etc.
Bearspaw Drive
Beaupre Crescent
Beil Avenue
Bell Street (S.W.)
Bell Street (N.W.)
Bennett Crescent
Benton Drive
Blackfoot Trail
Blakiston Drive
Blow Street
Boulton Road
Bowlen Street
Boyce Crescent
Braden Crescent
Brantford Crescent, etc.
Braxton Place, etc.
Brazeau Crescent
Brecken Road
Breen Crescent, etc.
Breton Bay, etc.
Brisebois Drive
Brockington Road
Brown Crescent
Bulyea Crescent, etc.
Burbank Crescent, etc.
Burgess Drive
Burns Avenue
Butler Crescent
Cabot Street
Cadogan Road
Cameron Avenue
Canmore Road
Cannon Road
Cardell Street
Cardston Crescent
Carleton Street
Carlyle Road
Carmangay Crescent
Carnarvon Way
Carney Road
Cartier Street
Casson Green

Cavanaugh Place
Cayuga Crescent, etc.
Champlain Street
Charles Avenue
Cherokee Drive, etc.
Cheyenne Crescent
Chilcotin Road
Child Avenue
Chippendale Drive
Chippewa Road
Christie Road
Churchill Drive
Clarke Road
Cleveland Crescent
Cochrane Road
Colborne Crescent
Coleman Road
Coleridge Crescent, etc.
Collicutt Street
Colonel Baker Place
Columbia Place
Comanche Road
Conrad Crescent, etc.
Constable Place, etc.
Constance Avenue
Copithorne Road
Cornell Place, etc.
Cornwallis Drive
Coronado Place
Cosgrove Street
Costello Boulevard
Craig Road
Crawford Road
Cromwell Avenue
Cross Crescent
Crowchild Trail
Crowfoot Way, etc.
Deerfoot Trail
Dorchester Avenue
Dr. Carpenter Circle
Durham Avenue
Edinburgh Road
Edison Drive
Elizabeth Road
Elizabeth Street
Exshaw Road
Fisher Road, etc.
Fleetwood Drive

Flowerdew Avenue
Foster Road
Fountain Road
Fowler Drive
Franklin Drive
Fraser Road
Frobisher Boulevard
Frontenac Avenue
Fulham Street
Fullerton Road
Gainsborough Drive, etc.
Galbraith Drive
Garden Crescent
Garrick Drive
George Craig Boulevard
Georgia Street
Gissing Drive
Gladstone Gardens, Gladstone Road
Gladys Ridge Road
Goddard Avenue
Graham Drive
Grant Crescent
Grier Avenue
Harcourt Road
Hardisty Place
Harley Road
Harmon Place
Harris Place
Harvey Place
Hastings Crescent, etc.
Healy Drive
Hogarth Crescent
Holden Place
Hooke Road
Hoover Place
Hope Street
Hudson Road
Hunter Street
Jackson Place
Jamieson Avenue
John Laurie Boulevard
Joliet Avenue
Kananaskis Drive
Kelsey Place
Kendall Place
Kennedy Drive
Kerfoot Crescent
Ketchen Avenue

Kirby Place
Klamath Place
Kootenay Street
Lacombe Way
Laird Court
Lake Cameron Drive
Lake Fraser Drive, etc.
Lake Louise Way, etc.
Lambert Avenue
Lancaster Way
Lane Crescent
Lansdowne Avenue
Lassiter Court
Lathom Crescent
Laurier Court
Laval Avenue
Law Drive
Lawrence Court
Lawson Place
Layzell Road
Leduc Crescent
Leeson Court
Lefroy Court
Legare Drive
Lepine Court
Lethbridge Crescent
Levis Avenue
Lewis Drive
Liddell Court
Linden Drive
Lindstrom Drive
Lismer Green
Livingstone Drive
Lloyd Crescent
Locke Court
Lodge Crescent
Logan Crescent
Lorne Place
Louise Road
Lowes Court
Lyle Avenue
Lynch Crescent
Lysander Crescent, etc.
Macdonald Avenue
MacDonnell Avenue
MacKay Drive
Mackay Road
MacKid Road, etc.

MacLeay Road
Macleod Trail
Maddock Crescent, etc.
Maggie Street
Maitland Crescent, etc.
Manning Close, etc.
Margaret Avenue
Markerville Road
Marquette Street
Marquis of Lorne Trail
Marsh Road
Marshall Road
Massey Place
Maunsell Close
Maynard Road
McCall Drive
McCall Way
McKinnon Crescent, etc.
McKnight Boulevard
McNeill Road
McPherson Road
McTavish Road, etc.
Middleton Drive
Millar Road
Miller Avenue
Millward Place, etc.
Montcalm Crescent
Moodie Road
Morley Trail, etc.
Morrison Street
Motherwell Road
Mount Norquay Gate, etc.
Mount Robson Circle, etc.
Mount Victoria Place
Munro Drive
Murphy Road
Murray Place
Nanton Road
Nelson Road
Nesbitt Road
Newcombe Place
Nickle Road
Niven Place
Noble Road
Nolan Road
Nordegg Crescent
Norquay Court, etc.
Norris Road

Northcote Road
Osborne Crescent
Palmer Road
Palmer Road
Patton Court, etc.
Peigan Trail
Pennsylvania Road
Queen Alexandra Close, etc.
Queen Anne Road, etc.
Queen Charlotte Drive, etc.
Queen Isabella Close
Queen Tamara Place, etc.
Radnor Avenue
Rae Crescent
Ramsay Street
Reader Crescent
Richard Road
Richardson Street
Richardson Way, etc.
Riel Place
Robson Crescent
Ross Road
Rouleau Crescent
Rupert Road
Russell Road
Sackville Drive
St. Monica Avenue
Samis Road
Sarcee Trail
Scurfield Drive
Seattle Drive
Selkirk Drive
Seymour Avenue
Shannon Avenue
Shaw Road
Shepard Road
Sherman Avenue
Shillington Crescent
Sifton Boulevard
Simons Crescent, etc.
Simons Valley Road
Sinclair Crescent
Snowdon Crescent
Spiller Road
Spokane Street
Steele Avenue
Stephen Avenue Mall
Stoney Trail

Strathcona Street
Sydenham Road
Tache Avenue
Talon Avenue
Taylor Crescent
Tecumseh Road
Thacker Street
Thomas Street
Thomson Avenue
Thornton Road
Townsend Street
Travis Crescent
Tregillus Street
Trelle Drive
Underwood Place
Usher Road
Valois Avenue
Vancouver Crescent
Vandyke Place, Road
Van Horne Crescent
Varley Drive
Vercheres Street
Virginia Drive
Wainwright Place, etc.
Walrond Road
Watson Road
Wedgewood Drive
Wellington Place
Wilcox Street
Wilde Road
Wilkinson Place
Willard Road
William Street
Willingdon Boulevard
Wilson Road
Wolfe Street
Woodsworth Road

 Subdivisions

Albert Park
Burnsland
Christie Park
Currie Barracks
Dalhousie
Dover
Franklin Industrial Park

Harvey Barracks
Hawkwood
Haysboro
HMCS Tecumseh
Hounsfield Heights
Lincoln Park
MacEwan
Marlborough
Mayfair
Mayland Heights
McKenzie
Millican Estates
Mills Estates
Montgomery
Ogden
Palliser
Patterson Heights
Point McKay
Radisson Heights
Ramsay
Richmond
Rundle
St. George's Heights
Shawnee
Shawnessy
Stanley Park
Strathcona Park
Temple
Victoria Park
Windsor Park

Selected Bibliography

1. Bolton, Ken. The Albertans. Edmonton: Lone Pine Media Productions, 1981.

2. Boote, Walter H. S., co-ordinator. Ogden Whistle. Calgary: Ogden Area History Committee, 1975.

3. Delaney, John J. Dictionary of Saints. Garden City, New York: Doubleday and Company, 1980.

4. Foran, Max, and Heather MacEwan Foran. Calgary, Canada's Frontier Metropolis. Burlington, Ontario: Windsor Publications (Canada) Ltd., 1982.

5. Foran, Max, and Sheilagh Jameson, eds. Citymakers. Calgary: The Historical Society of Alberta, Chinook Country Chapter, 1987.

6. Fraser, William B. Calgary. Toronto: Holt, Rinehart and Winston of Canada,1967.

7. Harrison, Tracey and Aphrodite Karamitsanis, eds. Place Names of Alberta Volume III. Calgary: University of Calgary Press, 1994.

8. Holmgren, Eric J., and Patricia M. Holmgren. Over 2000 Place Names of Alberta. Saskatoon: Western Producer Prairie Books, 1976.

9. Karamitsanis, Aphrodite. ed. Place Names of Alberta, Volumes I and II. Calgary: University of Calgary Press, 1992.

10. MacEwan, J.W. Grant. Calgary Cavalcade, from fort to fortune. Saskatoon: Western Producer Book Service, 1975.

11. MacGregor, James G. A History of Alberta. Edmonton: Hurtig Publishing, 1972.

12. Morrison, Elsie C., and P. N.R. Morrison. The Story of Calgary 1875 - 1950: A Souvenir of Calgary's 75th Anniversary. Calgary: Calgary Publishing Company, 1950.

13. Rasporich, A.W., and Henry Klassen. Frontier Calgary. Calgary: University of Calgary, 1975.

14. Shiels, Bob. Calgary, a not too solemn look at Calgary's first 100 years. Calgary Herald, 1974.

15. Sparks, Susie, ed. Calgary, a Living Heritage. Calgary: Junior League of Calgary, 1984.

16. Surplis, Herb, ed. Communities of Calgary: from scattered towns to a major city. Calgary: Century Calgary Publications, 1975.

17. Ward, Tom. Cowtown: An Album of Early Calgary. Calgary: City of Calgary Electric System and McClelland and Stewart West Limited, 1975.

What's in a Name...Calgary?
CENTENNIAL CONTEST

In 1992, The City of Calgary invited community groups, businesses and individual citizens to present project ideas for the celebration of the Centennial of our incorporation as a city in 1994. After consideration, over 140 projects received The City's endorsement as official Centennial celebrations. The cornerstone of these activities became the "What's in a Name...Calgary?" Centennial contest.

During the first part of 1994, Calgarians were introduced to a number of outstanding citizens, past and present, who helped to make Calgary the caring, vibrant city that it is. They were then invited to nominate, in ten different categories, people who they felt should be honoured as outstanding Calgarians.

After thousands of nominations were received, the results were tabulated and the top three or four nominees in each category were announced during Stampede Week. Ballots became available for citizens to vote for their favorites. Voting was active over the next few months and by the deadline of November 11, over 50,000 votes had been cast. The winners were announced at the First Night Festival on December 31, 1994, the last night of Centennial celebrations.

The "What's in a Name...Calgary?" Centennial contest was developed by three city firms: The Image Brokers, SuperMarketing and White Iron Film and Video Productions, and was sponsored by many Calgary businesses: CHANNEL 3 CFCN, QR77, The Calgary Sun, Hook Outdoor Advertising, Shaw Cable, The Calgary Stampeders, The Calgary Cannons, The Calgary Rad'z, Agfa Film, AGT Talking Yellow Pages, Calgary Co-op, Calgary Copier, Calgary Ford and Mercury Dealers, Calgary International Organ Festival, Canadian Airlines International, Colour Four Graphic Services, Earl's Restaurants, Echo Video Productions, Gala Homes, Phoenix Press and the Royal Bank.

Sponsored by...

Contest Winners

1. Category: **Sports**
Winner: **Lanny McDonald**
Nominees: Sugarfoot Anderson
Deerfoot

Lanny McDonald was born in Hanna, Alberta in 1953. He began his professional hockey career when he was drafted by the Toronto Maple Leafs from the Medicine Hat Tigers in 1973. He also played for the Colorado Rockies before coming to the Calgary Flames in 1981. McDonald retired from the Flames in 1989, the year he scored his 500th goal and his 1,000th point, and won his first Stanley Cup ring when the Flames defeated the Montreal Canadiens. In the final game of that series he scored the go-ahead goal. In 1992 he was inducted into the Hockey Hall of Fame, the first Calgary Flames player to be so honoured. He currently serves as the Flames Vice-President Marketing and Broadcasting. But McDonald's contributions to the city of Calgary do not lie only in his athletic achievements. He is also involved with many charities, most notably the Special Olympics, Ronald McDonald House, Alberta Children's Hospital and the Children's Miracle Network Telethon.

2. Category: **The Arts**
Winner: **W.O. Mitchell**
Nominees: Betty Mitchell
Jack Peach
Marilyn Perkins

W.O. Mitchell became a household name in Canada when his book, Jake and the Kid, became a CBC radio series which aired from 1950 to 1958. His humour and wit have made him probably the best known western Canadian author. Mitchell has been awarded the Leacock Medal for Humour, a Doctor of Laws degree from the University of Saskatchewan, Regina, a Doctor of Letters from the University of Ottawa, and an Officer of the Order of Canada. For further information, see W.O. Mitchell Elementary School.

3. Category: **War Heroes**
Winner: **Fred McCall**
Nominees: William McKnight
             J.G. Pattison

Once called a one-man fighting squadron, Fred Robert Gordon McCall was one of Canada's top-ranking wartime flying aces during World War I and was decorated four times for gallantry during his wartime service. He served again during World War II as a squadron leader, training new young flyers. He was inducted into Canada's Aviation Hall of Fame in 1977. McCall came to Calgary in 1906, where he died in 1949 at age 54. For further information, see McCall Drive.

4. Category: **Civic, Business and Political Leaders**
Winner: **Ralph Klein**
Nominees: Jack Leslie
             David E. Mitchell
             Larry Ryckman

A native Calgarian, Ralph Klein worked as a reporter for CFCN radio and television for 11 years before making his first bid for political office. In 1980, with next to no political experience aside from reporting on civic issues and running on a platform of improved communication between city hall and the public, he won the position of mayor with a 15,000 vote margin over two political pros. As mayor he oversaw the building of Calgary's light rail transit system and the preparations for the 1988 Winter Olympics. He was extremely popular, receiving over 90 per cent of the popular vote in the 1986 civic election. He left his post as mayor in 1989, when he switched to provincial politics and became environment minister in the province's Tory cabinet. He became premier of Alberta when he assumed leadership of the Progressive Conservative Party in December 1992.

5. Category: **Volunteers**
Winner: **Mary Dover**
Nominees: Frank King
             Georgette Thrasher

Daughter of pioneer Calgarian A.E. Cross, Mary Dover served both her city and her country, as a volunteer, politically and in wartime service. She spent a lifetime living up to her father's admonition to, as she says, "contribute as much as we could and not expect anything but to do what we could for other people." Her volunteer efforts included work with the Canadian Club, both locally and nationally, the TB association, Red Cross, Philharmonic Society, Canadian Legion, Calgary Tourist and Convention Association, Community Chest (now the United Way), and many other worthy causes. For further information, see Dover subdivision.

6. Category: **Scientists and Academics**
     Winner: **Howard Gimbel**
     Nominees: Jessie Connal
                   Dr. Howard McEwen

Born in Calgary in 1934, Howard Gimbel was raised on his family's farm near Beiseker, Alberta. He almost decided to make a career of farming, but instead chose the high-tech field of ophthalmology. He began his career as a doctor in Calgary in 1964 and was soon specializing in cataract surgery. In 1974 he became the first Canadian surgeon to remove cataracts by use of ultrasound and has since developed a number of surgical techniques which are now standard in modern cataract surgery. He opened the Gimbel Eye Surgical Centre in 1984 and has personally operated on more than 40,000 eyes. Surgeons from around the world have come to Calgary to learn Dr. Gimbel's techniques and the Centre's unique method of outpatient care. The Gimbel Eye Foundation, also established in 1984, is a charitable organization devoted to training and overseas surgery missions. Dr. Gimbel is a Clinical Assistant Professor at the University of Calgary and in 1992 received the Alberta Order of Excellence.

7. Category: **Environmentalists**
     Winner: **Grant MacEwan**
     Nominees: Tom Baines
                   Cliff Wallis

Environmentalist is only one of the many hats that Grant MacEwan has worn during his many years of service to Calgary and the province of Alberta. He says of himself: "I'm not by nature a proselytizer, but I felt it was my duty to try by influence, practical example, to get the message across that we're not here for very long and we have no particular claim as a generation to the good things of nature and we should learn to share before we use up too much of our resources as such." For further information on his life, see Grant MacEwan Elementary School.

8. Category: **Spiritual Leaders and Philanthropists**
     Winner: **Father Patrick O'Byrne**
     Nominees: Allan Dunber
                   Stanley Pallesen

Born and raised in Calgary, Patrick O'Byrne attended Sacred Heart School and St. Mary's Boys High School before attending St. Michael's College at the University of Toronto from which he graduated with honours in 1936. He was ordained a priest in Calgary in 1940 at age 25. He spent the early years of his priesthood working with youth and served on the board of directors of the local Don Bosco Home. However, his major concerns were for ecumenism and social action. He has worked tirelessly to improve those conditions which lead to welfare and unemployment. Father O'Byrne was instrumental in establishing Calgary's Interfaith Community Action Association, only the second such venture of individuals of various faiths in North America. He retired as its executive director in 1977 after a 19-year tenure. He has since served as chaplain at the Calgary Remand Centre. Even in retirement, at age 79, Father Patrick O'Byrne is still an active force in the inner city community and continues to entertain and make new friends of all he meets.

9. Category: **Emergency Rescue Heroes**
Winner: **Richard Sonnenberg**
Nominees: Lorne Morgan
Cappy Smart

Richard Sonnenberg was born in Coaldale, Alberta in 1966 and moved to Calgary in 1974. He was educated at Louis Riel and Henry Wise Wood schools. He always aspired to be a police officer and enlisted in the force in February 1990, graduating from the training academy that June. His desire as a police officer was to make Calgary a safer place for its citizens. He was killed in the line of duty on October 8, 1993. Known to his colleagues as "Lurch" because of height, Constable Sonnenberg is remembered for his fun-loving zest for life. He touched many lives with his caring nature, as a police officer and in his involvement with youth at Emmanuel Lutheran Church.

10. Category: **Characters and Personalities**
Winner: **Ed Whalen**
Nominees: Ron "Buckshot" Barge
John Costello
Margaret MacDonald

Born in Saskatoon, Saskatchewan, Ed Whalen planned to become an obstetrician. To earn extra money while he pursued his studies, he took a part-time job at a local radio station and discovered where his heart really lay. He quit university in 1948 to work for CFQC Radio in Saskatoon. Although childhood illnesses kept him from actively participating, he always had an interest in sports and it was sports that brought Whalen to Calgary in 1955. He has been a sports announcer, hosted other television shows and written a newspaper column. Whalen is known to local sports fans as the voice of the Calgary Flames and became an international personality through his ringside work on Stampede Wrestling, which is syndicated in over 20 countries. Aside from his popularity as a media personality, he is also involved in numerous charity organizations. He and his wife, Nomi, were instrumental in the formation of the Calgary chapter of the Variety Club in 1981. He is also a board member of the Alberta Children's Hospital, is involved with the Special Olympics and has served as president of the Rotary Club.

WE GO BACK A LONG WAY, TOO.

THE LORAM GROUP OF COMPANIES is a privately owned organization headquartered in Calgary, Alberta. Its roots go back to 1898 when Frederick Stephen Mannix—a young man in search of his fortune—left his home in Stonewall, Manitoba.

As he worked his way across the country with a team of horses and a scraper, constructing branch lines for the Canadian Pacific Railway, F. S. Mannix soon found himself part of the transformation of the Canadian West. From this humble beginning grew one of Canada's largest construction companies. This enterprise helped build the country's infrastructure through the construction of roads, highways, railroads, subway systems, bridges, dams, airports, power projects and pipelines.

THE
LORAM

PHOTO: CONSTRUCTION OF CALGARY MUNICIPAL AIRPORT
          FRED MANNIX & CO. LTD., 1939

TODAY, THROUGH MORE THAN NINETY-SEVEN YEARS OF GROWTH AND diversification, the Loram Group of Companies is engaged in

► oil and gas exploration, production and pipeline transportation,

► railway maintenance,

► coal mining,

► real estate and investments.

THE LORAM GROUP OF COMPANIES

MANALTA COAL LTD.

Prairie Coal Ltd.
Gregg River Coal Ltd.
Gregg River Resources Ltd.
Line Creek Resources Ltd.

PEMBINA CORPORATION

Pembina Resources Limited
Pembina Exploration Limited
Pembina Pipeline
Peace Pipe Line Ltd.

LORAM MAINTENANCE OF WAY, INC.

Loram, Pty. Limited
Loram Rail Limited
Loram S.r.l.

BOWFORT LAND LTD.

BOWFORT CAPITAL LTD.

MHL HOLDINGS INC.

GROUP
COMPANIES

PROUDLY CELEBRATING OUR CENTENNIAL IN 1998

The Best Shot

Winner of the "What's in a Name...Calgary?" Photo Contest sponsored by Afga Film.
Taken by Felix deSouza, the picture is of the bronze sculputure "The Winner" found in Century
Gardens (8 Avenue and 8 Street S.W.).